Reflections Upon
A Sunny Day

Reflections Upon A Sunny Day

Part One

An Autobiography by Murderer and Death
Row Escapee Fred H. Kornahrens III

Fred H. Kornahrens III
M. Scott Steedley
Joseph Wilkerson Kornahrens

Cover Image Credit: M. Scott Steedley
© 2017 Fred H. Kornahrens III, M. Scott Steedley, and Joseph Wilkerson Kornahrens
All rights reserved.

ISBN: 069299100X
ISBN 13: 9780692991008
Library of Congress Control Number: 2017918742
Manna Feast Productions, Walterboro, SC

*Although the author and publisher have made every effort to ensure that the information in this book was correct at press time, the author and publisher do not assume and hereby disclaim any liability to any party for any loss, damage, or disruption caused by errors or omissions, whether such errors or omissions result from negligence, accident, or any other cause. Some names and identifying details have been altered to protect the privacy of individuals. Identifying characteristics and details such as physical properties, occupations and places of residence may also have been changed, but it is our attempt to present the information as it was written. Any opinions expressed are the opinions of Fred H. Kornahrens III and are noted as such unless otherwise proven as fact.

Foreword
By:
M. Scott Steedley
and
Joseph Wilkerson Kornahrens

Charleston, South Carolina is one of the oldest and most diverse communities in the United States. European settlement of the area began around 1670, and this "Holy City" of Charleston soon became the gem of the thirteen original colonies. From its beginning until the present, it achieved wealth from rich soil and vast waterways, which allow the import and export of valued goods. The marshlands and tidal creeks reach out like fingers throughout the region and teem with an abundance of wildlife revered by everyone blessed enough to call the "Lowcountry" home.

For centuries, the wealth of the natural environment surrounding Charleston has been cherished by locals for its beauty and life-sustaining resources. Today, the riches of the Lowcountry are also valued by tourists, who come from far and wide to experience these wonders while learning the heritage that weaves throughout its history. This history is riddled with stories, old and new, stories that are deep and long and sometimes darker than the black water rivers common to the area. Perhaps unsurprisingly, some people wish some of these stories were never told.

If some secrets seem meant to remain unspoken, they nevertheless are present for those who have lived them. For such people, it often seems imperative to acknowledge the past without allowing it to predict our future. Yet this acknowledgment of the past can become more difficult when the stories are tied to mental illness. On the other hand, individuals often inherit genetics that predetermine the possibilities of how they interact with life. Other times, the details and stresses within an environment can contribute to a cycle of action and reaction already informed by mental illness. "Civilized" society today is populated by a huge number of individuals who seem to function "normally" but harbor deep-seated and unsettling aspects at the core of their being.

It is to be hoped that all who live experience the gift of love. Love comes in many forms. It can be felt by simply viewing nature or by sharing emotions with another human being. If we are lucky enough to engage in lasting relationships we find purpose for our lives outside of ourselves and seek opportunities to foster and cherish our relationships, which are, indeed, a gift of living.

If privileged, we're introduced to this supportive feeling from our parents who are our heroes. They model proper roles for us to lead in order to navigate successfully through the ups and downs of daily existence. Many less fortunate individuals grow up in homes of complication, instability, mental illness and violence. The mirror into which they stare casts reflections of horror and tragedy. For just this reason, many raised in such environments attempt to change their personal worldview and often envision a fairytale alternative to the pain they have witnessed previously.

Through life lessons, individual choices, or divine order- people sometimes succeed in securing their dreams of happiness and longevity. In other cases, no matter how hard they strive towards this goal, there is a predisposition that seems to follow them, a shadow that lurks around waiting for the chance to expose itself. Who do we blame for these haunted lives that fail to match reality to dream?

Ultimately as individuals, we are responsible for our actions. Life consists of a collection of past, present and future experiences, each life is a summation of genetic inheritance, things witnessed, information gathered along the way, stresses endured and accompanying side effects. If we are lucky, our lives also include moments of love.

Yet, even amid love, society presents numerous obstacles that seem to muddy the waters pointing to goodness and nobility. As we strive to maintain peace and security in our loving relationships, we face a variety of demands—physical, financial, spiritual, and emotional—that weigh heavily upon us affecting our ability to reason properly and act accordingly. When this occurs, actions can reflect the state of disharmony that plagues the human.

Each case is unique but there are common and recurring themes that link us together. Imagine all the happiness you yearned for to escape your previous pain was realized; you get a good job, find a partner, vow to spend life together eternally, start a family by birthing healthy children into this world and build a home within one of the most pristine, unspoiled areas on God's earth.

Now, try to comprehend for yourself those things you hold so dearly falling apart and slipping away. For some this may seem like the end of the world. For others it is a new beginning. Either way, it is a situation more prevalent today than at any point in history. Over half of marriages end in divorce. This is a hard reality.

What makes this difficult situation more trying is when children are involved. This is as hard for children as for adults. Sometimes it is a needed sense of relief for everyone as the continued union between parents creates a painful and negative pattern in no one's best interest.

Lawyers can get involved in the legalities of dissolving a binding marital partnership including assets and children. Often this worsens an already fragile situation. Many times, they do not help soften the blows but drive a wedge between parties and become mouthpieces that don't say much of true value. The people who may benefit most are the lawyers themselves.

The autobiography contained in the following pages tells the story of one spirit plagued by disharmony. Sadly, the turmoil that affected the life of Fred Herman Kornahrens III also resulted in loss of life and the destruction of innocence. Although Kornahrens's story takes place in the Lowcountry of South Carolina, it received media coverage across the nation. In offering this book to the public, we hope that it reaches within many hearts and potentially prevents the unfolding of similar tragedies.

This book is the first half of an autobiographical manuscript written by Fred. H Kornahrens III while living on Death Row in South Carolina. The other half of the manuscript is to be released at a later date. We have made few efforts to change the document in attempts of presenting it as it was written. To complete this Foreword, Joseph Wilkerson Kornahrens, the eldest child of Fred H. Kornahrens III, expresses his feelings on what he hopes to gain by sharing his father's version of a family's suffering:

"I now know the true meaning of the biblical saying that the sins of the father shall be carried by his son. Life is a test of strength and morality. I believe that every story has more than one side and this is my father's story.

Reflections Upon A Sunny Day

Blaming our past for the things we do is not an excuse for our failures. I believe that we are what we choose to be at the end of the day. It is a test of our strength.

I also believe your past is there to help guide you through life. I have written a story of my life in a book named <u>Weeds in the Garden</u>. It will take you into a child's view of this family. Some memories were good and some were not.

I hope when you are reading my father's autobiography you understand this is a one sided story. He tries to justify his crime in his head. My father found God in prison, but he should have found him sooner.

I also hope that these writings may help someone who has lost their way and that they also can learn from my father's mistakes and shortcomings.

I miss my family everyday and I want to tell you their story. This is my burden that my father left. He left me with the sins he committed. I live with them every day."

Joseph Wilkerson Kornahrens

Reflections Upon A Sunny Day
Author's Preface

Writing about my life history has been a very difficult task. Depression caves in upon me each time I search the corridor of my mind; that archive of memories, and relive my past. My story is of salt water, of boats and shrimp, of storms and many tears.

There is merit in forgetfulness. It is one of the gentle forms of healing and one of the most dangerous. I am a prisoner of memory and have a need to clear out the debris of the bad years. I have been jotting down memories since 1985. My notes have been very helpful in assembling this history. Some of the events may be out of sequence, but I am reasonably sure they happened in the year I say they happened. Sometimes one memory would trigger another. If one memory brought the remembrance of another, I wrote it down while it was still fresh in my mind.

I am sure there are things that I have forgotten to explain. Many actions, feelings and emotions carried over from one year into the next even if I did not mention it. My problems ran long and deep.

Most of what I have written in this story is the painful events of my life that caused me much heartache and grief. Between these times of anguish, there were times of happiness…or of hope.

My childhood left me with many deep emotional scars. I hold no bitter feelings against my parents for their shortcomings. I will always love and honor them. I cannot judge them nor anyone, for we all make mistakes throughout our lifetime.

In my midlife every familiar pattern was shattered. My wife tormented me with her lover and the aspect of taking away everything we owned. The abuse resulted in divorce – scattering of friends, loss of home and financial security and the loss of my three children.

No one has the patent on human suffering. People hurt in different ways and for different reasons. Each of us are individuals with different family backgrounds, religious training, education, experience and physical and mental capabilities. We each have acquired different levels of resilience or ways of responding to the different kinds of problems, losses or setbacks in life. And, each of us as individuals has a breaking point. All it takes is enough pain, torment, or stress and pressure, and we can all go over the edge.

We protect the ones we love, but unfortunately we sometimes hurt them. It has been a slow healing process for me with lots of time to think about my problems. I realize many things now that I could not before. I have reflected upon my past. Only during the years of prison, isolated from others and alone most of the time, have I taken my life apart and seen things I never understood before. Over and over I asked myself, "Where did it all begin?" With answers to prayer and the help of Dr. Diane Hamrick, I found that it started back as far as I can remember. That is why I am going back into my childhood memories

Reflections Upon A Sunny Day

I wish I had no history to report. I've pretended for so long that my childhood did not happen. I held it tight within me. I could not let it out. It's an act of will to have a memory or not, and I chose not to have one.

It had always been difficult for me to face the truth about my childhood because it requires a commitment to explore the outline and features of a history I would prefer to forget. For years, I did not have to face the memory of my youth. I made a simple choice not to and sought solace in the gentle faculty of forgetfulness, a refuge in the dark gloom of the unconscious. But, I was drawn back to the history of my childhood and the failures of my adult life.

My writing preserves the particulars of my life. I fill the pages with hard facts and nothing else. They are my rose windows into the past. REFLECTIONS UPON A SUNNY DAY

1986--Reflections Upon A Sunny Day

It was an early summer morning and the shimmering rays of sunlight were penetrating through my bedroom window. In the peaceful silence I could hear the bantam cocks beat their breast with flapping wings and crow. The sun was rising, like a day of creation, bringing light to a new day.

As the morning brought forth meaning and purpose, I stretched my sleepy body between the soft linen covers and looked around the room. There were patterns of light reflecting upon the oil-finished furniture. I gently slipped my feet out of bed and set them on the old hardwood floor. Stepping gingerly to the window, I looked outside. Oh, what a beautiful day it was going to be!

The sky was soft blue and there wasn't a trace of a cloud anywhere. The Spanish moss was hanging limp from the large Southern Live Oaks with their shadows, cast like a painting, on the idle water of Swinton Creek.

As my family slept, I quietly slipped into a pair of jeans and stepped out onto the porch. From the wooden porch my senses caught the smell that is cherished by all who have grown up on the unspoiled coastal waters; the marsh, the oysters, and all the marine life within the salt water giving off its particular, but pleasant aroma.

As I was enjoying deep breaths of this fresh air, the bantams and my dog, Spade, came running to greet me. Spade expressed his great happiness to see me and leaned his heavy body against my leg for affection. I spoke to him with gratitude, as I scratched him gently behind his long black ears. Spade was elated with happiness

The bantams were clucking, bobbing their heads, and scratching the ground at the bottom of the steps. It was their way of telling me they wanted a treat. I had enjoyed this ritual many times. I opened a handy bag of feed and tossed them a handful of cracked corn. It was a pleasant sight to watch the cock express his leadership and care by pointing out the kernels of corn as if the hens were too far sighted to see.

The grass was still wet with dew and shining like crystals in the early morning light. And, as I walked with Spade to the dock, small centipede grass seeds peppered my wet feet. The tide was low and some places there were small patches of fog still lingering over the water. Marsh Hens were bobbing and weaving around the edges of tall grass and there were a few Summer Ducks swimming off in the distance. The tide was beginning to flow in, and I noticed a crab at the water's edge easing around in the shallows trying to catch minnows.

As I watched the crab scurry around the bank, I became aware of my reflection upon the water. I smiled and thought how nice it would be to spend this sunny day on the river with my family.

Years have passed since that beautiful morning and the shimmering rays of sunlight no longer shine through my bedroom window. As I awoke this morning on a narrow steel bed, it was still dark and dreary. Instead of peaceful quiet, there was the sound of harsh screaming voices and steel beds banging hard against the cement floors. There was no fresh air or pleasant aroma, only the smell of fire and smoke and the constant roaring of a fire alarm.

Reflections Upon A Sunny Day

At 6:00 A.M., a rough voice could be heard above the other noise shouting, "COFFEE! MILK! JUICE! The coffee is always black and syrupy sweet. I placed my cups in the door slot for milk and watered-down juice. The milk and juice were sloshed into the cups with a near miss and spilled all over the door and floor.

At 7:00 A.M., the prison workout yelled, "CHOW! – CHOW! – CHOW" The chow, slopped on a foul looking tray, was shoved to me through a hole in my door. The breakfast consisted of powdered scrambled eggs, which had turned green, cold grits, two hard biscuits, and the milk was sour.

As I tried to eat the insipid meal, I had to defend it from the abundance of roaches crawling everywhere. After taking a small bite into the hard biscuit, I lost my appetite and slid the tray under the door.

The previous night had been exhausting. Men ceaselessly screamed nonsense and profanities from their doors. Televisions and radios blasted at full volume. The noise was so intense and loud that I could not listen, read, or even think. All I could do was survive and bear another night of the constant clamor and deafening noise.

The noise began to lessen in intensity at 2:00 A.M., and as I laid back to rest, the rats entered my cell through the holes in the wall, in search of food. A big one tried to jump into my bed, and in its attempt pulled the sheet off me. Throughout the night, I could hear them chewing on things.

There is a 60-watt light bulb enclosed inside the rear wall behind steel wire, but it is still dark in here. And, as I watched the fat bellied roaches wobble up the walls in the dim light, I thought about my first day in this drab cell. It smelled like a public outhouse. Waste matter was caked on the cement walls. When I attempted to wash the cell, the stench was so bad that it burned my eyes and nose. It took nearly a week to melt and scrub the fecal matter from the walls and the rusty antique toilet. In addition to the organic filth, there were sadistic pornographic pictures drawn on the dingy white walls. The cellblock supervisor promised to get me some paint within two weeks. After six months of asking, I gave up my plea for the paint.

Sections of this prison were built during the Civil War, thus rendering an almost medieval likeness to a dungeon. The rusty toilets on this tier are below many of the old sewer lines. The sewer from other cells backs up into my toilet, and for several months the sewer lines were broken loose from one of the tiers above. The sewer frequently splashed behind my cell wall and the stinking smell passed through the small vent located near the floor on the rear wall. I often could not eat the spoiled and monotonous prison food because of the terrible smell of sewer.

A few hours have crept by since breakfast and the drone of noise has increased. In another hour or two the noise will elevate to a full roar.

There will be no short exercise period today or tomorrow, nor any shower in the filthy little metal shower stalls where women are free to stare at our naked bodies. There is no privacy or respect granted in this kennel for human beings.

I used to look forward to leisurely weekends of camping and fishing. All of my weekends and holidays are now spent locked up in a small grimy cell without any personal hygiene privileges.

There are some people who think I don't suffer enough. This cell has a floor space of less than five by nine feet. With the bed, footlocker, toilet and sink, I have a walking space of eighteen inches by the length of the cell – three short steps. On days when I yearn to walk down a long

Reflections Upon A Sunny Day

dirt road, through a lovely forest, or up a grassy hill, I am limited to three short steps. And, when I need someone to talk with or a warm hug and kiss, it can only be found in a memory that seems unreal, because it happened in a different world…so long ago.

Zoo animals, even man-eaters, are treated more humanely than prisoners. Animals are given more room to walk and they are granted companions for company. Animals are provided with vitamins and their favorite foods by their human keepers. On the other hand, prisoners are fed food that is often spoiled and contaminated. And, when a prisoner becomes hungry, he has no refrigerator to explore. No matter if the prisoner has a strong craving for a glass of milk, a sandwich or a piece of fruit he has to do without and remain hungry.

Is it humane to lock a human being in a small cage, keep him isolated, feed him bad food, and provide little or no medical care? Should a man be made dependent on the prison system by robbing his will and motivation, by treating him like a beast strapped in chains and shackles, or by taking his self-respect with humiliating rectal inspections by anyone wearing a tin badge? Is it humane to be publicly displayed in chains and cages as something less than human by the media for exploitation, then strap that member of the human race into a machine, which was invented for profit, that barbarically kills prisoners by burning flesh, bone, and boiling their blood with high electric voltage?

Humans have been very skillful in the art of torture for thousands of years, and it continues today because people have an appetite for induced suffering. Today's prisons are very adept in the use of both physical and mental torture.

I have been reading in this dim light since early this morning, and it is time for the next meal. I can hear the clatter of trays and food boxes over the noise in the building. Someone is screaming about something and officers are teasing him. And, here's that shouting again, "CHOW! – CHOW! – CHOW!" The food is the same thing I ate yesterday and the day before; cold baked meatball with bland rice or potatoes. The meat stinks. It smells awful, and officers have just sprayed a man in his cell with tear gas. The gas rapidly spread throughout the building and my eyes are burning. From the end of the tier, the workout screams, "TEA! – ICE! – MILK!" The tea and milk are spilled all over the door and floor as usual. The milk was sour again, so I flushed it down the toilet. My eyes burn. The meal stinks. I gave up my attempt to eat and slid the tray under the door.

Many of the men rebelled against the idea of gas being sprayed during chow time. The screaming, barking, and bed banging escalated into a hot frenzy, then someone set a fire. The building grew dark with thick black smoke. I covered my mouth and nose with a washcloth until some of the smoke was cleared away by the exhaust fan. I was surprised to see the dark smut on the cloth where I was inhaling. I was even more surprised, when I saw my face and blew my nose. The officers extinguished the fire with CO2 and sprayed the man down with the chemical until he was white as snow.

Most of the incidents that are heard about, concerning this cellblock, are not caused by Death Row Inmates but rather by the [Substantial Security Risk] SSR Prisoners. They are the most dangerous prisoners in the state. Some of them were responsible for burning the Kirkland Prison to the ground. Their bizarre and violent behavior brings hardship and suffering to all.

There have been numerous shakedown inspections. When this takes place, the cells are torn apart by officers in search of contraband. Depending on how much personal property you have and how bad they mess up your cell, the cleanup and rearranging can be very frustrating;

moreover, the officers sometimes confiscate items that have been purchased from the prison canteen.

It has been hot. It has been so hot in this cell that even the roaches have been looking for a cool place to lay. The heat must drive them crazy because they sometimes run around like their behinds are on fire. If I leave any water in my wash bucket, they do their best to get into it. If the bucket were larger I'd get into it myself.

The temperature took a sudden drop last week. It was a pleasant relief from the heat, but almost everyone got sick with a cold. I believe the food handlers were responsible for the widespread contamination of the virus, and it surely took its toll on those who smoke. They sound as if they are going to cough up their lungs. And, during the short exercise period, they cough up phlegm that looks like yellow bird guts and spit it all over the small exercise area. The cement is covered with these sickening obstacles.

The temperature is back up and roaches are on the run again. When it's hot like this they become super energetic, and they seem to have excellent vision, too. They know when I'm watching them, for they stay close to an escape route – a crack or hole. If I pretend to be sleeping or act like I'm busy reading, they will come out far enough so I can get an open shot at them with my shower shoe. Even then it helps to be a bit of an athlete to chase these fast moving prison roaches.

The temperature is soaring to over 100 degrees outside today and this small cement cell is cooking me like an oven. The air is so heavy that it is difficult to breathe, and the sweat and oil is dripping from my body as if it were a side of beef roasting over a fire. And, just as the temperature is rising; the tempers of hot and miserable men are flaring.

While the hours pass with a man yelling for an officer to respond to his need, the officer is shouting, "YOUR LEFT, YOUR LEFT, YOUR LEFT RIGHT LEFT, 1 - 2 - 4, LEFT, RIGHT, LEFT." Over and over the guard carries on this shouting of cadence. And, an officer is asked to stop the constant clicking and grating of his handcuffs. The noise is nerve wracking, so he speeded up the monotonous clicking. Tempers boiled over and the banging of things against cell doors began again. Someone popped the pin on one of the large prison fire sprinklers, sending hundreds of gallons of water per minute flooding down the tier.

At 4:00 P.M., the clatter of those crusty trays began again. "CHOW" is shouted down the tier several times. The same sour milk is served again and on the tray is some kind of greasy tough meat that I cannot identify. I will have to eat it like an animal, for all I have is a flimsy plastic fork.

I am suffering here in prison, but my heart is at peace with my Lord. I realize that I must enter into the Kingdom of God through many tribulations; that my faith may be tempered. I have given an account of myself to God and there have been many tears for the wrong things I have done. There has been deep sorrow and sincere grief. There has been sadness instead of laughter, and gloom instead of joy. Then when I realized my worthlessness before the Lord and repented of my sins with all my heart, with all my soul, and with all my mind, I put my faith in Jesus as my Lord and Savior. God healed my heart, lifted me up, comforted me with His Holy Spirit and made me a new creature – an heir to the Kingdom of God.

I have been healing mentally, emotionally, and spiritually since I was put into prison. This healing process has enabled me to see things more clearly than before. I feel like a man who has healed from a long serious illness. However, this hospital (prison) is keeping me alive in a cage specifically to kill me in front of spectators who either hate me or have no compassion in general for fellow human beings.

God has used sorrow in my life to turn me away from sin and love of the world. He sent His Holy Spirit to teach me His Word, to give me strength and peace, to give me love and understanding…to seek the spiritual gifts of God and eternal life. All those things of the world I once thought very worthwhile – now I've thrown them all away so that I can put my trust and hope in Christ alone. I don't worry about anything; instead, I pray about everything asking God for my needs and thanking Him for His answers. His peace keeps my heart and thoughts quiet and at rest as I trust in Christ Jesus my Lord and Savior.

This day on Death Row began with the angry banging of beds against hard cement floors, but it is about to end with a moment of silence… As I close my Bible and step to the door, I grasp hold to the bars and slowly bow my head. I look down into the water surrounding my feet, and during this moment of silence, a moment of peace, my thoughts drift back to those Reflections Upon a Sunny Day.

The death penalty is for the politicians. Prosecutors use it for publicity in their political careers. Of the hundreds of murders that happen, only a select few are tried for the death penalty. Nearly every murder could be tried as a capital case with the flexibility in the laws; especially in the kidnapping and burglary laws.

Over ninety-five percent of this country's executions take place in the southern states. And, each state can use different methods of killing its prisoners. Each state can also use different reasons for sentencing a man to death. For instance, in Texas the aggravating circumstance is "Can the criminal be rehabilitated?" Texas has a state psychologist who is known as Dr. Death. He has sent over a hundred men to death row because he claims to know without a doubt who cannot be rehabilitated.

His interview with criminals may sometimes be for less than ten minutes. There have been instances where Dr. Death has given his determination without ever laying eyes on the defendant. The state pays him a hundred thousand dollars annually for his handy talent of getting juries to believe him and send people to their deaths.

Unless you have a friend or relative on death row, it is highly unlikely that you will care anything about a death row prisoner. The public media thrives on shocking the public with dirty gossip. They can make or break you with the pictures they paint for everyone to see. The general public is gullible enough to believe its politicians, lawmakers, and all down the line know what they are doing. And, if they say it's okay to execute prisoners, it must be okay. All too often society doesn't think for themselves. As long as they have a car in the driveway, a TV in the den, and food on the table, most people don't care and have little interest in what the government does.

If people truly had faith in Jesus and knew His love and teachings they would know that it is wrong to take the lives of prisoners. But, most of the people in this country live for its pleasures, think only of themselves, and have no love for their neighbor; especially a man in prison.

Small Craft Warnings

A long...long time ago my ancestors, a Semitic people, lived near the Great Sea. On the eastern shore, they fished where ancient cities were built. The fertile land was farmed by oxen drawn plows and the abundant game was proficiently hunted by arrow and spear.

For many generations this rich land was successfully defended from invaders, that is, until the Assyrians swept down in a national invasion and conquered the land, captured my people, and took them as slaves. For more than a hundred years they remained in captivity. Then came the Chaldeans, and they conquered the Assyrians. My Semitic ancestors left their land and migrated north and northwest across Europe to other countries. Thus, my people were scattered among nations.

They survived the Chaldean Empire 625-539 B.C., the Persian Empire 553-330 B.C., the Greek Empire 333 B.C., the Roman Empire 31 B.C.-476 A.D., the Ostrogoths 493-554 A.D., the Imperial Restoration of the Justinian Empire under the German – Otto the Great 962 A.D., the Habsburg dynasty 1530 A.D., Napoleon's Kingdome 1804 A.D., and on through the ages to the present time.

A few members of my family settled on the shore of the North Sea in a land that eventually named: The Kingdom of Germany. In this new land they cultivated the soil and grew crops. Later, the village where they lived was called Drangstedt. And, in the era of chivalry, the Bederkesa Castle was built a few miles away in the 12th century.

Based on information gathered, my people came from Thuringia country, which is southwest from Berlin. It was in the time of the beginning religious reforms caused by Martin Luther. They may have left their native land for this reason. In this time it was also a custom to change the German family name into Latin. In 1535 A.D., the administration officer in Bederkesa Castle sent his clerks into all villages around to note all people who had to pay taxes. The clerks asked the farmers what their names were and wrote them on a list. My first mentioned family member in 1535, in the village Flogein, answered that his name was Johann Carnarius. My people, with the Latin name Carnarius means butcher in English, may have spoken another Lower German dialect. Obviously, the clerk couldn't understand Latin and may have had a problem understanding the Thuringia dialect; therefore, he wrote the name Johan Carnarens into the register – thus the name was born. The same event happened seven years later in 1542 in Drangstedt. The first mentioned member of the Kornahrens Family here was Marten Karnarens. In 1562 the Archespicopal of Bremen and Verden got a new bishop; therefore, the administration had to celebrate a great welcome-party. Such a big party cost a lot of money, so the administration made a new "welcome-tax". This time the bishop's office sent its own clerks into the county to note the people, and all the Carnarius (Carnarens) declared once more their original names. This time the clerks from the church-administration could understand Latin, and this time they wrote all the names the right way. Caused by this tax register from 1562 it is known today that Drangstedt had a population of 57 and eight of these people were named Carnarius. There still lives a Carnarius Family in Hamburg. This family hasn't changed their name in the past five hundred years.

Till the end of 1700 A.D., nearly 300 years, the name continued to be written Carnarens. However, it appears that the officeholder of the

Reflections Upon A Sunny Day

Hannover Kingdom administration didn't like this form of the name, and they changed it into the nowadays "Kornahrens". In the original administration document from 1816 the officeholder wrote the name "Kornarens", but the family members signed it "Carnarens" as they had learned it from their parents.

My family became known as Kornahrens, meaning: RECORD KEEPER OF THE CORN HARVEST. (German, lit., corn - seed, grain; nahren - nourish, feed, nurse, live or feed on) In 1590, some of my relatives moved to the little village of Kuhrstedt, three miles from Dranstedt. Farmer Kornahrens had to pay taxes in Kuhrstedt since this time and the same farm place is in our family until this day.

Nearly always, the eldest son inherited the farm. The other children had to look for business elsewhere and some went to America.

Today, you will find the name KORNAHRENS in Germany only in these four villages: Drangstedt, Kuhrstedt, Ringstedt, Wustewohlde. And, in America, you will find the name KORNHARENS scattered across the nation from Carolina to California.

My great, great, great-grandfather, George Henry Kornahrens of Drangstedt, moved to America with his wife, Anna Catherine (Lohmann) and they had eleven children: J. Nicholas Kornahrens ran a grocery store in Summerville, S. C.; John L. Kornahrens lived in Jacksonville, Florida; Peter Kornahrens ran a grocery store on Meeting Street in Charleston, S. C.; Frederica Kornahrens married a baker; Catherine Kornahrens had the first kindergarten in Charleston, S. C.; Anna Kornahrens was a doctor. A female doctor in that day was unusual. Sophie Kornahrens lived in Washington, D. C. My great, great-grandfather, Johann Henry Kornahrens, had the first soda works in Charleston on Coming Street. The Kornahrens Soda Bottles are now collector's items. Carl Ludwick Kornahrens, also, had a soda water business on Hassell Street. Gerhardt

Hinrich Kornahrens had engraved on his tombstone: "A Christian should always set an example as being steadfast and fearless and even though death threatens all times, he should never be discouraged. Death can only extract our ghost and release it from the torments of life making way towards the peace of Heaven."

My great, great-grandfather, Johann Henry Kornahrens, Johann Henry Kornahrens, married Rebecca Young and they had four children. Their son, John Jacob Kornahrens, my great-grandfather, married Sarah O'Neil and they had seven children. Their son, Fred Herman Kornahrens (June 5, 1891-April 22, 1984), married Hattie Carter (August 22, 1894-February 7, 1974), and they had five children. Fred and Hattie were my grandparents.

I called my grandparents, "Mama and Papa." They had a grocery store and a farm. I can still recall my childhood experiences with them. My grandfather was a thin wiry man who went about taking care of work on the farm at a steady pace. I helped gather eggs or work in the fields on occasion. He also had a kennel and raised Cocker Spaniels. In the evenings, he would lite up his pipe and rest in an old comfortable rocking chair.

My grandmother was a short woman with endless energy. She always had something cooking in the kitchen, and that delicious aroma of country cooking still lingers in my memory. Her okra soup was unique as were other recipes. She was spry and active; a ceaseless conversationalist. She often told me stories at night as I helped her shuck corn and shell beans. I remember her telling me that she cooked the big red rooster that had dumped on me in the chicken yard. I'm not certain if she cooked him, but that big, mean rooster wasn't in the chicken yard anymore.

My grandparents had five children. Their son, Fred Herman Kornahrens, Jr. (August 25, 1920-June 30, 1979), married Mary Anne (Cirosky), and they had two children. They were my parents.

Reflections Upon A Sunny Day

My father was born in Charleston, S. C. He grew up on the farm and became a strong, young man. Having had eight years of education, he joined the U. S. Coast Guard and served in WWII as a Chief Bosen Mate aboard a Navy Ship.

Prior to his meeting my mother, he had a daughter by a previous marriage. I have never met my half-sister, nor do I know if she is still alive.

He was employed as a lineman with the South Carolina Electric and Gas Company in 1947. Later that year, he met my mother and they were married. My father continued working for the power company until he had an accident on the job in 1963. It happened while hanging a heavy transformer to a forty-foot utility pole. The pole uprooted from the earth and fell across the SCE&G Company truck while he was still safety belted at the top of the pole. The impact seriously hurt his back. He signed papers releasing the company of responsibility, and they signed papers releasing him of his job.

After much pain and suffering, he opened Fred's Auto Electric in Summerville, S. C.. I worked with him on weekends and during the summer. Then after a brief business endeavor with his brother in North Charleston, he opened Highway 61 Auto Parts near our home in Pierpont. After establishing a successful business in the community, the Atlantic Richfield Company proposed to buy his business out if he would manage their newly built station on the corner of Pierpont Avenue and Highway 61. My father accepted the offer. During this time he also opened the Brentwood Seafood and Steakhouse. The restaurant was a failure. He later sold both of these businesses and became a federal government employee at the Charleston Naval Shipyard as an electrician.

My mother was born in Charleston on September 19, 1926. Her father was an immigrant from Czechoslovakia and opened a slaughterhouse business in Charleston. My mother had eight years of education and worked at the Cigar Factory for a short time. When she was nineteen years old, she had a nervous breakdown. I feel sure that in 1945, mental health care was still in the dark ages.

Having looked upon old photographs, I found that both my parents were quite attractive when they met. They were married in the small town of Moncks Corner on December 24, 1947. Ten months later, I, Fred Herman Kornahrens III, was born on October 19, 1948.

It was the year of the biggest election surprise in U.S. history; the 1948 Presidential Race in which Democratic incumbent Harry Truman beat Republican New York Governor, Thomas Dewey. Polls predicted a Dewey landslide. The newspapers printed the wrong headlines stating that Dewey defeated Truman. The U. S. population was 146,631,000 and the average American income was $3,187.00. I am sure my father made considerably less.

My parents were renting a duplex in Saint Andrews Homes. It was a housing project of wood frame houses built in Charleston during the war.

The Bowman's lived in the other half of the duplex home. They were newlyweds, too. They became friends of my parents, and I was told that I rocked my crib against the wall. The Bowman's used to think it was the headboard of my parents' bed.

In 1949, my father bought two acres of land near Orange Grove Road and began building a small cement blockhouse. Me and my wood crib were moved to this new location the following year. He continued to work on our new home, and for some time there was an outdoor shower and an outhouse in the woods. My mother took a photo of me as I pretended to catch fish in a depleted sand pile.

Reflections Upon A Sunny Day

My sister, Loretta Anne Kornahrens, was born on January 8, 1952. I was only three years two months old when she was born, but I remember the day my father took me to the hospital to bring my mother and baby sister home. My mother got in the back seat of our 1948 Chevrolet with Loretta swaddled in a blanket. Loretta's face was pink and my mother cleaned some kind of mucus from her nose. Loretta slept in my old wooden crib that had pictures on the headboard.

My mother had a nervous breakdown. She was admitted into the Columbia State Hospital from February 15 to April 26, 1952. My sister and I lived with relatives during this time. While at my grandmother's, I hid under her house because I was confused and afraid. When my mother returned from the hospital, she was not well, but she was better.

I read somewhere that a child will know half of what he's going to know as an adult by age five. I was old enough to understand some things. My father flirted with women, and mother was sick with jealousy. My parents had violent fights.

My father did not know how to deal with my mother's mental illness and treated her badly. My mother's obsession and nagging was not tolerated by my father. His frustration came out in anger and violence, and I became a victim of physical cruelty. I found out in my adult life that my beatings began when I was a baby in my crib. It's a sad fact, but more children under five years of age are killed by their own parents than die of disease.

Both of my parents had violent tempers. They fought while I cried for them to stop. I tried to get in the middle and separate them, but I simply wasn't big enough and got slapped across the room. Knives were wielded and objects were thrown. As a result of one of the fights, my mother had to have her lip stitched together. She was ashamed of the scar for many years.

The frustration and anger of my parents led to my many beatings. I would bleed from the wounds left on me from his leather belt. When my mother intervened, she became a victim of the hard lashes too. She would curl up like a hurt dog and the licks would take her breath away.

My father drank occasionally and visited the local bars. My mother was insanely jealous of a woman, named Fowler, and sent me with my father as a spy. My father took me with him to the bars. He sometimes got drunk and sick. I was a worried child. The fear of losing my family was deeply planted in my heart.

I was beaten very badly with a rough oak stick for playing with the other children in the Nickolson's yard. I believe my father had a disagreement with the Nickolsons. They threatened to call the police about the beatings. My father told me that his father had beaten him with a bullwhip. Abused children often grow up to become brutal parents themselves, inflicting similar pain on their own children.

Our cement blockhouse was white-washed as were the tree trunks in the yard. Green metal awnings were over the windows and the roof was covered with green slate tiles. It was cold inside our house in the winter. The concrete floors and cement walls seemed to absorb the cold winter weather. My father bought a Sears and Roebuck kerosene heater and placed it between the kitchen and the bathroom. On the very cold winter nights, many heavy blankets were piled on my bed. My mother tucked the blankets in tight to keep me warm.

I helped feed my baby sister and remember her first steps. Her crib was in the front room near the door. I don't know why, but my father built two front doors on our house like a duplex. He later did away with one of the doors, and when he added onto the house I helped by carrying cement blocks to him. He put some coins in the wall and sealed it up.

Reflections Upon A Sunny Day

Where we lived was considered to be country even though we were only about three miles from downtown Charleston. There were only a few homes around and all the roads were dirt except for the main highways. My best friend was Kessler Groves. He lived with his grandmother, Mrs. Ruth Grooms, on Orange Grove Road. I wrecked my tricycle at her house and hurt my head on the edge of a brick in her flower garden. The wound bled profusely and a doctor closed it with a metal clamp.

One afternoon a small SCE&G utility truck ran over a very large Diamondback Rattlesnake near our house. The driver parked the rear wheel of the truck on the snake. The snake bit the tire again and again.

Autobiography of Fred H. Kornahrens III

1948

My name is Fred Herman Kornahrens III. I was born in Charleston, South Carolina on the 19th day of October 1948. My father, Fred H. Kornahrens Jr. was born in Charleston on August 25th, 1920. Prior to meeting my mother, he had a daughter by a previous marriage. I have never met my half sister, nor do I know if she is still alive. My father had eight years of education and served in the U.S. Coast Guard during WWII. He began working for the South Carolina Electric and Gas Company as a lineman in 1947.

My mother, Mary Anne Cirsosky, was born in Charleston on September 1st, 1926. Her father was an immigrant from Czechoslovakia and began a slaughterhouse business in Charleston. My mother had eight years of education. When she was nineteen years old, she had a nervous breakdown. I feel sure that in 1945, mental health care was still in the dark ages.

Looking upon old photographs, I found that both of my parents were quite attractive when they met. They were married in December 1947. Ten months later, I was born in an era referred to as: The Baby Boomer Years.

It was the year of the biggest election surprise in U.S. history: the 1948 Presidential race in which Democratic incumbent Harry Truman beat Republican New York Governor, Thomas Dewey. Polls predicted a

Dewey landslide. The newspapers printed the wrong headlines stating that Dewey defeated Truman. The U.S. population was 146,631,000 and the average American income was $3,187.00. I am sure my father made considerably less.

My parents were married in the small town of Moncks Corner. They rented a duplex in Saint Andrews Homes. It was a housing project of wood frame houses built in Charleston during the war.

Mr. and Mrs. Bowman lived in the other half of the duplex. They were newlyweds too. My parents formed a close friendship with the Bowmans.

I was born while my parents lived at Saint Andrews Homes. I was told that I rocked my crib against the wall at all hours of the day and night. Bob and Ruth Bowman used to think it was the headboard of my parent's bed.

1949

Age 1 – I don't have a lot of information to report for this year. My father bought an acre or two of land near Orange Grove Road. He began building a small cement blockhouse.

1950

Age 2 – We moved to Orange Grove Road. My father continued to work on our home.

The cement blocks were whitewashed and so were the tree trunks in the yard. Green metal awnings were over the windows, and the roof was covered with green slate tiles.

It was cold inside our house in the winter. The cement floor and concrete block walls seemed to absorb the cold winter weather. And, for some time, there was an outdoor shower behind the house and an outhouse in the woods of our backyard. My father bought a Sears and Roebuck kerosene heater and placed it between the kitchen and the bathroom. On the very cold winter nights, many heavy blankets were piled on the bed. My mother tucked the blankets in tight to keep me warm.

1951

Age 3 – I had a wooden rocking horse. I pretended to catch fish in the sand pile behind our house. There were not many homes around, but Kessler Groves became my best friend. He lived with his grandmother on Orange Grove Road.

1952

Age 4 – my sister, Loretta Anne Kornahrens, was born on January 8, 1952. I was only three years two months old when she was born, but I remember the day my father took me to the hospital to bring my mother and baby sister home. My mother was hot in the backseat of our 1948 Chevrolet with Loretta swaddled in a blanket. Loretta's face was pink and my mother cleaned some kind of gross mucus from her nose. Loretta slept in my old wooden crib that had pictures on the headboard.

My mother had a nervous breakdown. She was admitted into the Columbia State Hospital from February 15th to April 26th. My sister and I lived with relatives during that time.

While at my grandmother's, I hid under her house because I was confused and afraid. When my mother returned from the hospital, she was not well but she was better.

I wrecked my tricycle at Mrs. Grooms' house and hurt my head on the edge of a brick that was in her flower garden. Mrs. Grooms was Kessler's grandmother. The wound bled profusely and a doctor closed it with a metal clamp.

I am old enough to understand some things. My father flirted with women, and my mother was sick with jealousy. My parents had violent fights. My sister and I were born to a house of complication, drama and pain. We were southern.

1953

Age 5 – My father did not know how to deal with mother's mental illness and treated her badly. My mother's obsession and nagging was not tolerated by my father. His frustration came out in anger and violence.

I was a victim of physical cruelty. Both of my parents had violent tempers. They fought and I plead for them to stop. I tried to separate them, but I got slapped across the room. Knives were wielded and objects were often thrown. As the result of one of the fights, my mother had to have her lip stitched together. She was ashamed of the scar for many years. My father's frustration and anger often led to my many beatings. I would bleed from the wounds left on me from his leather belt. When my mother intervened, she became a victim of the hard lashes too. She would curl up like a hurt dog and the licks would take her breath away.

My father drank occasionally and visited the local bard. My mother was insanely jealous of a woman, by the name of Fowler, and sent me with my father as a spy. My father took me with him to the bars. He sometimes got drunk and sick. I was a worried child.

My father beat me very badly with a stick for playing with the other children in the Nicholson's yard. I believe my father had a difference of opinion with the Nicholsons. The Nicholsons threatened to call the police about the beatings. A stick broke off in my leg. My father told me that his father had beaten him with a bullwhip.

I helped feed my baby sister and remember her first steps. Her crib was in the front room near the door. I don't know why, but my father built two front doors on our house like a duplex. He later did away with one of the doors. When he added onto the house, I helped by carrying cement blocks to him. He put some coins in the wall and sealed it up.

Where we lived was considered to be the sticks even though we were close to Charleston. There were only a few homes around and all the roads were dirt except for the main highways. One afternoon, a small SCE&G utility truck ran over a very large diamondback rattlesnake. The driver parked the rear wheel of the truck on top of the snake. The snake bit the tire again and again. The tire was wet with venom. My father took me to see this. After the snake was killed, someone measured it to be a little over eight feet long.

This year was the end of another war. The Korean War was declared from 1950 to 1953. Some 54,246 Americans died as a result.

While playing in the yard, it was very common to see a blimp or a group of old war planes fly over from the airport. Sometimes early in the morning, an odorous stink would settle in with the fog from the West Virginia Pulp and Paper Company. The Paper Company was located on the other side of the Ashley River as was the Charleston Airport.

During thunder storms, I observed the toads coming out of their hiding places and enjoyed the refreshing smell of ozone from the open windows. The sound of rain beating against the awnings was relaxing. After the rain, everything seemed to take on an aspect of new creation. The hummingbirds would visit the Mexican rose bush, the birds would sing, the frogs would chirp, and the bumblebees and butterflies would rush from one moist flower to another. Both plant and animal seemed to be pleased and sometimes a beautiful rainbow, in all its grand colors, would arch across the sky.

1954

Age 6 – I attended my first year of school. My mother, a Catholic, enrolled me into the Blessed Sacrament Catholic Elementary School. On my first day of school, I worried more for my mother than for myself. The nuns, dressed in black, seemed nice enough. My mother stayed on the school grounds for most of the day. I assured her that I was okay. I had not attended preschool or kindergarten.

After the first day, I began riding the school bus. It was a lonely experience to ride the bus and attend the catholic school. Kessler and all my other friends got on one bus, while I got on the parochial school bus all alone. I wanted to go to school with my neighborhood friends. I knew none of the children at the Blessed Sacrament School. Most of the children, who attended the Catholic School, lived in the Avondale area. They played with one another after school. When they made plans or spoke of their activities, I was not part of it. I felt alien to my school. At home my neighborhood friends would discuss their activities at the public school. Again, I felt the gap of difference between us. I wanted to be accepted but it seemed that bridges were being burned between the relationships.

During that first year of school, I caught the mumps, measles, chicken pox and a few other viral infections. I also had my tonsils removed. I sensed many peculiar odors at the hospital. Dr. Wilson put me to sleep for the operation by placing what appeared to be a kitchen strainer, filled with cotton, over my nose and dripped ether into it. After the operation, my throat was very sore. My parents bought me a toy PT boat.

My parents bought my sister and I a white rabbit for Easter. One evening our dogs, Muff and Puff, killed the rabbit in the front yard. My father lost his temper and told my mother to take me and Loretta inside the house. While I stood beside my mother in the kitchen, I heard my father fire his shotgun twice. Sometime later, I heard my father say he wished he hadn't killed the dogs.

One afternoon, when my father returned from work, he was carrying a little Chihuahua puppy. We named her Tiny. I became very attached to that little dog. When she was old enough, she was mated with a male Chihuahua. I didn't understand why the two dogs were hooked together. I asked my father and he told me that he tied them together with a rubber band. His answer made me believe he was being cruel to Tiny.

For some reason my father had to go to the radio station on Orange Grove Road. My mother insisted that I go along, so he took me and Tiny with him. While outside at the station, Tiny browsed around. A big tomcat stalked her, probably mistaking her for a rabbit or something, because she was so small. The cat pounced on her and she fought back with all her might. We rushed to break up the fight. Tiny had a lot of spunk. My father treated her many wounds with mercurochrome.

Our house was built quite a distance from the road. Some dogs, from the neighborhood, had a habit of knocking over our trashcans and scattering the garbage. My father opened some shotgun shells, poured out the pellets, and refilled the empty shells with raw rice. He fired the rice-loaded shells at the dogs and ran them away.

My father worked hard and sometimes he and other men would stop by the house with the big Dodge Power Wagons. There were times when

Reflections Upon A Sunny Day

I went to work with my father. The big powerful truck and FM radio was quite impressive. I noticed that there were times when my father did not get along well with his boss. My father had to work in all kinds of weather. When the weather was at its worst, my father had to work all the harder. Sometimes my father would be gone for days at a time to repair broken lines during ice storms.

Every year, the South Carolina Electric and Gas Company held a party at their clubhouse on the Isle of Palms. Loretta and I would play with the other children for hours during the party. I enjoyed the party, but I did not like the route we took to get there. We would always have to cross the high Cooper River Bridge. I sat in the back seat, and I was too small to see much over the front seat. When we started up that tall bridge, my father would shift up into second gear and the front of our 1948 Chevrolet nosed up into the air. All I could see was the sky. The bridge had two-way traffic and all the cars were big as tanks. All the cars seemed to take up more than enough of the road.

I tried to stop my parents from fighting. I cried and pleaded with them. The front room was a mess. My father went outside and got in the car. My mother followed him with a brick in her hand. She slammed her hand through the car window with the brick. Her hand bled badly and required stitches.

I was often beaten and did not understand why. I felt a need for a safe place. I hid under my bed, and I had a special place in the woods that felt safe and peaceful.

My father made homemade beer. He had an old Coke chest cooler and a machine that sealed bottle caps. He used Nehi bottles for containers. It was a dark beer with a good taste.

My father took me to a Big Top Circus. The circus was set up on a dusty field. At the entrance of the big tent, my father bought me a large bag of popcorn. Before we went inside the tent, my father stopped to talk with someone he knew. There were some huge elephants standing behind me. The only thing separating me from them was a single strand of rope. It was late in the evening, so I stood near the rope to get a good look at the elephants. The elephants were taking a good look at me too. When I turned around to check and see if my father was still there, a huge elephant grabbed me and picked me up over the rope. It had me off the ground and its mouth was wide open. I thought the elephant was going to eat me. I yelled and one of the circus men made him put me down. My father was on the scene quickly. The man said the elephant wasn't going to hurt me; that it just wanted some popcorn. I held out the bag and the elephant grabbed my large bag of popcorn and tossed it in his mouth. He ate the whole thing.

1955

Age 7 – I repeated the first grade. It bothered me that I did not advance in the grade with my classmates.

My sister was three years old and still sucking a bottle. My mother gave Loretta and I beatings, but we did not bleed from them. Loretta's arm was sprained from a beating. I was afraid of my father's temper. I was a nervous child and bounced in the back seat of the car and rocked in my bed.

Sometimes when we had visitors, I was teased with the possibility of my parents selling my sister. It upset me.

Loretta tore up my comic books and personal things. When I fought with her, my father beat me. There was a strong division of love in my family. My father was devoted to my sister, while my mother was devoted to me.

While playing in my backyard, I tied a rope around two trees and twisted the handle of a sling blade between the rope very tightly. With a dozen or more twists of tension, the sling blade spun around and hit me in my head. It hurt me so badly that I feared I would die. I became sick and could not eat. I mentioned my accident to my mother in case I did die, but I did not let her know how seriously ill I felt. I was afraid of getting into trouble and being beaten.

I had to dig the septic tank lines for the sewer system with the fear of physical punishment if I did not make significant progress.

While the Bowman's were visiting, six-year old Patty Bowman fell into the open septic tank, which was half full of thick sewer. Patty, dressed in a pretty white dress, sank to her armpits in the awful mess. I feared the trouble and the beating that might come, but I ran to my parents and the Bowman's for help.

My father gave me strict orders to cut the grass in our large yard. I feared a beating if I could not start the lawnmower. It did not start easily for me. If I failed to satisfy my father, I was beaten and told to dry it up and be a man.

I was alone at home sometimes and got very hungry. I felt angry when I got hungry. I usually found a pack of wienies in the refrigerator.

My father bought me a Daisy pump BB gun for Christmas. I shot birds and cooked them outside on an open fire.

1956

Age 8 – I graduated the first grade. I wore Band-Aids and long sleeve shirts to school to cover the cuts of my beatings. My father's belt cut horseshoe prints in my skin. In the summer, when the sun tanned my skin, the scars turned white.

I feared my parents would get a divorce, and my mother would starve to death.

Reflections Upon A Sunny Day

I got a terrible headache after eating a burnt cheese sandwich. It may have been my first migraine.

I picked many bags full of blackberries. My feet were tough enough to walk over the thorny vines barefooted. I helped my mother roll dough for homemade pies. Loretta and I rolled out the leftover and cut out little pies with bottle caps. My mother baked them along with the blackberry pies. They looked like oyster crackers.

When Kessler and I got into an argument, my mother forced me to beat him up.

I accidentally caught a five-gallon can of gasoline on fire while making play candles in my backyard. I fought the fire with the water hose and put it out.

I felt sorry for the chickens when my father chopped off their heads. They flopped around spewing blood everywhere.

When our dogs came in heat, my father connected a 110-volt wire around the dog pen and set the ground with water. My father and I sat in the car when it was dark. He turned on the headlights when the male dogs touched the wire. They yelped and ran away.

1957

Age 9 – I graduated the second grade. The Catholic Nuns told my class that the round bread host was the real Holy Body of Christ and if we chewed it, the host would bleed in our mouth. My first Holy Communion was on March 2nd.

The nuns were very strict. We had to assemble in formation and march in ranks like the army. While in the classroom the nuns would not excuse the children to go to the bathroom, for it was a matter of discipline. The children were given orders to hold it. Many children wet their pants and cried. The nuns beat our hands with an oak ruler for punishment. It the ruler broke they really got mad. Sometimes they would turn the ruler sideways so the metal edge would cut your knuckles. The metal edge would sometimes separate from the ruler.

My parents' fights caused much frustration. My mother would get angry and say, "I'm gonna tell your daddy when he gets home." I would hide in the woods with the dread and fear of my name being called. When I did hear my name called, I reluctantly came out for fear of being beaten harder and longer if I did not obey. My mother would yell, "That's enough Fred," but he wouldn't stop until his anger ran its course. When my mother intervened, there were more fights and arguments.

My father sold our home on Orange Grove Road. In the process of moving, my father put me to work in the attic. He had me remove the

"Rock Wool" insulation from between the rafters. It was like fiberglass but worse. I itched like crazy.

My parents rented a duplex near Dupont Road. I missed my neighborhood friends a lot.

My grandmother, Cirsosky, died June 11th.

1958

Age 10 – I graduated the third grade. One of the children got sick in class. The nun made the little girl clean up her own vomit while everyone else watched.

Mrs. Flanigan drove my school bus for years. The catholic school had Mack school buses and the carburetors were not governed as were the public school buses. Mrs. Flanigan drove like a bat flying out of hell. On straight roads, she would stretch the Mack bus out to speeds over 75 miles per hour. She took curves so fast that children were flung from their seats, if they didn't hold on. When she hit holes in the road, the children riding in the back seat would bounce to the roof. One day, when she came flying into the schoolyard, she ran over a little boy. The bumper knocked him skidding across the asphalt. He bled a lot and appeared seriously injured. The boy was in the hospital for a long time.

On March 11th, an Atomic bomb fell from a B-47 on Mars Bluff, a farming community six miles from Florence, South Carolina.

I had an argument with my sister. My father beat me. I hid in my bedroom closet. He beat me again.

The lady next door was nice. Her infant baby choked while lying on its back. I ran in the kitchen and quickly warned her.

I helped my father nail the flooring down in the new house he was building. He built two front doors on this house too. We moved to Magnolia Ranch on May 3rd. My dog, Tiny, died that night. I cried and my heart hurt so badly. I prayed that she would be in heaven when I got there. My father made a cement tombstone marker for her grave.

Bobby Smoak was my age and lived next door. Bobby became my best friend, but I still thought of Kessler often.

Hewitt Beauvea lived in Magnolia Ranch and attended the Blessed Sacrament School. We were in the same grade. Hewitt did not play with Protestant children. I played with him sometimes, but his parents were not friendly.

Hurricane Gracie hit Charleston, South Carolina. The floodwaters reached our back porch and many things floated away.

The teenage boys in the neighborhood called my father "Bigfoot." He threatened to kick their ass' to the moon.

On a rare occasion, my sister and I played in bed with my father. He smothered me. I could not breathe and feared he would kill me. He released me only after I scratched his nose. I felt that he did not want me to play with them.

I crawled under the house and found the space under the back porch that gave me a sense of peace and security.

1959

Age 11 – I graduated the fourth grade. The nuns told my class that we should hate the Jews because they killed Jesus Christ. They also told us not to play with the Protestant children in our neighborhood. The nuns told my class that you cannot go to heaven unless you are a Catholic. They told us, if you did not believe in the teachings of the Holy Catholic Church, you were a heretic. I was taught to be prejudice.

I had a religion class everyday. My class was marched to the church several times a week for mass, stations of the cross and confession. We were taught to confess our sins to the priest and he would forgive them by giving penance – assigned repetitious Hail-Marys and Our-Fathers.

We were taught, from the Catholic religion books, that sins were broken down into two groups: Venial and Mortal. If you died with venial sins on your soul, you went to Purgatory until you suffered enough for your sins to be accepted into heaven. If you died with a mortal sin on your soul, you went to Hell.

The Catholic Church had bingo games and an annual bazaar. We were given serial numbered collection envelopes and coin cards to take home and be filled. We were told of the special blessings we would get if we left our belongings to the church when we died. And, there was a collection box under the votive candles, so you could pray to your patron saint.

The boys in my neighborhood teased me about my school. They asked me why I prayed to a statue on the school grounds. My class had to march outside to a shrine and pray to the statue of Virgin Mary.

The nuns were rigid. They trained us to sit, stand and kneel on command with a metal clicker called a cricket.

The TV show, the Untouchables, was popular with my classmates. Hewitt made a silencer for his .22 caliber Crossman air rifle out of hardware, cloth and cotton.

I was self-conscious about a mole on my face. I did not feel good about myself. Sometimes I felt sorry about ever being born. I sat in the chair on the back porch and rocked for hours.

I was trained from birth to love Jesus and to hate niggers with all my heart.

1960

Age 12 – I graduated the fifth grade. I had great difficulty paying attention in class. My attention span was very short. My teacher, Mrs. Sykes, made fun of me. She made me do things that had nothing to do with what was going on in the classroom.

Someone made fun of the way I laughed. I didn't want to ever laugh again. I never wanted to cry again either.

My parents took me and Loretta to the Magnolia Drive-In Theater. My father sent me to the concession stand. I bought the items and returned to the car with everything packed in a small box. The ice cream was soft and practically falling off the stick. My father asked me if I had been fooling around playing and let it melt. He was mad and ready to beat me. I had come straight from the concession stand and I told him so. I followed him back to the concession stand. He threw the food at the cashier, in front of dozens of people, and cursed everyone out.

Aunt Louise and Virginia, my mother's sisters, visited our home. They flirted with my father in the kitchen. My father flirted back and teased my mother. My mother got mad and had a violent fight with Virginia. They broke a chair and rolled and fought on the floor. It was a terrible scene.

My mother became sick and wandered around in the front yard shouting and singing at the top of her voice. She blessed the flower bushes and everything with the sign of the cross. A stranger was standing at the pond across the road and saw her strange behavior. My father walked across the road to speak with him. My father told the man that my mother had lost her mind. The man said, "It is a shame." He said to my father "You look familiar to me." My father talked with the man for a while, then the man said, "I know where I've seen you before." My father asked him "where?" The man said, "You were the man raising hell about the ice cream at the Magnolia Drive-In." My father was shocked and I could tell he was embarrassed.

My mother had a nervous breakdown. She did strange and crazy things. My father hog-tied her in the bedroom and stuffed pills down her throat. I was shocked at the sight of my mother being tied up on the floor. She was thirsty and had defecated on herself. I untied her and gave her water. My father tied her up again. I was upset and he tied me up.

My mother was admitted into the Columbia State Hospital from June 6th to July 8th.

I lived with my grandmother for a while. I found an old Crack Shot .22 caliber rifle in a junk pile near her house.

While running on a wet slick cement walkway at Bobby Smoak's house, I flipped and landed on my head. The impact knocked me out. My sister helped me home. I was dizzy and everything looked dark and blurry. I had a concussion and could not stay awake. I lost my awareness of time and location.

Bobby, Danny, Drayton, John, Paul, and myself made wooden carts that looked like go-carts. We used whatever kind of axle and wheels we could find and steered the front axle with a rope. We took turns pushing them or pulled them with a bicycle. Occasionally, we talked an adult into pulling us with a car. One day, while we were all playing with the carts on Fruitwood Avenue, Mr. Brunson walked out to the road to watch us. He was holding a can of beer. His face was red and his nose was practically glowing. We crowded around him and begged him to give us a pull. He slurred, "Alright tie them all together and hokum up to ma trailer hitch". He backed his

1954 Chevy out onto the road and waited for us to hookup. We were all screaming in excitement, "Give us a fast ride, give us a fast ride." He gunned that old Chevy several times until it screamed and blew carbon out the tailpipe, then he started to pull us. The lead rope popped and we had to re-tie it. Then we took off again. He built up speed and when we took the curve at Mr. Woods' house, we were setting a new speed record. I was on the end and when my cart came around the curve, I slid off the road into Mr. Loveday's ditch but steered it out. Mr. Brunson slowed down to turn onto Parsonage Road. On previous occasions, Drayton's rope had a habit of breaking. His cart was the one tied to the trailer hitch, and now that rope held strong. Mr. Brunson made the turn and floored the gas pedal. In moments we were flying on the rock surfaced road. My rear tires spun with so much speed until the rubber expanded and left the steel rims. It was late evening, almost dark, and sparks were flying from my rims. Some of the other carts lost wheels and sparks, sand and exhaust carbon stung my face. My cart whipped from one side of the road to the other because I was on the end and my rims were skidding. It was a miracle I did not hit a mailbox. We were screaming to stop, but Mr. Brunson could not hear us. Drayton's brother-in-law saw us go by, when we had turned onto Parsonage Road, and saw we were out of control. He built dirt track racecars and his 1955 Chevy was souped up. Somehow he got around me and ran Mr. Brunson down. We stopped and disconnected what was left of our carts and never asked for a fast ride again.

1961

Age 13 – I graduated the sixth grade. I barely passed my grades. I have trouble learning and cannot concentrate. I feel stupid. The nuns made some of the children wear a dunce cap.

Reflections Upon A Sunny Day

Mr. Crowley took me deer hunting on a four thousand acre plantation in Ravenel, South Carolina. The caretaker of the property, Mr. Harry Lee Wilkerson, gave me a ride on the back of an 8N Ford tractor equipped with half-tracks. He took me to his house. Mrs. Wilkerson was washing dishes on the back porch. She gave me a glass of water. Some dirty little girls were playing behind the house. The wood frame house was painted dark green with a red tin roof. I hunted with my father's .410 pump shotgun. The shells were reloaded with 00 buckshot.

My family was different from the one's of my friends. Seldom did any children visit me or my sister to play. My father would not hesitate to beat me in front of my friends. My mother would not think twice about being very rude and ill tempered with my friends. My mother has visions and hears voices. She is suspicious and paranoid. She is schizophrenic; hallucinates; has delusions and suffers manic depression.

My mother became sick. My father tied her up and played doctor with her pills. He did not handle the situation properly. I wanted to help but did not understand my mother's illness. I did not know what to do, so I tried to comfort her. I begged her to lay down and try to sleep. I followed her around so she wouldn't get herself into trouble or hurt. I tried to quiet her down when she was outside in the yard screaming and singing at the top of her voice. She had mood swings from being as gentle as a lamb to being as offensive as a wildcat. She went outside naked and mumbled incoherently. Her illness left a deep impression on my life.

My mother was admitted into the Columbia State Hospital from September 7th to October 5th. While in the hospital, she had electric shock treatments. As a result of the treatments, part of her memory was erased from her mind.

My father took my sister and I to the State Hospital. It was not a pleasant place to visit. There were many locked metal doors and the presence of insanity was predominant. Men and women shuffled along with a faraway look in their eyes. Some of them wore straight jackets. My mother behaved like a child who was being mistreated. She wanted to come home so badly. My mother clung to me desperately with her blue veined hands and begged me not to leave her there. She pleaded with me to take her home. I wanted to help but didn't know how. I felt sick with grief.

1962

Age 14 – I graduated the seventh grade. My Catholic Confirmation Ceremony was on March 15th. My Confirmation name was "David". David was real and imaginary to me. For years, I often felt myself to be David, for he was intelligent, happy and without any problems.

I was fearful of being outspoken for fear of appearing stupid. Silence did not reveal ignorance, so I thought. I did not get a head start at home to be prepared for school and the world. My father taught only discipline. My mother fed and clothed me, but she could not teach me the things I would need to know. My mother did not know what country she lived in.

Reflections Upon A Sunny Day

I played football with the Saint Andrews Playground for a while, and my father told my mother that there was something wrong with me.

I worried and my heart ached when my mother showed signs of getting sick, I had migraine headaches.

I felt lonely and often sat on the back porch humming an unknown tune while rocking in the rocking chair. My cat and bantam chickens kept me company. They were my friends.

I caught a dog in the act of killing my ducks. My father was home. I asked him what to do? He said, "Shoot the dog!" I shot the dog.

At home and school, I was trained exquisitely in the fine art of obedience. My father did not like my friend, Paul Williams, and made me beat him up. I did not want to hurt Paul, but my father took his belt off and threatened to beat me if I did not obey.

On another occasion, my father tied my hands together and beat me in the garage. A great sadness bivouacked in my heart again. I burned with the despair that slips up on the powerless and disinherited. Something in me was dying, but there was nothing I could do about it.

Tears would flow out of my eyes but my expression would never change. I learned to grieve in silence.

1963

Age 15 – I graduated the eighth grade. It was my last year in the Blessed Sacrament Catholic School. I feared my father's command to get up in the morning for school. I got up quickly to avoid a beating.

My father got seriously hurt on the job with the South Carolina Electric and Gas Company. While hanging a heavy transformer on a forty-foot utility pole, the pole uprooted from the ground and fell with my father at the top. A canal had been dug nearby, which weakened the earth around the pole. The pole fell across the utility truck. The impact caused my father's head to strike the heels of his boots, as his safety belt whipped his back to a snapping stop.

My father signed papers relieving the SCE&G Company of all responsibility. The SCE&G Company gave him a small check and papers relieving him of his job. My father lost his job after working 16 years for the SCE&G Company. He was sick and weak from the accident. I feared my mother would have another nervous breakdown. I feared that we would not have the money to pay bills, the house payment, or to buy food.

My father went to an attorney and had papers drawn up to take my mother's name off the house and property. My father coerced my mother into a lawyer's office, but she refused to sign the papers. My father got mad and abandoned her downtown in the city of Charleston. My father got mad at me because I defended her. My mother was showing signs of getting sick again. The strain of it all had an effect on me. I feel that I had a mental breakdown.

This year of school was very confusing for me. I was disoriented and forgot where my classes were located. I couldn't remember if I had a wall locker, nor could I remember the subjects I was taking. I knew something was wrong but didn't understand what was happening. My reality seemed to be a dream. I was disoriented at home too. Sometimes I was David and for a little while things seemed better. My mother noticed that something was wrong with me. She had appetite pills prescribed for me by Dr. Wilson. My mother felt that food would cure whatever was wrong with me.

1964

Age 16 – I graduated the ninth grade at Saint Andrews Junior High School. I went to summer school for English.

My father had medical problems, headaches and weakness, from his accident. He re-mortgaged our home and went into business for himself. He rented an old building in Summerville and opened Fred's Auto Electric. The starter and generator repair seemed to keep him busy, but he moved his business to North Charleston with, J.C., his brother. He did not do well there, so he rented an old building in Pierpont and opened Hwy. 61 Auto Parts. This business was successful, but the building needed remodeling. My father did minor mechanic work, rebuilt starters and generators, and sold gasoline and auto parts. After the business was established, my father hired a man to operate the station and started working for the Charleston Naval Shipyard as an electrician. My father had to give up his job at the Shipyard and return to the station. The man he hired was stealing money from the business.

I did 600 consecutive pushups. Coach Kicklighter asked me to join the track team, but I quit to work for my father in the evenings. I worked for my father on weekends too. One Saturday morning, while at the station alone, a man sexually assaulted me. I fought him off. I felt sure about being stronger than the man, but was afraid of getting into trouble if I hurt him. I told my father about what happened, but he didn't do anything.

My friend Bobby Smoak moved away. His parents got a divorce. I missed Bobby. He gave me his black and white cat named Smoaky. He was always catching rats and dragging rabbits in the yard. I saw him catch a bird in mid-air when it got too close. When I was on the back porch watching the tide come in, he would climb up in my lap. My father spread some powdered chlordane on the ground in the garage, and Smoaky walked through it. Smoaky licked his paws and the poison went to work. It turned him into a skinny rack of bones. He ate a bird and it didn't digest. It came out of his bowls with the feathers still on the meat. Smoaky died a slow death.

After Bobby moved I tried to befriend Danny Murray, but in all the time we spent together he wasn't a trustworthy friend.

Pam Hudson was my new neighbor. She was about a year younger than myself. We spent some time together.

1965

Age 17- I did not graduate the tenth grade at Saint Andrews High School. I did not like my U. S. History class. The teacher assigned enormous amounts of homework and the class was tested on the assignments. There were no instructions or lectures in class, just a blackboard full of homework assignments each day. I worked for my father after school and didn't have the time for so much homework.

My father bought me a 1954 Ford. He paid thirty-five dollars for it. I completely rebuilt a 292 cubic inch Thunderbird engine and mounted it in the Ford.

There were thick wood timbers, with inch and a half holes bored at intervals, mounted on the wall of the High School Gym. Wood dowels fit into the holes. We called it a peg-board. It's purpose was to develop upper body strength by climbing up and down the wall with a wood dowel in each hand. You could not use your feet for support. I broke the school record in the consecutive number of times I climbed around the peg-board. I was also an undefeated wrestler.

I had been to a dentist only once in my life. When I broke my big toe in the surf at Folly Beach, I didn't have anyone treat it until it looked like it was going to rot off. I caught the Asian Flu and got very sick. When I asked for a penicillin shot, my father scorned me and made me feel guilty as sin.

Throughout the years, my mother had episodes of becoming sick and getting better. It was a lonely and depressing experience for me. I worried in concern for her, for if she pulls through this time it seems only a matter of time before it happens again.

My mother became sick again. My father did not believe in wasting money on doctors. He continued to tie my mother up and stuff pills down her throat. I pleaded with him to take her to the doctor. My mother had another nervous breakdown and was admitted into the Columbia State Hospital from July 4th to August 14th.

I dated Sylvia Kennedy.

Society took cancer and heart disease seriously but largely ignored mental illness; moreover, a high degree of emotional tumult in a family is prone to cause relapse.

There were times when I could not carry on a conversation without changing from one subject to another with a frenzy of words and wild ideas.

1966

Age 18 — I graduated the tenth grade at Murray Vocational High School. I took Social Studies; Machine Shop; Metallurgy and Blue Print Reading. The U.S. History Class was a lot better.

I was too strong to accept anymore of my father's beatings, so I ran away from home. I slept in my car or at a friend's house. I came back home when my father got over his rage.

When my mother became sick, I became very concerned for her. My heart was filled with worry, and I followed her around to make sure she didn't get hurt. She trusted me and would listen to my persuasive suggestions. I helped her but she became sick and had a nervous breakdown. She was admitted into the Columbia State Hospital from January 8th to February 9th. My mother was assaulted and raped at the hospital.

My father had an argument with a man at Moody's Bar and wanted me to beat up his son.

I felt so alone. I felt nothing inside and took extraordinary and dangerous risks without fear of dying. Nothing mattered anymore.

I could use the boat anytime, so I spent a lot of time in the river. Every sandbar and oyster bank was familiar to me. One day, while running the boat at full speed near our house, my father hit an alligator. The alligator was hit with such force that it broke the motor loose from the transom and flipped it into the boat with the propeller spinning at six thousand revolutions per minute. It could have been a fatal accident. Bill Windam killed the alligator and ate its tail. The motor had cut the gator's front leg off. My father had to get the motor clamp welded back together.

I dated Sylvia Kennedy, Pat Robinson and Linda DeMille.

I grew up a river boy with the smell of the great salt marsh predominant in sleep. My childhood was one of disorder, peril, and small craft warnings.

I felt there had always been a problem with me when I was growing up, but an unmentionable one, my terrible secret. I had always felt different, unsafe, and alone because of it. I became a prisoner of lost time and unremembered days. I tried to give the appearance of normality even though I was different from the very beginning.

1967

Age 19– I graduated the 11th grade at Murray Vocational High School. The draft board had an interest I me.

Before my senior year, I was acutely aware of the distinct possibility that I might die in Vietnam for reasons that were rather unclear to me. Vietnam did not make any sense to anyone. Thousands of young Americans were dying there for no reason. I went to the National Guard Armory and placed my name on their waiting list.

The Atlantic Richfield Company built a new station in Pierpont and offered to buy my father's business and give him management of the new Atlantic Station. My father accepted their deal.

When the Sewage Plant was built in Pierpont and Springfield, the public was told the waste would be clean and would actually help the water. That was a lie. I saw the raw sewage, turds and prophylactics, churning in the tides. There was a major fish kill but it didn't make any news. The tide flowed in and out with tons of fish floating belly up.

I bought a 1957 Chevrolet. It was a classic Bel Air two-door hardtop. The engine was removed and torn down. I completely rebuilt it and had many high performance parts to use such as: port and polished heads, special valve springs, solid lifters, Duntov .030 - .030 camshaft, Delco dual point distributor, high velocity oil pump, lightweight flywheel, high-rise intake manifold, and a modified Carter AFB 4-barrel carburetor. The car ran very well. Brown and Brown Body Shop painted it with the original colors: aqua-blue with a white top.

For nearly a year a cherry bomb lay on top of my bedroom dresser. One afternoon I decided to get rid of it. I carried it to the back porch and prepared to light it. I noticed that the fuse was short. I put a box of matches between my teeth and struck a match. I lit the fuse and the cherry bomb exploded almost immediately in my hand. It made me angry. My neck was cut and my hand was in shreds. It took a long time for my hand to heal.

I dated Pat Robinson and Wanda Purmort.

I was filled with an inconsolable loneliness. On weekend mornings, I got in the car and went for a drive. I drove around and in a way I felt I was searching for something.

1968

Age 20 – I graduated the twelfth grade of Murray Vocational High School. I enrolled in the Trident Technical Education Center. My subjects were Tool and Die, Trigonometry and Metallurgy. I also worked at Avco Lycoming as a machinist. I went to school during the day and worked nights at Avco.

I traded my 1957 Chevrolet in and bought a 1968 Dodge Super Bee. I drove this car 160 miles per hour on country roads. The new Dodge gave me a lot of mechanical and electrical problems.

I became physically ill, when I thought Wanda was pregnant. She was good to me and with much regret, I am sorry I wasn't satisfied with her.

In November, Patty Jo Wilkerson visited the Atlantic Station and left her telephone number with my father for me to call. I called the long distance number and we made a date. I knew Patty Jo's sister, Janet, who was married to Ira Byrd. Ira was a regular customer of the Atlantic Station, and we often met in the river when boat riding and water skiing.

I had no idea where Patty Jo lived. She gave me directions to follow 162 through Hollywood, South Carolina. I stopped at a small gas station and asked someone for further directions to find her house. I found the dirt road that I was looking for and followed it for over a mile. I couldn't believe my eyes. It was the same dark green wood frame house with the red tin roof that I had been to years before. My previous visit to this house was from Hwy 17 – the opposite direction on the dirt road.

I met Patty Jo's parents again. Mr. Wilkerson was hot and dirty from control burning a section of the woods.

On our first date, we went to the Sea Side Pavilion on the Isle of Palms. Patty Jo was engaged to a man in Greenville, S. C. at the time.

My friend, Bobby Smoak, had moved away but we saw one another every once in a while. We had shared a lot of time together in the sand pile playing with toy trucks and the like, when we were neighbors. I saw Bobby one last time. His head was swollen and caked with make-up as he lay in a coffin. Bobby had put the barrel of a .22 caliber rifle in his mouth and pulled the trigger. I was a pallbearer at his funeral. His death disturbed me greatly.

1969

Age 21 – I was enrolled in the Trident Technical Education Center. I worried about the serious threat of being drafted into the Army. I went to the Federal Building and took the US. Air Force entrance exam. I passed the test and was making plans to join the Air Force.

In February, SFC Sam Ramsey called me and asked if I was still interested in joining the South Carolina Army National Guard. I enlisted in the National Guard on March 8th. When I received my orders for active duty, I dropped out of TEC, took a leave of absence from Avco, sold the Dodge and bought a 1962 Chevy Super Sport. I worked for my father until it was time for me to report for active duty.

Patty Jo worked for the South Carolina National Bank as a new accounts clerk. She visited me everyday at the Atlantic Station during her long lunch break. Patty and I were engaged in May.

In June, I reported for active duty training at Fort Bragg, N. C. with the 82nd Airborne Division. When I arrived at the Basic Combat Training Company, the Drill Instructors fell on us in a crazed venomous pack, when we stepped off the bus. They put their hot breath against our necks and ears and roared into them, abusing, loathing, hitting and violating us trying to break us down to creatures less than human — less than they were. The DI's plan was to rip civilization from our backs as through it were nothing more than strips of skin. Their aim was to change us by breaking down every single vestige of civilization and society we had brought to protect and sustain us. They would tame us like a beast of the field before they remade us in their own fierce image and trained us to kill in a hundred different ways.

The training was hard, but I earned a weekend pass for firing the highest score in the battalion with a M-14 rifle. Patty Jo came to see me during my training and again with my parents, when I graduated combat training. After graduating BCT at Fort Bragg, I received orders to report to Fort Lee, Virginia for Advanced Individual Training. In October, I completed the courses of Stock Control and Accounting and Special Automotive Supply. After graduating AIT at Fort Lee, I received orders to report to Support Company 1st Battalion 118th Infantry stationed at the SCNG Armory in North Charleston, South Carolina.

In November, Patty Jo and I rented an apartment in Pierpont. On November 15th, we had a large Church wedding in the Ravenel Baptist Church. We visited the mountains of North Carolina on our honeymoon.

1970

Age 22 – I changed my entire life for my wife. I joined her church – the Ravenel Baptist Church. I gave up my friends for her friends, and I rarely saw my relatives but were with hers constantly.

Reflections Upon A Sunny Day

My father and Mr. Smoak opened the Brentwood Seafood and Steak House. I don't know if Mr. Smoak invested any money in this venture, but he was to manage the restaurant while my father continued to operate the Atlantic Station.

Patty Jo withdrew $2000.00 from our savings account at SCN and made a down payment on a 64- foot mobile home. Somehow, the withdrawal was shown as a deposit. I don't know if she corrected the error. We set the trailer up in Ravenel near her parents. Her father was caretaking a 4000-acre plantation for Mr. Malcolm D. Haven.

We sold our cars and bought a new Volkswagen. The Buchanan VW dealership charged us for valve cover gaskets each time the valves were adjusted during warranty services. The car began burning oil. Sand, from the long dirt road we lived on, got into the engine through the top of the valve cover. The engine was dismantled at the dealership. The valve cover proved to be the original equipment gasket installed at the factory in Germany. The dealership cheated us. I had to pay $300.00 for the repair, because they did not replace the valve cover gaskets I had been paying for all along. After they rebuilt the engine, it still burned oil. They probably left sand in the oil pump. I took it back to the dealership. They wanted me to pay more money, but I refused. Mr. Buchanan agreed to work on the engine again but advised me to get rid of it.

Patty Jo talked about the assistant manager of SCN everyday. She wanted Pam Ohlant's job at the bank.

I shot a 12 1/2 foot alligator after it ate our German shepherd dog. I counted thirteen alligators in the twenty-five acre pond next to our trailer. Also, a wild black hog habitually rooted up our driveway during the night. I got hurt, while hunting hogs, and thirteen stitches were needed in my face.

Avco Lycoming was laying off a lot of people. I began looking for another job. The S.C. National Guard had an accepted federal civil service job opening in North Charleston. I applied and was hired as a federal employee under the Department of Army for the SCNG. I worked with Sam Ramsey as an AST – Administrative Supply Technician. A few weeks later, the U.S. Customs Agency called me to start working with them. I regret turning them down.

While at Joyce Avant's, Patty Jo's sister, I saw Jon Avant for the first time. As we were leaving her house, I noticed that Patty Jo had an interest in him.

Patty Jo became pregnant in June. She became very irrational and hostile towards me. She blamed me for her misery.

Patty Jo constantly talked about her friends. She had paranoia about her social standing in the community, and she felt that she was better than anyone in her town.

Mr. Wilkerson and I had a very close relationship. We helped one another, and we hunted and fished together. Mrs. Wilkerson was lazy and complained a lot.

I raised a baby squirrel that had fallen from its nest. I let him go when he was fully grown.

My job with the SCNG was demanding and the paperwork was overwhelming.

I could not hold my parents accountable or indict them for crimes they could not help. They, too, had a history – one that I remembered with both tenderness and pain. In families there should be no crimes beyond forgiveness. I wanted to re-create "my" family, make improvements, succeed where they failed. I wanted to change history.

1971

Age 23 – My wife went to Dr. Wilson for birth control pills before we were married, but she did not take them as prescribed. Her term of pregnancy was difficult, and I fell prey to her frequent attacks of verbal abuse. During her contractions, she squeezed my hand with a strength that surprised me. I stayed at her side comforting her until it was time to go into the delivery room.

My son, Joseph Wilkerson Kornahrens, was born on March 27th. I decided between naming my son, Joseph or Fred, with the flip of a quarter. The middle name of my son, I gave from a man whom I admired as a father-in-law and a dear friend who was not blessed with a son of his own, Mr. Harry Wilkerson.

We called our son Joey. His leg was a little crooked at birth. We put a brace on his leg at night until it straightened. I was proud of my son.

We sold our mobile home to Scooter and Shirley Simmons. Patty Jo and I rented a house on Savage Road.

We traded in the Volkswagon and bought a 1969 Chevelle. I also bought a Honda SL-350cc motorcycle.

Jack Parker came to our house in a hysterical state of mind. He was troubled about his failed marriage. He told me that he took an overdose of pills. I took him to the V.A. Hospital. My sister quit school and married Jack in 1969.

Mr. Smoak talked a good story about how he could manage the Brentwood Seafood and Steakhouse, but all he did was sit in the back of the restaurant drinking whiskey while the employees carried off all the food and money. My father repaid his first bank loan, but he suffered a big loss in the restaurant business. He sold his lease with Atlantic Richfield and borrowed more money to reopen the restaurant.

1972

Age 24 – We bought a brick home in James Island. Patty Jo's half brother, Carl Southwell, lived on the same street.

I sold my motorcycle to my brother-in-law, Ira Byrd, and we bought a 1969 Ford Fairlane

Someone stole my 20 hp Mercury outboard motor.

Patty Jo became pregnant in February.

I was admitted into the hospital for emergency kidney surgery Dr. Paul Sanders removed a kidney stone. I had trouble with my kidney for a long time.

Patty Jo was working at the First National Bank. She worked there for a while and quit. Patty Jo told me that she didn't like the people who worked there. (In 1985, Attorney William Runyon told me she was fired for stealing over $2000.00).

I changed jobs. I transferred to Summerville for a promotion. I worked at Det 1, Co B 1st Bn 118th Infantry alone as an AST.

Patty Jo was pregnant and had the mumps. She went into labor, and I took her to Dr. Stosnoski. He gave her a shot to try and stop the labor. It did not work. I held her hand in the labor room. Her face was swollen like a frog.

My son, Fred Herman Kornahrens IV, was born November 13th. Patty Jo was contagious and had to be quarantined in a private room. She got little care from the nurses. They had to handle all objects: clothes, sheets, food, trays, etc., with gloves and facemasks. My son, Freddy, was born immune to mumps.

I watched Dr. Wilson circumcise Freddy in the hallway. I would have said something if I had know the procedure. Dr. Wilson had a nurse open Freddy's diaper and hold his hands back. Dr. Wilson pinched the end of Freddy's penis and cut the flesh off with a pair of scissors without any anesthetic. I guess doctors figure babies can't complain. Freddy's face turned blood red as he screamed. Then Dr. Wilson stitched him up carelessly.

Patty Jo said, "Let's call Joey and see who he will come to?" When Joey came to me, Patty Jo was more than displeased.

1973

Age 25 – Charleston had a rare snowstorm. We built a snowman in the front yard. The Summerville National Guard Armory was opened for stranded motorists. Army equipment was used to clear the highways and I-26.

Patty Jo stayed on the road a lot. Her family had a name for her, "Ramblin' Rose".

Joey was admitted into the hospital to have two lumps removed from the top of his head that looked like sprouting horns. He was two years old on March 27th.

My father's business, the Brentwood Seafood and Steakhouse failed. He lost a lot of money. He started working, again, for the Charleston Naval Shipyard as an electrician.

I sold the Chevelle and bought my father's 1967 Plymouth Sports Fury. It was in like new condition.

Occasionally, my parents kept our children while we went out for supper or a movie. Patty Jo had a strange habit of making the boys cry before we left. If the boys were content, Patty Jo would go to the door and say, "Mommy is leaving you." If the boys didn't respond with screams and tears, she would say it again more earnestly. They were sure to cry before we left, and then she would console them.

Patty Jo told me her sister, Linda, died of carbon monoxide poisoning a couple of years before we were married. Patty Jo told me that, after her death, Linda visited her a few times while in her bedroom.

Patty Jo told me that she lived with her sister, Joyce, in Greenville for a while. It was at that time she became engaged to a man named, Herman Stroud.

Patty Jo called little Freddy, "Fee Fee". He was one year old on November 13th.

I was a proud father. I dreamed of the days when my sons would play sports, of days we would toss a football around, and of days we would hunt and fish together as father and sons. I looked forward to each day, to see my boys grow and learn to be a success in life. I wanted a special love and bond between me and my children. I wanted to share their joy and sorrows. I wanted to be a father they could trust and share their innermost feelings with. I wanted their unwavering love.

1974

Age 26 – My grandmother, Hattie Carter Kornahrens, born August 22, 1894, died on February 7, 1974. She was "Ma-Ma" to me and I loved her. There was a rumor that she was beaten, at the Columbia State Hospital, and died from the injuries.

We sold our home in James Island and bought a seventy-acre farm in Walterboro, South Carolina. The property was fenced with barbed wire. Approximately twenty acres was cleared for farming or pasture. There was a deep well, a utility shed, a stable and a two-story house under construction. The house was in need of brickwork outside and finish work inside.

Patty Jo's aunt died. We bought her estate consisting of an acre lot in Ravenel and an old house trailer. We sold the land for a profit, but the buyer still owed us three hundred dollars. We moved the trailer to Walterboro to live in while we worked on the house. We sold the trailer when we moved into the house.

My sister Loretta, remarried. She married, Thomas Osborne, a Sergeant in the Air Force. While Patty Jo and I were at the hospital waiting on my sister to have her first child, our dog, Bruno, mauled our neighbor's hogs.

Patty Jo stepped out the back door and saw a large rattlesnake on the ground. I watched the snake while she brought my gun. I shot the snake's head off.

Mr. Crosby planted my field in corn and it made a fair crop. I had farm animals and bought a Farmall Super "C" tractor for a thousand dollars. It was old but ran like brand new.

I received a telephone call from the Walterboro Police Department. My wife, Patty Jo, was arrested for check forgery. I went to the police department and they released her. Patty Jo was gruff with me when I asked her what happened. She later told me that she opened a checking account in her dead aunt's name and was caught writing checks in a store. I don't know why she did it.

Patty Jo received a credit card in the mail from the SCN Bank. About a month later, I received a bill from the bank for five hundred dollars. I asked Patty Jo about the bill. She told me that she had run into the back of Isaac Newton's car with the Plymouth while in Hollywood. I didn't know an Isaac Newton from Hollywood. Patty Jo told me she gave money to Mr. Newton and used the rest to repair the Plymouth. I inspected the Plymouth very carefully. It had not been wrecked. I didn't pursue the matter.

Patty Jo got legal custody of a teenage girl. Sandy had been in Reform School, and she was related to the Crosby Family. Patty Jo had a feud with the Crosby's. Sandy babysat our children for Patty Jo. When I came home from work, I often found Patty Jo and Sandy screaming at one another. I was tired of it and told them all the screaming and arguing would have to stop. Sandy buckled down and started making good grades in school. Patty Jo and Sandy had an argument about the Crosby Family. Sandy took an overdose of pills and was admitted into the hospital. Sandy didn't live with us anymore.

I sold the Fairlane and bought a 1968 Mustang. I sold the Mustang and bought a 1970 Chevrolet pickup truck.

Patty Jo worked the night desk at the Ramada Inn. I asked her not to work at night, but she would not listen to me. When the new Howard Johnson opened, she changed jobs and continued to work the night shift. The owner of the Howard Johnson hired an elderly couple that were his good friends, to manage the motel. Patty Jo shrewdly tried to alienate the owner's relationship with the elderly couple, so she could get their job as manager.

Patty Jo had a thirteen-year old black girl baby-sitting our children. The little girl was pregnant. Sometimes, Patty Jo left our children at the baby-sitters house. I went there one afternoon to pick up our children, and the stench coming from inside the house was awful. It smelled like they had been defecating on the floor for a long period of time.

I returned home from work and found my 14-foot fiberglass boat burnt to a crisp. It was a windy day. Patty Jo had a fire going in the fireplace and a spark flew out the chimney and set the field on fire. My boat and trailer were propped up on a fat-lighter pine tree stump to keep the rainwater out. The stump burned like an old truck tire and my boat went up in smoke with it. The boat was not insured.

My mother had a nervous breakdown. She was admitted into the Charleston County Hospital from October 23rd to October 28th. She was then admitted into the Medical College from October 28th to November 11th.

1975

Age 27 – Patty Jo told me about the prostitution that was going on at the motel. She told me about a highway patrolman who hung around her desk all the time. She told me he had a crush on her and often followed her home from work.

Captain Fuller W. Avant became the supervisor of the AST's in the First Battalion. No one liked his philosophy or personality. He had two AST's bury ammunition in the ground at Headquarters. An investigation was conducted when it was uncovered by a backhoe, while digging for gas lines. Captain Avant lied and swore the AST's buried the ammunition without his knowledge or consent. If there had not been a witness, the two AST's would have lost their jobs. Captain Avant received a week's suspension. He told SFC Ammons, of St. George, he could not go to church on Wednesday nights because it would be a conflict of interest with his job. He told SSG Pruett, of North Charleston, that he should give up being the leader of a boyscout troop for the same reason. And he told me I had to get his permission to plant a vegetable garden. Captain Avant gave me a lot of heartburn.

My mother had a nervous breakdown. She was admitted into the Columbia State Hospital from March 4th to March 18th.

The wires behind the stove caught fire. My brother-in-law, Carol Murdaugh, repaired the wire. He informed me that the wires in the house were a mess of loose splices everywhere. The switches in the den were always giving trouble.

I received a phone call one night from Shirley. She was crying and told me that my wife was with her husband. I called the Howard Johnson Motel and Patty Jo was not there. When Patty Jo came home, I asked her where she had been. She said, "At work all night." I said, "I called and you were not there." I was already upset from the long wait for her to come home and when she fired back with a mouthful of venomous lies, I slapped her face. She yelled with defiance that she was at work and had not seen Kenneth. I said, "Let's go over to the Kenneth and Shirley's and get to the bottom of this". Patty

Jo did not want to go, but I insisted. At their house, Patty Jo and Kenneth admitted to being together in a barn but swore they didn't do anything.

My father bought our Plymouth. Patty Jo had put a lot of miles on it I bought a 1972 Ford Pinto.

Patty Jo's half-sister Rae Edmondson, moved in our home. Rae was divorced, wild and liked to party. She was going out with a lot of men. Rae came home tired and drunk, and told Patty Jo about the wild time she was having. Patty Jo envied her sister and started following her around. Rae started dating Jerry Baldwin. He owned a shrimp boat.

Patty Jo was spending a lot of time away from home. I didn't know where to look for her. Jack Parker told me he knew and took me to a small brick house in Walterboro. I went inside and there were about eight half naked teenage boys and girls drinking beer, whiskey and smoking marijuana. I had never smoked marijuana and the thought of it appalled me. The house belonged to Jerry Baldwin. Jerry was about 45 years old. He walked into the room, wearing gold chains around his neck, without a shirt. I asked him if Patty Jo was there. I was told that she had left. I didn't see her car so I went home. I didn't know Patty Jo was hanging around with this crowd.

Rae Edmondson starting dating Billy Baldwin, Jerry's brother. Billy was married and owned a shrimp boat too. I was told that Billy was a board member on Colleton County Counsel. Billy told stories about himself, Saidi Limehouse and Governor Edwards. Billy often flew his plane over our house at treetop level.

Patty Jo was hanging around with a crowd that was smuggling drugs.

I sold the Farmall Super "C" and bought a Ford 2000 tractor. I sold the Farmall for $1200.00 and paid $2500.00 for the Ford.

Patty Jo talked in her sleep. She was talking to someone named Ted. I asked her about her dream, but she told me she didn't remember.

I went to Camp Shelby, Mississippi for two weeks active duty, with the National Guard. When I returned home, Patty Jo was not there. Rae and Billy told me that Patty Jo had left me for another man. I didn't know what to think. Billy and Rae attempted to line me up with another woman, but I could have no part of it. I wanted Patty Jo back.

Rae and Billy told me that Patty Jo ran off with a man who lived in Columbia. They told me his name was Ted. I later received a call from Patty Jo, and she told me she was at Myrtle Beach. I plead with her to come home. She agreed to meet me in Greenville at Frank and Millie's house. I drove straight to Greenville, with my heart in my throat, and waited for her at Millie's house. I was emotionally shattered. Patty Jo arrived late. She was obscure about her activities.

Patty Jo and I spent the night at Millie's house. We headed back home in the morning. Patty Jo followed me in her car, but to my surprise, she swung off the interstate at the Columbia exist. I went home. Patty Jo arrived much later and told me she had to stop and talk to Ted.

I woke up in the middle of the night with chest pains and couldn't breathe. I got up and the pain eased up. I went to the Summerville Hospital that morning. The doctor examined me and told me that I probably hyperventilated.

Patty Jo said, "Let's clear out of Walterboro." Patty Jo had made some enemies. I knew she didn't get along with the Crosby's, but this was something more. I asked Patty Jo about it, but she wouldn't tell me.

Patty Jo and I were at Mary Douglas' house in Charleston. We received a phone call and were told our house was on fire. We went to Walterboro and found our home burnt to the ground. The house was fully insured. We did not have a homeowner's policy. The insurance company told us it was an electrical fire. After the insurance company paid, I still owed money on the mortgage.

We rented a trailer at the Cloverleaf Trailer Park in Summerville. After a couple of months, we bought a home in Dorchester Regency, which was about a mile out of Summerville.

I visited my parent's home and found my mother tied up on the floor. I took her home with me and called her doctor. I took her to the hospital.

My mother had a nervous breakdown. She was admitted into the Charleston County Hospital from September 11th to September 19th.

1976

Age 28 – My son, Freddy, came to me, while I was shaving in he bathroom. His face was turning blue. I grabbed him quickly and dislodged a piece of candy from his throat.

I traded in the Pinto and bought a 1972 Ford LTD. I sold the truck and bought a 1971 Jeep. I bought a used Holiday Rambler Camper for $1000.00.

Jack Parker was attending TEC. I went there and used a shop lathe to make a rifle silencer for shooting deer in Walterboro. While there I met the supervisor of the U. S. Army Reserve AMSA Shop. (AMSA –Area Maintenance Support Activity)

I was still working as an AST in Summerville. The National Guard OMS 13 Shop had a job opening. Captain Avant and the overwhelming paperwork was a lot of pressure. I started working for WO Harold Way at the OMS Shop in Mt. Pleasant. (OMS – Organizational Maintenance Shop)

Patty Jo took the Camper to Edisto Beach, while I was on two weeks active duty. Patty Jo stayed at the beach for six weeks. On a warm night in June, my third child was conceived on a park table in the sand dunes. I believe Patty Jo would have stayed at Edisto Beach all summer.

My mother had a nervous breakdown. She was admitted into the Charleston County Hospital from June 28th to July 15th.

While Patty Jo was at Joyce Avant's house, her boys involved my children in homosexual acts.

My mother had another nervous breakdown. She was admitted into the Charleston County Hospital from November 27th to December 8th. It always upset me to see my mother get sick. On future occasions I was able to repress her sickness by taking her to the doctor for shots and medication.

1977

Age 29 – Patty Jo was pregnant. Billy Baldwin told Patty Jo that he would give her a thousand pounds of shrimp if she would name the baby after him. Patty Jo talked about those shrimp all the time. When Lisa was born, she had a birthmark on her leg. The birthmark looked like a shrimp.

My daughter, Lisa Michelle Kornahrens, was born on March 13th. She was born in the labor room of Trident Hospital. Dr. Perry was not there for the delivery. He cursed the nurse and told her she should have held Patty Jo's legs together until he got there. The delivery room was dirty. Dr. Perry cleaned Patty Jo out while she screamed in pain. He called her names and told her she couldn't feel a thing with the anesthetic. The nurse corrected Dr. Perry and told him there had been no anesthetic given to Patty Jo. He then blamed the nurse. The private room was dirty. Patty Jo told me that Dr. Perry had to appear before a hospital board of review.

Mr. and Mrs. Wilkerson moved next door. Tommy and Pam moved to Dorchester Regency too. Laura was separated from her husband. Patty Jo went off with her at night a lot.

Patty Jo's uncle Reuben stayed with us for a while. Patty Jo helped him spend his money. Reuben would chase old women all day and holler with heart pains at night. I had to ask him to leave.

I came home from work and an old woman sitting at the table fell out the chair onto the floor. The baby-sitter was stone drunk. Patty Jo had many different baby-sitters. I complained about things missing from the house.

When Reuben died, his children were angry with Patty Jo. It had something to do with his will. I never found out the details.

I transferred from the National Guard OMS in Mount Pleasant to the Army Reserve AMSA in Charleston. Both jobs were federal civil service. I, also, transferred to a new military unit in the U.S. Army Reserve.

With my problems with my wife, I dreaded going to the annual two weeks of active duty. My new unit, the 941st Transportation Company, consisted of 160 blacks and 5 white soldiers. The AMSA Shop and this unit had an on-going feud and I got caught in the middle.

Patty Jo had worked at banks, but she was terrible with a checkbook. She didn't maintain a balance, and she would forget to record the amount for checks written.

Patty Jo was not a housekeeper. She hired women to clean the house for her. On one occasion, I picked up an old black lady at her house and for some reason I had to go inside her house. Her house was immaculate. I shuddered to think about taking her to my pigpen called home.

Patty Jo would not stay at home. Her family called her, "Ramblin Rose". I sold the Holiday Rambler Camper.

While visiting Rick and Janice, we saw a house and property on the water for sale on Yonges Island. On our way home, we stopped and spoke with Shirley and Scooter Simmons about the house that was for sale.

Patty Jo promised she would stay home more, if I bought the house on Yonges Island.

We put our home up for sale, in Dorchester Regency, and signed the paperwork to buy the house on Yonges Island on October 19th.

Mr. Wilkerson loaned us ten thousand dollars on the Yonges Island property with the agreement he could move a doublewide mobile home on the property.

I built a go-cart, a Christmas gift for the boys. Patty Jo and I went to two Christmas parties: first to George Ridgell's and later to Joan Murdaugh's in Walterboro. My brother-in-law spiked my drinks too strong. I got drunk and sick.

Jack Parker was married to Mary Douglas.

1978

Age 30 – We moved to Yonges Island. The property had bushes growing five feet tall. I cleaned and landscaped the property with the tractor. The house was in need of interior work. I spent the equity from the sale of our home in Summerville to remodel. I also, borrowed additional money against the property in Walterboro, and we worked hard to fix up our home. It was a beautiful place.

Patty Jo started working for Chuck Long at Saint Paul's Academy. My boys went to a private school. Freddy won the Mr. Hollywood contest. Mark Armstrong's little girl won Miss Hollywood. Joey was seven years old on March 27th. Freddy was six on November 13th. Lisa was one on March 13th.

I sold the Ford tractor for $5000.00 and bought an Allis Chalmers diesel tractor for $7000.00.

Reflections Upon A Sunny Day

Patty Jo's promise did not last. She would not stay home. She put more miles on a car than a bus driver put on a greyhound. Her late hours out at night continued.

Patty Jo had a hysterectomy. She said, "Now I can screw anyone I want to and not worry about getting pregnant". I didn't know what to think about her comment. I hoped it was some kind of sick joke.

Patty Jo introduced me to her friends, Jon and his wife. Jon was related to Hubie and Joyce Avant. Hubie married Patty Jo's sister, Joyce.

Patty Jo could not get enough of Jon and his wife's company. She wanted them over all the time. Jon and Patty Jo paired off on each visit.

When Patty Jo wanted to go to Jon and his wife's, she would tell me to hurry up and get dressed or she was going to leave without me. They cleverly sent me off on errands with Jon's wife. Patty Jo told me they were married. On another occasion, she told me they were divorced and living together. I didn't know what to believe.

Everywhere Patty Jo and I went, Jon was there whether it was out to a movie, bowling, supper, the beach or to a party. Beverly was not with him.

Patty Jo continued to stay out late at night. Every time we were with Jon and Jon's wife, Jon and Patty Jo paired off together. I complained about it. Patty Jo said, "If I didn't like it, I could leave."

I warned Jon to keep his distance from Patty Jo. He acted smug about it. Jon never had much to say. He didn't seem to have a good personality or any personality at all. I really didn't see why Patty Jo was so interested in Jon.

The stress and worries were eating me up. I was not over Patty Jo's last affair yet. I lifted weights. It seemed to relieve some of the stiff muscles in my neck and shoulders. I had a lack of self-confidence, low self-esteem and I was very naïve. I waited for Patty Jo to come home at night, for I couldn't sleep for worrying about her. I felt lonely and depressed. I felt angry and jealous. I felt inadequate.

Patty Jo often denied me sex. I got frustrated.

I made love to DeAnne, who was one of our baby sitters. It was the first time I had cheated on my wife.

Patty Jo rented a beach house at Edisto Beach and invited Jon and his wife to spend the week. I had to work but took a couple of days off. I watched Jon and Patty Jo pair off together.

Reflections Upon A Sunny Day

I talked with Jon, and he told me how he avoided paying state income taxes by claiming his residence in Ohio.

At some point in time, Jon's wife moved out on Jon. He was living in a small trailer on Johns Island. Jon worked with cement, building steps, sidewalks and swimming pools.

I complained about Patty Jo's late hours at night. She didn't want to hear it. I swallowed my frustration and tried to make believe it didn't exist.

The telephone rang repeatedly during the night with Chuck, Rae, Joyce, Mrs. Wilkerson and others wanting to speak with Patty Jo, but she wasn't home often.

While in bed late at night, my stomach hurt from worry and I could not sleep. Patty Jo came home at 3:00 A. M. I got up and met her at the door. I asked her where she had been. She stiff-armed me in my chest and said, "None of your god damn business." I followed her to the bedroom and demanded to know where she had been. She said, "I've already told you, none of your god damn business." I pushed her on the floor and repeated my question. She told me she was at Rae's, her sister's trailer. I later called Rae and she told me Patty Jo had not been there.

The following day, Patty Jo went to see Joe Runey. I did not know it at the time, but Jon Avant had sent her to the Offices of Rawl and Runey, Attorney's at Law. Jon was familiar with these lawyers. They handled his divorce.

After Patty Jo talked with her lawyer, Joe Runey, she told me I had to pack my clothes and move out. She told me she had filed for a divorce on the grounds of physical cruelty. I pathetically threw myself at her feet begging for understanding. I crawled around on my knees crying and pleading with her. She laughed at me.

I became sick with this turn of events. I ate Tums and Rolaid tablets like candy. I tried to reason with Patty Jo, but I didn't know at the time she would have done anything to get me out of the way, so I couldn't interfere with her coming and going where and when she pleased.

We continued to live and sleep together for over a week. I begged her to forgive me. She said, "I'll think about it." Patty Jo decided we would spend the night at Joyce Avant's. Jon was there. Patty Jo said, "If you are completely honest with me, I will forgive you." She said, "You must be honest or we can't get back together." She asked me if I had ever cheated on her. I told her that I cheated on her once with DeAnne. She said, "I forgive you."

Reflections Upon A Sunny Day

I spoke with Jon Avant about Patty Jo again that morning. Afterwards, I went to work. Patty Jo went to her attorney, Joe Runey, and filed for a divorce on the grounds of adultery with DeAnne.

Patty Jo and I went to Joe Runey's office. We had come to a reasonable separation agreement but Joe Runey was totally unreasonable. He said, "I'm going to make the terms of the separation." Without my knowledge, he went to the Family Court and arranged it so I was to pay $900.00 a month support. It was more than I brought home in a month.

I had to move out of my home. I was totally devastated and suffered an emotional collapse. After being married and having my own family for nine years, I had to pack my clothes and move back home with my parents.

About a month later, I rented an apartment. Sometimes, I went to Jack and Mary Parker's for their company. Don't know why, but soon after I arrived, Mary would get dressed up and say something sarcastic to Jack and leave. I asked Jack if I was the reason she got mad. He said, "No". Then I asked, "What was the reasons for her actions". He said, "I don't know and don't care."

I went to the office of attorneys" Goodstein, Mims, and Keith Kornahrens. My attorney was Michael Mims. When I had to go to court, I was informed that my attorney was now a Judge. I went to court with a new attorney. In court, my new attorney sat beside me staring into space with glassy eyes. He sat there on cloud nine, while Joe Runey slandered me for the lowest scum on earth. I was humiliated and degraded. I complained to Keith about the lawyer. (In 1985, Attorney Runyon told me this lawyer was disbarred for his persistent drug use)

My apartment was lonely and too quiet. I could not stand the silence – no sound of my children or my complaining wife. I was lonely and hurting beyond all explanation, I felt like I could curl up and die. I tried to do positive things; moreover, I tried to bury my grief in a flurry of activity.

I sold some timber, from the property in Walterboro, so that I could afford the apartment and pay the house payment at Yonges Island. I gave money to Patty Jo for support and groceries. I bought some cheap furniture for the apartment and bought a used Ford Granada. Patty Jo had the Ford LTD.

I spent hours driving aimlessly up and down highways. The only thing I was sure of was that I felt desolate inside. The emptiness was tearing me apart. I considered slamming the car into an oak tree.

The Granada was a rust bucket in disguise. I traded it in on a 1978 Cutlass Supreme. It had been wrecked but expertly repaired.

Reflections Upon A Sunny Day

I couldn't work. I paced the floor of the AMSA shop in circles I could not think about my work or what I was supposed to be doing. I made some near fatal accidents, that I did not tell anyone about. I could not concentrate. My mind was constantly thinking about my family. I took a thirty-day leave of absence from the AMSA shop.

I took a leave of absence from the 941st Transportation Company, my military unit.

I lost weight and had to force myself to get out of the apartment. I hated to eat out alone. I had food in the apartment, but I was too depressed to cook just for myself. I went out to eat and felt bad about it. I felt insecure and lonely.

I didn't believe I could get sick like my mother, but I thought maybe there was a medicine that could make me feel better – something that could possibly take my troubles away. I felt the need for help, but I didn't understand what kind.

I went to Dr. Reynolds, about my nerves, and he put me on medication. I took a pill and tried to drive my car. I stopped at a stop sign, as a big cement truck approached from my left. My head said, "Remain stopped," but my foot said, "Go". I pulled out in front of that big heavy truck and was almost killed. I had another close call, before I got back to my apartment. The following week, I went back to Dr. Reynolds, and he prescribed another medication. I took it, but it didn't help the way I was feeling. I felt worse and stopped taking it.

I met Cathy McDonald, at the Seven-Eleven Store, in Pierpont. We were friends from our school days. Cathy told me she was divorced. We dated a few times.

I went to Dr. Reynolds and told him I was impotent. He explained it was because of my nerves, and when I was feeling better my problem would go away.

In August, I noticed Patty Jo driving past my apartment during the day and at night. My apartment was 25 miles from Yonges Island.

I dishearteningly went alone to the Western Sizzlin' Steak House for supper. To my surprise, Pam Hughes was working the cash register. Pam told me she left Tommy. She gave me her phone number and we dated a few times. Patty Jo was jealous of Pam Hughes. Patty Jo had a fit. She looked for Pam's car and started knocking on my door.

Patty Jo envied my car and apartment. Patty Jo thought I was having a great time and she was jealous. She didn't want me home, and she didn't want anyone else to have me either.

Patty Jo's nephew, Arnold, was baby-sitting my children. I checked on them and found my children soaked in urine sleeping on the floor. Patty Jo was out with her boyfriend.

Patty Jo and Jon spent the weekend in Atlanta and attended an Atlanta Falcons football game.

Patty Jo had a teenage boy move in the house with her at Yonges Island. He lived there for several weeks.

Pam was a tall attractive twenty-one year old woman. She worked at the Charleston Naval Shipyard and drove a new Mustang. I caught a case of scabies from her. I had to go to a dermatologist and he prescribed quill lotion.

Patty Jo continued to drive slowly past my apartment. One evening, she stopped and wanted to come in. She slept with me and told me not to tell anyone.

Patty Jo and I went out together. We went to Yonges Island and Jon's truck was parked on the road in front of the driveway. I smoked marijuana for the first time. I got high and slept with Patty Jo.

Patty Jo continued to sleep with me at my apartment. Our divorce was nearly final. She wanted to make a deal. She said, "Let's go through with the divorce and you move in with me." I said, "No". She relented and agreed to stop the divorce and for me to come home.

I moved back home in December. I was very glad to be back together with my family. I did everything possible to please Patty Jo.

Christmas was coming in a couple of weeks. Patty Jo told me she could have had a big Christmas. I apologized and told her I would do the best I could. She said, "I'm not sure I did the right thing by asking you to come home." She could have torn my heart out and stomped on it with her foot and it would not have hurt me any less than the sound of her words.

Patty Jo parked the Ford LTD and took the keys to the Cutlass Supreme.

1979

The AMSA Shop continued to feud with the 941st Transportation Company. The Company Commander of the 941st, Captain Brock, was grateful for my correcting the major problems he had in the motor pool. He told me of his plans to make me his new Warrant Officer in charge of the motor pool.

Reflections Upon A Sunny Day

There was a change of command during my leave of absence. The AMSA Shop supervisor deceitfully went behind my back to have his friend, who had worked against the unit for years, put in for the Warrant Officer position in charge of the 941st motor pool. SFC Macon asked me to teach him how to do the job. I told him to learn by experience. I had worked hard for the unit, while the AMSA personnel refused to help. The AMSA was supposed to support the 941st, but would not because the AMSA supervisor and the motor sergeant of the 941st resented one another. After the supervisor's friend got my job, the AMSA started supporting the unit.

Mr. and Mrs. Wilkerson moved a doublewide mobile home on the property at Yonges Island. Patty Jo's parents complained about her late hours at night.

I know Patty Jo had a boyfriend. Patty Jo tried to throw me off by telling me he lived out of town and she didn't see him anymore. For some reason, she seemed to think I didn't know about her affair with Jon.

Patty Jo wore a MISPAH charm on a bracelet. Jon wore the other half on a chain. She told me her boyfriend wanted to buy her a Lincoln Continental.

I tried to overlook Patty Jo's comments. I asked Jack Parker for advice. He said, "Kill her with kindness".

I stayed home and cleaned house, washed dishes and clothes. I did everything possible to make her happy.

I received hang-up phone calls nearly everyday. Patty Jo wrote Jon's name, over and over, on paper. His name and phone number was left around the phone.

I knew Patty Jo was having an affair with Jon, but I wanted to deny it and think it was not happening. I hoped her affair wouldn't last; that she was just infatuated and my problem would just go away. My family was my life and I didn't want to lose it. My hope was for Patty Jo to love me more, so she would soon grow tired of Jon.

Jon's wife shot herself in the head with a pistol. Patty Jo told me she survived the gunshot but was left with the mind of a child.

Jon called my house and asked for Patty Jo. She was at Rae's trailer. I found out later that Jon was trying to get in touch with my wife to tell her that Ira Byrd was killed in a helicopter crash. Ira was married to Patty

Reflections Upon A Sunny Day

Jo's sister. We attended the funeral, but Patty Jo overtly brushed me off several times to be with Jon.

My father had a fight, under the Ashley River Bridge, with Marty Sowell. My mother later told me that my father was disappointed in me because I didn't seek retribution.

Patty Jo gave me hell for no reason. She started arguments about DeAnne and other things in the past. I didn't know what to expect when I came home from work. One day she acted fine, and the next day she was on my case as soon as I stepped in the door.

Patty Jo showed me a gold bracelet she was wearing and told me her boyfriend paid $500.00 for it. It was in the Sam Solomon catalog for $29.00.

Jon sent cards and letters to Patty Jo. I found them everywhere. Jon didn't sign the cards but the envelopes had a Johns Island postmark. Jon lived on Johns Island. He sent flowers to where Patty Jo worked and she brought them home.

I tried to cope with the affair Patty Jo was having, but it was taking its toll.

Patty Jo said to me,"Men are so childish, give them some pussy and they fall in love".

Patty Jo stayed on the phone gossiping about other people. She couldn't look or pay attention to the children for having the phone glued to her ear. On several occasions, the food was still raw when it was served on the table.

When Patty Jo would meet one of her old friends, she would act like she had missed them dearly. She would smile and laugh, but when they were out of earshot, she would talk mean and nasty about them.

When I returned from work, Patty Jo would scream at me if I petted the dog before entering the house.

Patty Jo said to me, "My boyfriend loves my children more than you do".

I returned home from work and found Jon Avant sitting at my table with Patty Jo and Rae Edmondson. Rae was Patty Jo's half sister. I said, "What's going on?" Rae said, "I just got here." My son, Freddy, showed me a handful of money that Jon had given him to go play outside. Rae made a joke of it.

Reflections Upon A Sunny Day

My son, Freddy, later told me that he was given money to play outside when Patty Jo went to Jon's trailer. Freddy was seven years old. Joey was eight and Lisa was only two years old.

I lived out my childhood thinking my father would one day kill me. I dwelt in a world where nothing was explained to children except the supremacy of the concept of obedience. It was hard to grant amnesty to the man who did not touch me as a child except when he was beating me.

On Sunday the 30th of June, I took Patty Jo, Joey, Freddy and Lisa out boat riding in the river and we had a picnic on a sandbar. That afternoon, after we returned and were preparing supper, my mother called. She said to me, "Your daddy has had a terrible accident". I asked, "What happened and how bad is he hurt?" She told me that he had an accident while out in his boat. I asked, "He is going to be okay, isn't he?" She said, "No, Freddy, it killed him". I was stunned. A blur of thoughts rushed through my mind.

I wasn't prepared for his death nor was my mother. My father loved my children and enjoyed spending time with them. He was so proud of them and now he was gone. He had even bought a pony for my children to ride. Seeing a smile on his face with my children warmed my heart. My children were so young and I wondered if they would remember him.

My mother told me that he had been sleeping on the couch earlier that day as if dead. When he woke up, he told her that he wanted to go fishing. My mother packed him a lunch. My father kept his twelve-foot aluminum boat with a 9.8 Mercury outboard in the boat ramp ready to launch. My father was still suffering from an injury at the Navy Yard. He left the house by way of Church Creek to fish in the Ashley River, but he didn't have a chance.

While on his way, a fast speeding boat ran over his little fishing boat, from bow to stern, and chopped my father up with the oncoming propeller and crushed his skull.

Somehow my father pulled himself to the mud bank and there he died. The speedboat, with its occupants, stopped but did not render any assistance. They left the scene and hastily trailered their boat at the Parsonage Point public landing.

After my father's body and boat were removed from Church Creek, that same speedboat returned to the scene at midnight and the occupants searched the area of the collision. The persons responsible for my father's death were never charged or convicted. I gathered my facts slowly, for people were reluctant to become involved. And over the years, I continued to receive pieces of information. One of the occupants of the speeding boat was married to a County Policewoman. Another was a neighbor who once lived on Parsonage Road. The owner of the boat was a known drug dealer and had a prior record of colliding into another boat while under the influence of drugs and alcohol. I was also told that one occupant of the speedboat bragged about how he ran the old man down. My father's death was a painful blow to me, and they left my mother a very lonely woman.

I was torn between comforting my mother and keeping Jon away from my wife.

I took care of my father's burial and arrange my mother's finances. She had no money or access to the bank account. My mother told me that my father did not plan to leave me anything in his will.

Detective Paul Hawkins was the investigating officer of my father's death. We sat in my mother's living room and discussed the facts. (In 1985, during my trial, Detective Hawkins stated that he did not know me)

In August, the eye of Hurricane David passed over Edisto Beach. The tidal water of Swinton Creek swelled over its banks and flooded our house. The Ford LTD was parked on a hill, but the high water still reached the steering wheel. Everything in the tool shed was deluged with salt water. Our insurance policy did not cover all the damage.

I accompanied my mother, during the night of the storm, to comfort her in her new loneliness. She talked about dying and my heart ached for her. My wife was at Joyce Avant's, which was a convenient place to have companionship with Jon.

Scooter and Shirley Simmons lived about a quarter-mile from us in our old trailer. They often visited us. Patty Jo and Shirley were always scheming and plotting something. They smoked a lot of marijuana together and they were up to no good most of the time.

Patty Jo started arguments for an excuse to leave the house. There wasn't anything in the present to argue about, so she picked things from the past.

Patty Jo seemed to have some dirty gossip about everyone. She was obsessed with bad mouthing everybody behind their back. She would talk about her friends Shirley, Sally and Mary. She talked about other friends and even her own family. I know she did the same thing to me behind my back.

Patty Jo habitually lied about things. She often told on herself or got caught in her lies.

Patty Jo said, "I have to visit a friend in the hospital." She came home late. The following morning, I found more cards and flowers in the car from Jon.

Age 32 – I had severe migraine headaches. I went to the Hollywood Clinic and the doctor prescribed Florinol.

Patty Jo was a liar of the first order with oak leaf clusters all over her. She was as adapt with small lies as she was with lies that could destroy lives.

Patty Jo told me she didn't want to live in the house anymore; that she wanted live in an apartment with tennis courts and swimming pools.

Jon had moved, from the trailer, to an apartment. I didn't know the location of the apartment, but I drove around and looked for Patty Jo and Jon.

Patty Jo started a conflict between me and my children. They heard her shout, "I favor Freddy and don't love Joey." She drummed this into Joey's head repeatedly. Joey was hyperactive and it was Patty Jo who usually ordered Joey punished. Patty Jo had screamed and screamed at the children so much that they paid little attention to her. She often bribed them to get her way.

Patty Jo demanded that it was my responsibility to discipline the children. When I tried to explain to her that it was just as much her responsibility, she got mad and vindictive towards me. When the children did something wrong and I disciplined them, Patty Jo jumped in and cursed me out in front of the children to make me look wrong. When the children did something wrong and I didn't say anything, Patty Jo would curse me and tell me it was my job to handle it. She worked long and hard to turn my children against me.

Patty Jo said to me, "I don't know why I get so much pleasure being mean to you. I just can't help myself."

At one point, it seemed that Patty Jo was making an effort to quit with Jon, but he was persistent and wouldn't leave her alone. He called her at home and work. The hang-up calls continued for me. Jon kept her head messed up. He told her everything and anything she wanted to hear in order to break up my home and family.

Patty Jo told me she knew someone who was madly in love with her and would buy her anything she wanted.

Somehow, Patty Jo still didn't think, I knew about her and Jon's affair. I didn't tell her I knew, but she tormented me with little bits of information about someone who loved her. Patty Jo asked me if it were possible to love two men at once.

Reflections Upon A Sunny Day

Patty Jo was so busy with herself and gossiping on the phone; that she never noticed what the children were doing. They could be choking to death and wouldn't notice.

Joey was beaten badly by a baby-sitter. We went to the police department and filed a report of the incident.

Jack Parker wanted to borrow my truck camper shell, so we went to the farm in Walterboro and put it on his truck. I took a look at my equipment and decided to move it. I returned three days later, on Saturday morning with my tractor on a lowboy trailer, to load the equipment and move it. When I checked on my equipment again, I discovered that everything was missing. I checked the tracks on the ground and with a neighbor. The neighbor told me that someone, in a red pickup truck and another person in a logging truck, backed a big log-skidder off onto the road in broad daylight and entered my property. They loaded all of my tractor equipment on the logging truck and left like they owned the place. My equipment was not insured.

I was bitten by a pygmy rattlesnake. It struck my ankle. My son sucked the wound for me and spit out the venom.

Friends and family members call nightly and asked me where is Patty Jo? I tell them I don't know. They called her Ramblin' Rose.

I wouldn't argue with Patty Jo. On many occasions, I would go for a drive hoping that things would be better when I returned.

Patty Jo had no respect for the truth. I suspected that she believed her own lies.

When it was time for me to leave for work in the morning, Jon would call the house. He would talk with my wife at home and work. Everywhere Patty Jo and I went we saw Jon there too.

Patty Jo said, "Hurry up and get dressed or I'm leaving you." We were going to the Western Sizzlin Steak House. I told her they wouldn't run out of food before we got there. She pitched a fit and raised hell with me. I hurried to the Steak House. Jon was there and Patty Jo picked the table next to him.

Patty Jo told me that Jon screwed Mary Parker. I told Jack but he didn't care.

We often went out in the boat to fish, shrimp, gather oysters and clams or just pleasure ride. In July, when I began working on the boat for a trip to the Beaufort Water Festival, Patty Jo threatened to leave me if I did any work on it. When it was time to leave, Patty Jo was the first person in the boat. Scooter and Shirley Simmons accompanied us on the trip. We joined other boats on the way and we spent the night on board when we arrived. When the water festival began the next morning and all the boats gathered at the Beaufort Bridge, I noticed that Jon was sitting in a boat nearby. After the regatta, we headed home. On the return trip, a drunk man crashed his boat into mine. It took a year and court to make Julius O'Neal Barfield pay for the damage.

Patty Jo said, "I'm going to sue Dr. Perry." Dr. Wilson had died, so she went to his wife and found out that the medical records were burnt in a fire.

Patty Jo's method was unclear to me. She was looking for lieutenants, for business employers, for friends and relatives to believe her lies. She had a plan of attack of indefinite shape and structure, which she planned to initiate at some future time.

While a neighbor, Mack McGrady, was visiting, the telephone rang. We were having a pleasant conversation and Patty Jo answered the phone. It was her mother calling. Patty Jo told her mother we were having a fight. I turned to Mack in sadness and said, "She is trying to make me look like a villain to her family and friends.

Janice Baldwin called and told me she had an excellent job opportunity for Patty Jo. She worked for Dr. Paul Sanders and there was an opening for a desk clerk.

Patty Jo and Janice went to school together. Janice and her husband, Rick, were our friends.

I told Patty Jo about Janice's phone call. Patty Jo took the job at Dr. Sanders' office. Patty Jo talked about Janice everyday and plotted to get her job. Patty Jo manipulated Dr. Sanders and succeeded in getting Janice fired. Patty Jo got her job. Patty Jo then turned Dr. Sanders against me with lies.

Janice later told me that Jon was calling Patty Jo at Dr. Sanders' office.

I took our children to school every morning and picked them up in the afternoon at my mother's house. After I enrolled my children into the Springfield Elementary School, Jon enrolled his children there too.

Patty Jo stayed on the go. She often told me she had to go shopping. I drove around, with my children, but couldn't find her. If I asked her any questions about her activities, she got mad and started an argument.

Jon called my house at 6:30 A.M. every morning. I was usually on my way to school, with my children, and work at that time. I caught him on the phone several times, but he stopped talking.

Patty went to Joyce Avant's a lot. Jon was there. Joyce and her husband, Hubie, encouraged Jon's affair with my wife and joined them for nights on the town.

Joyce had a party. My nerves were so bad; that I got sick and had to lay down. Jon was late getting to the party. He got drunk and passed out.

Patty Jo went to the doctor for diet pills. She also bought black-beauties from her friend, Margo. After taking those pills her attitude became worse. She got mean as hell.

She threatened me and dared me to touch her. She jabbed her fingernail into my chest while screaming at me at the top of her fierce voice. Patty Jo screamed, "I'm glad your father is dead and I wish the same for your mother."

Joan Murdaugh had a party at her house in Walterboro. Joan is Patty Jo's sister. Jon was at the party. I was torn between hurt and anger. I asked Joan, why is Jon here?

Patty Jo and Shirley called and harassed the Deanne's family at all hours of the night.

Patty Jo stacked Jon's cards and letters on the shelf in the hallway.

Jack Willard told me there was talk going around about my father's death. Jack told me they were bragging about it. He pointed out one of them for me.

Bobby Owens told me my father was run down twice. I heard other people say the same thing.

Patty Jo started arguments, but I refused to argue back. She would say, "I know what you're thinking!" I must have heard this a thousand times.

Reflections Upon A Sunny Day

Patty Jo made excuses for her self to justify what she was doing. In a fit of rage she said, "I'll fuck your friend, Mack McGrady."

Patty Jo might have been new to conspiracy, but she mastered its tricks and stratagems with a felicity that indicated she carried a natural affinity for it. She swore a thousand times that she was going to take everything I owned.

When Mack visited, he and Patty Jo flirted with one another. With a sly grin, he would say to her, "Are you happy?" It was a secret between them. I told Mack that I was having enough trouble with her already and didn't need any more.

Patty Jo argued and dared me to hit her. While jabbing me in the chest with her finger, she cursed and screamed in my face with an insane viciousness. I didn't touch her. She went outside and sat on the back steps. While I watched through the window, she picked up a rock from the flower garden and beat herself in the arm with it. All I could think was, I wondered who she was going to tell I did it?

I stayed out late shrimping. The next day, Patty Jo and I went boat riding with some friends. I had a terrible headache. Patty Jo said, "Here, take this pill." I thought it was for a headache. My heart began beating wildly. I thought I was going to have a heart attack.

I was unhappy with so many things in my life. Jon was sabotaging my marriage. The doubts that I had been trying to deny for years would no longer stay hidden. There were so many things in our relationship that was wrong.

Patty Jo was out late. I answered the telephone and a woman said, "Jon's screwing Patty Jo," and hung up.

Most of Patty Jo's skirmishes were like games of war, with the souls of our children serving as the ruined captured flags in the campaigns of attrition. She didn't consider the potential damage when using something as fragile and unformed as a child's life. Patty Jo told them I was no good. She often screamed at me and played dead on the floor.

In a fit of anger, Patty Jo threatened to kill me. She told me she had a drug, Inderal, at Dr. Sanders' Office that would kill me and it would look like a heart attack.

Patty Jo would get in my face and try to provoke me into a fight. She said, "I wish I was stronger than you, because if I were I would beat your ass."

George Ridgell said, "You better look out. Your buddy is slipping around on you." I asked, "Are you talking about Jon Avant?" He said, "Yes, I saw him and Patty Jo together in Summerville the other night."

While I was at work, someone stole my trolling motor and tools from my tool shed. A few days later, Mr. Singletary stopped by to tell me what he heard about my stolen property. He said, "Mr. Carol Smoak told him about the robbery and described who did it." I never met Mr. Carol Smoak, but I spoke with Wilkie Tanner and he was able to tell me who the boys were. A couple of weeks later, while Patty Jo's niece was baby-sitting and our cars weren't in the yard, some boys drove a car up the driveway. When the baby-sitter opened the door to see who was in the car, they turned around and tore through the yard and left.

It was a Saturday morning, and desperately hoped that Patty Jo would not start an argument and leave the house. My head hurt, as I fried myself an egg in the kitchen. The telephone rang and Patty Jo answered it. Laura called to ask Patty Jo to stop calling their house at all hours of the night and something about Laura's husband. (Laura and her husband, Lally, were back together after a separation) Patty Jo cursed her with every breath. Patty Jo told her that she was going to screw her husband and DeAnne's husband. (DeAnne was Laura's daughter) Patty Jo hung up the phone and turned her rage of anger on me. She demanded that I call and curse them out. I told Patty Jo that I hadn't spoken with the Futch's in over a year. I said, "It wouldn't do any good for me to get on the phone with them. It would be like throwing gasoline on a fire. It would make things worse. Why don't you leave them alone?" Patty Jo cursed me and told me her divorce was still open. She said, "I'm calling my attorney, Joe Runey, and have you kicked out of my house and you'll leave with nothing but the shirt on your back." She said, "The courts always favor the woman, so you don't have a chance against me." She said, "I'll see to it that you don't get to see my children". And, she said, "I will take every dime you make." My head was pounding and my nerves were on end. I pulled my gun on Patty Jo and said, "You are a lying, cheating bitch, and I ought to shoot you." I told her I knew about the affair she was having with Jon. Patty Jo denied it. I told her, of times and places, when they were together. Patty Jo's mouth dropped open and then she said, "I don't love him and I'll stop seeing him". The next day, Patty Jo told me that she had spoken with Jon and told him not to call anymore. About a month later, I found a note, on the hallway shelf from Jon to Patty Jo, stating that he had missed her and was glad they were back together again.

Patty Jo told me, it was Debbie Chaplin who called me and said, "Jon's screwing Patty Jo." She told me Debbie was jealous of her and Jon.

Mary Parker told me that it was okay for Jon and Patty Jo to be together.

Reflections Upon A Sunny Day

I was in charge of the tool room at the AMSA Shop. It was necessary to sign for tools in order to maintain proper accountability.

One of the AMSA employees, Freddy Macon, was very rude and obnoxious. He was a redneck bully. I did not like his bigoted attitude or his hostile mouth. I tried to reason with Freddy, but he would not listen. I warned him that I would not accept his abuse. One day, Freddy stormed into the tool room like a brute and took tools outside without signing for them. I said, "Freddy, you have to sign out for the tools." When he raised a tool in his hand and said, "I'll shove this wrench up your ass". I beat him up.

The chief supervisor from Fort Jackson visited me at the AMSA Shop. To my surprise, he told me not to worry about the fight. He said, "Freddy's been asking for it a long time."

Patty Jo said, "Let's go bowling." I figured Jon would be there, so I called Jack and Mary Parker and asked them if they would like to go. Mary told me she had something to do but she suggested that Jack may want to go. I spoke with Jack and he wanted to go. While I was getting ready, Mary called me back and chewed me out because Jack was going bowling with us. She threatened to make trouble for me with Jon and Patty Jo.

When we arrived, at the bowling alley, I noticed that Jon was there.

I asked Patty Jo why she would always argue about things in the past. She always told me she was testing me. She said, "It's a test."

I began seeing Jon's face, when I saw other blond headed men. When I saw billboard signs like those for Marlboro cigarettes, I saw Jon's face.

Patty Jo often pretended to be Dolly Pardon and Barbara Mandrell. She began playing country music on the stereo. It was Jon's favorite music.

I found a twelve-foot cedar in the woods and cut it down for our Christmas tree.

1981

Age 33 – I brought to my adult life nostalgia for a lost childhood. I longed to raise my children in an atmosphere of love that did not exist in my childhood. Joey was 10, Freddy was 9, and Lisa was 4 years old. It grieved my heart to see them bicker, argue and fight. The discordance between them made me wonder if a shred of compassion existed in their hearts.

Reflections Upon A Sunny Day

When Patty Jo became irrational, she could be a very difficult person to live with. And when she screamed at me, I was frustrated with the inability to do anything about it.

On one occasion, my children asked Patty Jo not to scream at me. They asked her to leave me alone.

Mack McGrady and I went fishing at midnight and gigged 63 large channel bass. When we returned to my house at daylight, Scooter Simmons stopped by to look at the fish. While we were talking, a truck, towing a Ditch-Witch, turned into my driveway. It was Jon Avant. Without my knowledge, Patty Jo arranged for Jon to come over and dig a ditch for Mr. Wilkerson. Scooter told Mack to get me away from the house. Mack took me to his house.

Patty Jo and I went to Dr. Hill for marriage counseling. He was our children's pediatrician. We talked with him separately. I told Dr. Hill of Patty Jo's affair with Jon. Dr. Hill told me that Patty Jo denied having an affair with Jon. I told Dr. Hill that Patty Jo was living in the past and started arguments about things that happened years ago. We then talked with Dr. Hill together, and he told us to wipe the slate clean and forgive and forget the past. Dr. Hill said, "Starting today you will forget the past." Patty Jo agreed, and I agreed. We thanked him and walked back to our car. Patty Jo got in the car and started arguing about DeAnne and other things. I said, "You just promised Dr. Hill, that you would forgive and forget the past, and we aren't even out his parking lot yet."

My children told me that Patty Jo took them to a playground. Whatever this playground was about, I felt sure it had something to do with Jon. I drove around and looked for Patty Jo and my children at playgrounds. Patty Jo wanted to talk about Jon. She wanted to tell me how he was in bed. I said, "I don't want to hear it." She asked me about DeAnne and how she was in bed. I said, "I don't think about it and it's nothing to be talking about."

I returned home from work and Patty Jo commenced to yelling and wanted to know who the woman was I had in my jeep. I didn't know what she was talking about and I told her there had been no woman in my jeep. She said, "You were seen with a woman in your jeep this morning." I told her that I had been at work all day. I said, "If you want to check, call anyone at the shop." She said, "I wouldn't believe anyone where you work." (I believe Jon told her there was a woman in my jeep to stir up trouble)

Mr. Wilkerson came over and asked me to help him do something. Patty Jo started on me with her mouth. Mr. Wilkerson told her to shut up and leave me alone.

I was getting the children ready for school. Patty Jo started arguing and threatening to take every dime I made and have me kicked out with just the shirt on my back. I grabbed her by the arms and marched her to the bedroom and told her I was tired of her screaming at me in front of the children. I said, "If you want Jon so bad, pack your clothes and leave, but me and the children are staying here." Mr. Wilkerson walked into our bedroom and said, "What's going on?" I didn't tell him about the problem I was having with Patty Jo and Jon.

I returned from work and Patty Jo demanded me to beat Joey. I asked, "Why?" She said, "He has been picking on Lisa." I asked, "When?" She said, "About three hours ago, and he has been waiting in his room for you to come home." I asked, "Why didn't you take care of it when it happened?" I said, "It is just as much your responsibility to discipline the children". Patty Jo screamed at me and said. "It is your job and if you don't go in this room and spank him, I'm leaving and I don't know when I'll be back tonight." She said, "You do it or else." I went into Joey's room and asked him if he had picked on Lisa. He said, "Yes, sir." I said, "You know you are not supposed to". He said, "Yes, sir" I said, "I'm going to give you a spanking." He said, "Yes, sir." Patty Jo was standing at the door watching. I gave Joey a spanking. While he was crying, Patty Jo rushed over to Joey and picked him up. She comforted him and turned Joey's face to me and said, "Your daddy is a mean son of a bitch."

The hang up calls continued and Jon still called at 6:30 A.M. My neck and shoulders ached with constant pain and tension. The migraines increased in frequency and the depression permeated my soul. I was obsessed with saving my marriage, and I hoped that time would solve the problem.

Patty Jo was recruiting everyone possible to believe I was mean and the cause of all the problems.

Patty Jo didn't have to be at work until 9:30 A.M., but sometimes she would get up with me in the morning. While I shaved and brushed my teeth, Patty Jo showered and douched with a fruit flavored product. When I left the house at 6:15 A.M., with the children in the jeep, Patty Jo got in the Oldsmobile and pulled out of the driveway right behind me. (Patty Jo had an appointment with Jon)

Debbie and Lamont Chaplin had an oyster roast. Patty Jo was not home. I went to the oyster roast alone. Debbie asked, "Where is Patty Jo?" I said, "I don't know." Debbie said, "The bitch, I know where she is."

Patty Jo often told me she had to work late at Dr. Sanders Office. On other occasions, she told me she had to go shopping. I didn't know what she did with her money. She had her own checkbook and rarely paid a bill. She kept my checkbook a mess, and I paid all the bills.

I took our hog to the market. Patty Jo told our children that I murdered their hog. The children were very upset with me. I tried to explain where all the other hogs and cows went when they were grown. I explained the difference between dogs and hogs. I told them Uncle Carol's hogs went to the market. My children claimed to understand, but I could see in their eyes that Patty Jo had scored a victory.

We often went to church on Sunday, and as soon as we got in the car to leave, Patty Jo would talk about everyone there. And if Laura and DeAnne were at church, I really caught hell.

Reflections Upon A Sunny Day

I had sex with Patty Jo. She was cold, reserved and unresponsive. I got Joey and Freddy up and took them to school. Patty Jo called me at work and told me she would be working late again. After work, I went to my mother's house to pick up my children, but something about Patty Jo's working hours made me painfully suspicious. I asked my mother to let me use her car for a little while. I drove downtown and parked in front of the Medical University, facing Dr. Sanders Office. It was after working hours for Dr. Sanders Office, and Patty Jo's car was the only one in the parking lot. From where I was parked, I could see Patty Jo in the front office. She kept looking through the window blinds, and I wondered why? It wasn't long before I knew the answer. I saw Jon. He had parked his car down the street instead of parking in Dr. Sanders' parking lot. Jon walked the edge of the parking lot, between the bushes, instead of in the open and knocked on the door. Patty Jo let him in and closed the window blinds. I sat in the car frozen for a couple of minutes as a flurry of undiscerned images flashed through my mind. I didn't know what to do, but I couldn't help myself. I had to see what was going on.

At the edge of the office window, there was a space not covered by the venetian blind. I looked through the edge of the window and saw them embraced. Jon had his hand in my wife's pants. I knocked on the door and heard some shuffling inside. They were running out of the front office. I looked in the window again and they were gone. I beat on the door and they would not answer. I walked around to the side door and kicked it. I was furious and near-sighted, for I was aware of nothing around me except for obstacles in my way. The door was broken in half, but before it was passable Patty Jo came to the door and asked me what I wanted. I said, "Let me in." She unlocked the front door and let me in. I said, "Where is Jon?" Patty Jo said, "Jon who"? I said, "Jon Avant". She said, "I don't know what you are talking about." I said, "Where is Jon?" Patty Jo said, "He hasn't been here." I said, "I saw you together." Patty Jo said, "You must be crazy." I kept asking, "Where is Jon?" while shoving her towards the rear of the building. She kept saying, "You're crazy." I lost control and stuck her in the arm with my pocketknife. I lost awareness of time and space and my mouth was completely dry. I said, "Where is Jon?" Patty Jo said, "Look at what you've done." I stuck her in the leg. Patty Jo hollered, "Jon come out." Jon opened the door about an inch to peek outside and slammed the door shut. He had hidden himself in a private bathroom near the employee lounge. I broke through the door and cut his arms and legs. Jon screamed for Patty to help him. Jon said, "He is going to kill me." Jon was kicking and screaming like a hysterical pig. I dropped the knife and we fought for it. Jon was more afraid of my fists than the knife. I pinned Jon down on the floor, with the knife in my hand, and said, "I'm not going to kill you." I said, "I want you to leave my wife alone and get the hell out of town." Jon said, "Yes, Sir, I will." I picked Jon up and shoved him through the door. I looked for Patty Jo, but she wasn't in the building. I walked outside and policemen were on the street. I walked by them to the car and drove to mother's house. I was upset and misplaced my keys to the jeep. They were in the door lock, but I didn't see them or remember putting them there. I used my extra set. My sons, Joey and Freddy, got in the jeep and we headed towards home. I told my boys that Patty Jo and I wouldn't be living together anymore. I told them that Patty Jo had a boyfriend. My boys said, "We knew she had a boyfriend and we know who he is." I asked, "Who?" They said, "Jon." My boys told me that Patty Jo was with Jon in his apartment. They told me about their being outside on the tennis courts (the playground) and Patty Jo not giving them a drink of water when they were thirsty. I asked my boys who they wanted to live with. They said, "We want to live with you, daddy."

I went to Dolly Byrd's house to pick up Lisa, but I found out that Shirley Simmons had my daughter. I went home and Scooter Simmons arrived almost immediately to tell me I was in trouble. I said, "I know".

Reflections Upon A Sunny Day

We went to Scooter's trailer and within a few minutes, Mack McGrady was there too. Mack asked me to spend the night with him and his wife, Susie. Scooter and Shirley looked after my children. Mack and Susie helped me look through the phone book for an attorney. It took a long time to reach one, but I finally got in touch with Mr. Ben Peeples. He gave me a phone number to reach him in the morning. I did not sleep that night. Every time my mind started to switch off, the slide projector in my brain would click and another frame of the events that happened that afternoon would appear.

    I still loved my wife, but I hated what she became and what she did. My wife and family was my life – my purpose for living. Yet, there seemed to be no way to stop the inevitable divorce.

    I hired Mr. Ben Peeples as my attorney, but I had to pay his fee. My attorney told me my chances of getting custody of my children were slim and none.

    In April, Patty Jo said, "If you drop the adultery charges, I will not pursue the criminal charges." Jon signed a waiver stating that he would not pursue the charges.

    I was broke and hurt to the marrow of my soul with pain and unhappiness. I was heartbroken and lonely for my family. I was humiliated and afraid of the judicial system. I was depressed and lost weight.

My attorney, Ben Peeples, told me that I may still have to deal with the state concerning the criminal charge of assault and battery with intent to kill, even if Patty Jo dropped her charges. He said, "You could possibly get 10 to 20 years in prison. I told him all I could remember about the events that took place. I believed in the peace of truth.

I made an appointment to see Dr. Diane Hamrick, a psychologist in Charleston. I had several appointments with Dr. Hamrick, but I couldn't afford to keep going. I was broke. Dr. Hamrick told me to look out for number one – myself.

Patty Jo stayed with her parents for a week. I was still living in our house. I spoke with Patty Jo, while she was in the yard, but she was unreasonable.

I was worried and depressed. Mack and Susie fixed supper for me. Mack's mother gave me a hug, and I broke down and cried.

In public, Patty Jo overdid happiness. She volunteered for social or charitable functions for her own reasons. Most people considered her to be sweet, beautiful and industrious. She was all these things and a field marshal to boot.

Reflections Upon A Sunny Day

Jean Carson told me that Patty Jo could do no wrong. Jean was Patty Jo's sister from Greenville, S.C. Jean said, "If Patty Jo wants to be with Jon, it's none of your business. Patty Jo can do whatever she wants to." I told Jean a marriage doesn't work that way.

Attorney Joe Runey ordered me to pack my clothes and to get out of my house. It was Patty Jo's threat come true. I moved to my mother's house.

Patty Jo moved into an apartment on the same road where Jon lived. She had a completely furnished house to live in, but Patty Jo wanted the swimming pools and tennis courts of apartment living. Patty Jo grew tired of things quickly. It didn't matter what it was. She was never satisfied. Patty Jo left our children with countless baby-sitters, so she could ramble the roads. Patty Jo was not a housekeeper, there was no organization, and it was so frustrating. I may find the phone bill in the kitchen drawer or in the bathroom cabinet or maybe not at all. Patty Jo carried on so many times about Jon buying her a Lincoln Continental. When she took the keys to the Oldsmobile Cutlass Supreme, she trashed it in a matter of weeks. Soiled diapers were stuffed under the seat. In July, the powerful stench of rotting diapers in a hot car was overwhelming, and the sticky Coke syrup from the melted Hardee's cups filled the dashboard. Patty Jo grew tired of her children, the house, car and husband too. But, the main reason for her moving to an apartment was to escape the eyes of her parents, for they lived next door on the property. Patty Jo did not want them to see the truth or question her activities.

Mack McGrady told me he would go to court and testify that he screwed Patty Jo while I was at work. At first, I thought he was just saying this to help me – not because it was true. I said, "Wouldn't that get you in trouble with Susie and your mother?" Mack changed his mind. Months later, when I could think more clearly, I thought about the remarks Patty Jo had to say about Mack's penis and their secret comment: Are you happy? I also remembered Patty Jo said, "I'll fuck your friend, Mack McGrady." I believe she did.

Attorney Ben Peeples recommended me to withdraw my charge of adultery. I followed his advice. Patty Jo filed for divorce on the grounds of physical cruelty.

Foregoing the orders of Family Court, I continued to pay the house and car payments, and I gave money to Patty Jo for child support. I kept my cancelled checks and receipts.

From the time she filed for divorce to the date of court, Patty Jo wrote down the things she wanted as if it were a Christmas list. In the doorway of the courtroom Patty Jo said, "I almost forgot, I want your boat too". My attorney, Ben Peeples said, "Give her anything she wants." He said, "We don't need any trouble from her concerning the criminal charges." Patty Jo got the house and water front property on Yonges Island, the Cutlass Supreme, a house full of expensive furniture, my tractor, my boat and my children. I was to pay child support until they were 21 years old or married. I was to pay all medical expenses and maintain $50,000.00 worth of life insurance on the children payable to Patty Jo in the event of their death. I was also to give Patty Jo $10,000.00 from where ever I could get it.

I got my clothes, the car payment for the Cutlass Supreme, the bills, and property in Walterboro, which was mortgaged to remodel the house on Yonges Island.

I missed my children, and I thought about asking them if they would move to another state with me.

Jon Avant succeeded in destroying my 12-year marriage for lust and personal gain. My children were not allowed to live with me because, as a man, I was not equal as a parent. My property, possessions, my dreams and goals for the future were gone because I fought to keep my wife and family. The pain and agony of this total loss rendered me helpless, and a part of me died.

I didn't fit anyplace anymore. I wanted to belong somewhere and with someone. I saw myself as a failure.

I went to Patty Jo's apartment to pick up my children for the weekend visits. Patty Jo was at Jon's apartment. I was able to visit my children every weekend until June. Patty Jo was at Jon's most of the time.

Patty Jo called me at work and demanded me to pay her and Jon's medical bills. Patty Jo was covered by my government employee health insurance program and by the insurance she had working for Dr. Sanders. I was broke. I was paying her car payment, her attorney's fees, child support, the mortgage on the farm, and other miscellaneous bills.

I was lonely. I took my children fishing. My son told me I should find myself a girlfriend.

Patty Jo wanted the $10,000.00 without delay. I had to go to court several times. Attorney Joe Runey sent me his bill for any action he took for Patty Jo, and I had to pay it.

I had to sell the property in Walterboro to come up with the money Patty Jo wanted. The property was for sale at a fair price, but the market for real estate was slow.

In June, Patty Jo and Jon rented a house in the Springfield Subdivision. They moved in together. I asked my attorney, Ben Peeples, about this situation because our divorce was not final. He told me I could do nothing.

Patty Jo took Jon around to visit all our old friends.

Reflections Upon A Sunny Day

I visited Jack and Mary Parker. For some unknown reason, Mary insulted me and told me she was going to Patty Jo's and Jon's to have some fun. I stopped visiting Jack and Mary. Everything I said or did got back to Patty Jo. Jack would tell Mary something and she would hotline it to Patty Jo.

I changed real estate companies. I also ran ads in the Charleston News and Courier and the South Carolina Market Bulletin. I saved the ads. Real estate sales were slow and the broker offered to put in a good word for me in court.

At an oyster roast, Mary Parker asked to speak with me. She began crying and told me she was sorry for hurting my feelings. She kissed me and I cried. I said, "I think it is best that I stay away from you and Jack. You have become friends with Jon and Patty Jo and it just wouldn't work out."

Patty Jo's attorney, Joe Runey, had me back in court again. The judge told me I was in contempt of court for not paying Patty Jo the $10,000.00 as ordered. He sentenced me to serve two years in prison at CCI. I tried to explain to the judge that I was doing everything possible to get the money. I presented a folder filled with papers and ads to substantiate my efforts. The judge said, "You're dragging your feet." He suspended the sentence and gave me thirty days to come up with the money.

The real estate company found a buyer. The broker agreed to wait for their commission, so Patty Jo could get $10,000.00 cash. I didn't receive any cash from the sale. I was still broke. Six months later, I started receiving monthly payments from the buyer as agreed in the real estate contract. According to the State of South Carolina, on September 22nd, I was divorced from Patty Jo.

I received a bill from Family Court. The bill indicated that I owed over $17,000.00 to Patty Jo for delinquent child support payments. Attorney Joe Runey had me set up in Family Court to pay astronomical payments since 1978. Mr. Runey's maneuver was not legal. It was a tangled mess and I had to straighten it out.

I met Pamela Jane West. Pam was an attractive tall blond who enjoyed the outdoors.

Attorney Ben Peeples informed me that the charges against me for assault and battery with intent to kill were dropped. He told me that my record was removed from the police files.

In December, I rented an apartment and Pam West moved in.

1982

Age 34 – I had been defeated. All that I loved and cherished had been taken from me. I lost my family, and I never got over that total and absolute loss.

I was weak and broken from my losses. I was lonely and wanted someone to fill the terrible void that afflicted my soul. I desperately hoped Pam would be good for me. With all that had happened, I felt like giving up but something within me would not consent to surrender. I was desperate to get back on my feet and get my life back on course. I needed a decent woman in my life.

Pam shared my interests in hunting and fishing but the reason was surely a paradox. She would spend an hour in front of the mirror putting on makeup, mascara and lipstick, to go fishing. I enjoyed her company and she went out of her way to please me. Pam was good with my children and took up a lot of time with them. She helped them with their homework and took them to movies when I had weekend duty with the Army Reserve. Pam did not have a driver's license. She told me they were taken as a result of a D.U.I. charge. I made arrangements for her to get a drivers license.

Patty Jo called me on the telephone crying, "I can't do a thing with Joey." She said, "You were always so good with Joey and he always listened to you." She asked me if I would help her with him. I said, "Yes". The possibility of Patty Jo becoming civil with me became a wishful thought.

On the following weekend, Patty Jo sent instructions for me to punish the children during my visit for something they did at her house. I told my children we weren't going to play by her rules while you're with me.

Pam complained about Patty Jo calling our apartment. Pam told me that Jon flirted with her, when she took the children back to their house in Springfield. Jon stayed out of sight when I picked up my children.

Pam began hanging out at a local tavern to drink. I warned her that I would not put up with too much drinking. She slowed down but didn't completely stop. I sincerely thought I could change her bad habits.

I checked Freddy's homework. Patty Jo was signing incorrect work. She wasn't taking the time to check his work and he needed help.

Pam wanted a commitment. She claimed a commitment would make her more devoted to me. I wanted to fill an emptiness in my life and I wanted to take care of her needs. I conceived that the combination would produce a strong bond known as marriage.

We looked at a house that was for sale on Johns Island. It was a VA repossession in need of repair. I made a down payment. A week later, vandals set fire in the kitchen, broke the sliding glass door and broke all the back windows of the house. They knocked down the brick fence around the cement patio too. The neighbors told us they saw some young black boys throwing bricks at the windows. The real estate company repaired most of the damage.

Reflections Upon A Sunny Day

On May 5th, I married Pam West and we bought the house on Johns Island.

We had an unlisted telephone number, but Patty Jo somehow got it. She called and wanted money. Pam objected to the calls and accused me of trying to have an affair. I needed Pam's support, but all I found was discomfort.

Patty Jo called me at work and harassed me about money. The young clerk complained to the supervisor about my use of the phone.

Pam was very jealous of one of her sisters. Pam's sister, Sylvia, was better known as Sam. She was a self-employed prostitute.

Patty Jo launched another attack at me with her lawyer, Joe Runey, claiming I owed Family Court $57.00. I spent an entire weekend assembling a file out of a notebook. I taped my canceled checks and receipts to each page by month showing the amount paid each month and discovered that I had paid more than was required. I felt confident that my evidence would speak for itself.

I had to take another day off from work to go to court. While I waited in the hallway of the Courthouse, I spoke with a deputy. When I was called into the Family Courtroom, the deputy followed me. The Judge said, "The Family Court computer indicates that you owe $57.00," then asked, "Is that not so?" I said, "Sir, the computer may say that, but I have all my receipts in this book and it clearly shows that I do not owe the money." The Judge blew up and hollered at me. He got completely outrageous and screamed, "The computer record shows you owe it!"

The Judge had a file on his desk and opened it. He said, "I see here that you had a two year sentence to CCI suspended. I'm revoking the suspension. You will hereby be committed to CCI and serve two years in the South Carolina Department of Corrections." I was stunned by the Judge's behavior and my being sentenced to prison. I was a hard-working man just trying to make a living and make ends meet. I would lose my job. I would lose my freedom and be locked in an alien environment of cutthroats. I was overwrought by my sudden change in life. The Judge beat his gavel on the desk and ordered the deputy to take me into custody. The deputy escorted me to the hallway and shook his head. He said, "I can't believe the way the Judge acted". I said, "He wouldn't even look at my receipts."

I was sentenced to spend two years in prison. The deputy said, "If I were you, I would pay the $57.00 and maybe the Judge would change his mind about your sentence." The office was nearby, so I paid the money.

After paying the money, I stood beside the deputy at the Courtroom door. We waited a long time before being called back into the Courtroom.

The Judge said, "I see you have paid the $57.00, but I am afraid you are too late. The sentence stands. You will serve two years in prison for being delinquent in your support payments." He slammed his gavel on the desk and just stared at me. He did nothing but stare at me for a couple of minutes. Then he said, "I am suspending the sentence and fining you $250.00 for being in contempt of court." I had to call someone at the AMSA Shop and asked them to bring me the money, for I had to remain in the custody of the deputy.

I had to swallow my pride, anger and self-respect. I could not win when all the people in the system were corrupt.

The Judge gave me orders that any money I paid to Patty Jo, for whatever reason, would go through Family Court.

Patty Jo wanted money for Joey's glasses. When I paid it through the court, her attorney, Joe Runey, threatened to pursue additional legal actions against me.

Pam got her drivers license. She had nothing to do all day, but she refused to get a job. During the day, she hung out at bars drinking and playing pool. I tried to stop her from drinking but the more I tried the more hostile she became with me. I finally recognized that Pam was an alcoholic.

Pam drank beer, wine and whiskey. She drank straight whiskey on ice with a dash of water. She often came home drunk and accused me of her sister. I wasn't sure if she meant flirting or having an affair with her, but I had done neither. Pam didn't like to drink alone, so she often went to her sister's apartment and got drunk. Sam paid her bills and rent by her profession. Pam envied her sister's independence. When Pam did not come home in the evenings, I checked the bars and her sister's apartment.

On a particular occasion, I found Pam drunk at Sam's apartment. I asked Sam for her help, but Sam was also a drunk. Pam cursed me and wanted to fight. Without Pam hearing, Sam told me to park across the street and wait for her. About fifteen minutes later, Sam met me in the parking lot. I was expecting her help, but she had something else on her mind. I let her know my concern was for my wife. Sam said, "Okay, I'll speak with her." Sam told me to wait about ten minutes and stand outside the apartment door. I waited about two minutes and stood beside the sidewall of the apartment. The staircase was next to her apartment, so only a thin wall separated the distance between us. I could hear Pam and her sister talking. I heard Pam tell Sam all about how she fucked one of her old boyfriends for $70.00 and how she spent the money. Sam said, "You better watch what you say, Freddy might be standing at the door." I listened until I heard enough. When I knocked on the door, Pam opened it. I said, "Pam, I heard everything you said and we're finished." She stood there with a drunk, surprised look on her face, and I left.

In times of hurt and loss I usually withdrew into a self-made enclosure of impenetrable solitude. I drove around with no particular place to go, but I stopped by Jack and Cherice Willard's house for a few minutes before going home.

Pam called me on the phone at least a dozen times during the night begging me to forgive her. She promised me that she would never do it again. I forgave her. Two weeks later, I caught her again.

Pam was a violent and destructive drunk. She tore things up in the house and accused me of the immoral things she was doing herself.

I noticed Patty Jo driving past my house on several occasions. It couldn't have been a coincidence, because I lived about twenty miles from her.

I bought Pam a 1980 Toyota Celica. She got drunk and wanted to go off in the car. I took the keys and locked the car. She smashed the car's back window with a gasoline can. After she attacked me, I slapped her and made her go to bed. When she woke up the following morning, she started fighting with me again. I didn't want to fight with her, so I gave up and covered my face with my hands.

I went to see Attorney Jim Gonzales. I told him that Pam was an alcoholic, and having affairs with other men. I said, "At first I thought her drinking was a bad habit, but now I know it's alcoholism." I told him that Pam was a violent drunk, and I showed him the bruises from her attack. I showed him a picture of Pam. Mr. Gonzales said, "A Judge wouldn't believe she is a drunk. She looks too young and pretty." Pam was 26 years old.

When Pam wasn't drinking, she could be very pleasant to me. We were doing a lot of work to the house. We completely repainted the inside and outside of the house.

Pam asked me for credit cards and promised not to charge much. I gave her the cards.

Pam got drunk and aimed a .22 caliber Ruger semi-automatic pistol at me. She tried to fire it at me but it wasn't cocked. She said, "I don't want your little bastards over here anymore." I didn't want to fight with her, so I drove around for a while and returned after dark without her knowing it. I spent the night in my jeep.

While feeling the pain of more heartache, I heard the pistol fire inside the house. I sat up straight and wondered if she had shot herself. Then, I wondered if people would think I had shot her. The possibility of being arrested for shooting her entered my mind, too. I watched the house closely for a few minutes. Finally, I saw her shadow pass by a window. She had shot a hole through the bedroom wall and the pistol jammed.

Reflections Upon A Sunny Day

I tried to help Pam with her drinking problem, but she didn't want help.

Age 35 – I received a letter from the Federal Government Employee Health Benefit Program stating that Patty Jo filed a claim against my health insurance.

I found out later that Patty Jo was swinging a crooked deal with Dr. Devito for a breast implant. Patty Jo called me about the insurance claim and demanded me to pay for her breast implant. Pam gave me hell about it.

Jack Parker called me from Kings Bay, Georgia. He told me there was a man there who was bragging about how he killed my father. I called Detective Paul Hawkins and reported everything Jack told me. Detective Hawkins did not call me back. A month later, I called him again and still got no answers.

Jon Avant changed the name of the construction company. He was being sued for faulty work and filed bankruptcy. Jon put the company in Patty Jo's name and sold his old equipment. He bought new equipment under the name of the new company.

Patty Jo called and threatened me. She wanted me to give her money. She simply loved money more than she ever loved me. I told her to leave me alone. I said, "If you want money, get it from your boyfriend. You wanted him so bad! You took everything I had just like you said many times before. You have it all now, so just leave me alone." She said, "I'll sue you" I said, "I will get a good lawyer and fight you."

While on my job at the AMSA Shop, a deputy delivered papers to me. Patty Jo was suing me for $150,000.00.

I went to Attorney Jim Gonzales for his help in regard to the civil suit. After several trips to his office, he told me Patty Jo and her attorney, Joe Runey, might want to make a deal. Jim told me they wanted to settle out of court. I asked him to find out the details.

Patty Jo found out she needed more ammunition to get what she wanted.

SSG Leroy Linen was a magistrate in Charleston County and a member of the 3271st USAH Aug (300B). Leroy told me that Patty Jo couldn't collect on the civil suit until she had a criminal conviction.

Solicitor Charles Condon called me at work. He said, "I hate to be the bearer of bad news but your criminal charges are back. Get yourself a lawyer!" I couldn't believe it. My criminal charges had been dropped nearly three years ago.

I went to the Courthouse and spoke with Mr. Condon. He told me Patty Jo got a battered women's group to put pressure on him, and he had to do something.

I called Attorney Ben Peeples. He told me they could bring the charges back because it never went to court. He said, "Let me go to the Grand Jury in your place." I asked, "Shouldn't I be there?" Ben told me he did not want me to go. I thought he knew what he was doing, so I followed his advice.

Attorney Ben Peeples did not call to tell me the results of the Grand Jury. I called and asked him how did it go? He said, "Not good." He told me it had been three years since the charge, and he couldn't remember much about what had happened. He described to me what Patty Jo stated to the Grand Jury. Patty Jo had told a bunch of preposterous lies and the Grand Jury reacted to her every lie as if they were gospel. I was indicted. I never knew what to expect from Patty Jo. She was a master of lies.

Over the course of years, I attended many military schools in the eastern United States. I often worried about my wife and family while away at these schools. There was no peace of mind. I knew my wife was not faithful.

I had to go to Pennsylvania for the AMSA Shop. I didn't trust Pam, so I asked her to go with me. Pam was usually sweet and kind when she wasn't drinking. She reminded me of a juvenile delinquent who needed constant attention. Pam got drunk in Pennsylvania. On the return trip to South Carolina, I had to drive an eighteen-wheel tractor-trailer rig, along with other men from the AMSA Shop.

When we neared Charleston, Pam broke away from the convoy and left Interstate 26. I parked the tractor-trailer at the AMSA Shop in Charleston. Robert Goodale needed a ride home, so he rode with me. My jeep broke down before we reached Johns Island. The electronic ignition burnt up. We caught a ride and later towed the jeep to my house. Pam wasn't home. I borrowed a car and had an idea she would be at a bar in Goose Creek. I found her there drunk. The bouncer threw her out. She was mad at me and took off in her car and got into traffic before I could follow. I drove home and went to bed. Later I received a call from the Goose Creek Police Department. Pam was under arrest for DUI second offense.

I went to Goose Creek and got Pam out of jail. It was the week of the 4th of July. Pam and I decided to go to Florida for the 4th of July weekend. We went to Tampa and visited her brother in Jacksonville. When we returned late Sunday night,, we found our house burnt to the ground. It was raining and very dark, which added to the disheartening shadows of black ruins. We looked for our dogs, then drove to our neighbor's house. They weren't home, so we went to my mother's house. I asked my mother if she had heard anything about my house. She said, "No." We spent the night there. Early the next morning, my son, Joey, called my mother's residence to speak with me. He asked me about my house burning down. I'm sure Patty Jo put him up to calling me, and I believe she had something to do with it. Patty Jo and Jon were now living with Mr. Wilkerson in Yonges Island. Mrs. Wilkerson had died some weeks ago of poor health.

Pam and I went to the Fire Department to get a report of the fire. The person we spoke to was very sarcastic to us.

I felt sure the insurance company would take care of us. We spoke with the insurance adjusters, and I told them about my house in Walterboro. The insurance company refused to help. They told us they suspected arson. Everything we owned was in the house. We had no money for food, clothes or rent. We moved in with Pam's parents.

I went to Attorney Jim Gonzales and told him about my home and the insurance company refusing to honor the homeowner's policy. He knew something about the insurance company and accepted the case.

There was an article in the News and Courier about DUI cases. The paper had a story about an attorney, Reese Joy, who gave an effective defense against the accuracy of the breath analyzer. Pam wanted him to represent her in court. We called his office and made an appointment. Attorneys Reese Joy and Debbie Lewis took the case.

Pam had to appear for roll call at the Berkeley County Courthouse. I accompanied her. When Solicitor Stoney asked Pam who would be representing her, she told him Attorneys Reese Joy and Debbie Lewis. He said, "Oh! You're bringing in the Big Guns."

Pam was terrified in regard to the concept of going to court. I gave her encouragement and moral support. Pam gave me hell and accused me of flirting with Debbie Lewis.

Pam and I went to the Attorney's Office, who were on permanent retainer with the American Mutual Fire Insurance Company, to give a deposition. Attorney Jim Gonzales was present, to. We found evidence that the insurance company was notorious for cheating people.

I revised my assessment of Patty Jo almost daily. I feared the silence, because I had learned not to underestimate her.

Pam went to the bars and stayed out late drinking. She returned to her parent's house in a truck with her brother and another man. Her brother got out of the truck, but Pam remained in the truck with the man for quite a while before going in the house. Pam was drunk. I packed my few clothes and went to my mother's house. I returned at 9:00 A.M. for my aluminum boat. While I was changing the trailer hitch ball on my jeep, Pam came outside and told me she was going on a spending spree with the credit cards.

Reflections Upon A Sunny Day

Pam already had me in deep debt with the cards and her threat caused me great concern. I went into the house and picked up her pocketbook to get my credit cards and Pam attacked me. I held up my hand to hold her off. I wasn't aware of it, but her eye got hit with the crescent wrench that was still in my hand. I took the credit cards and left. Pam later told me that either she or her mother called the Mount Pleasant Police.

I didn't know it, but Pam had a black eye. We made up and rented an apartment in Mount Pleasant. We, also, rented some furniture and bought a few essentials.

My children were over less. They told me that Patty Jo knew where we lived.

When I returned from work each day, my stomach was in a knot. I wondered if Pam would be home or out drinking. I put a tape recorder on our phone line. I recorded Pam's telephone calls. I listened to her lover's frequent calls. It broke my heart, but I learned the truth. I listened to where she went and what she did. The recorder told it all.

When Pam would leave home to get drunk and sell her love, I would break down and cry. Crying seemed to help wash some of the pain away.

Pam went to trial in Berkeley County for the DUI charge. Attorneys Reese Joy and Debbie Lewis represented Pam. Several of Pam's old boyfriends from the Goose Creek bar were there, too. I took the witness stand for Pam. Solicitors Stoney and Charles Condon were there for the prosecution. Judge Hamilton Smith said things that he shouldn't have in trial. The trial ended in a hung jury. Judge Smith gave orders for a retrial.

Attorney Debbie Lewis called our apartment to tell us they can swing a deal. She said, "If Pam will plead to reckless driving, she won't have to go to court again". Pam agreed. The fine was to be $200.00 or more. I told Pam I would give her the money.

I listened to the tape recorder. Pam intended to collect $200.00 from me and $100.00 from one of her boyfriends.

I suspected Pam would be going to see her boyfriend. I left my job at 9:00 A.M. and went to my apartment to listen to the tape recorder. I listened to the recording and it told me that Pam had gotten dressed and left to service her boyfriend in Columbia for money. I listened to her recorded conversation and it tore me apart. I would have gone to Columbia, but the universal joints were worn out in my Jeep. I took the tape to work and let Robert Goodale listen to part of it.

When I returned from work, I confronted Pam about the affair she had that day. She didn't know how I knew about it. Pam said, "It was all your fault." A lifetime of practice had taught her to blame everything on me.

After several more trips to the attorney's offices, the American Mutual Fire Insurance Company paid for our home. Pam wanted her half of the money. She bought a $1000.00 diamond ring just like the one her sister, Sam, wore. We bought some new furniture and clothes, too. Pam continued to give me hell about her sister for no reason.

I had to go to the Courthouse about a dozen times concerning Patty Jo and the criminal charges. Some of the people at the Courthouse thought I worked there.

I spoke with Solicitor Charles Condon and he told me he didn't believe Patty Jo's story about being in Dr. Sanders Office with Jon after working hours. He said, "I believe Patty Jo has some loose screws in her head." I was surprised to hear him say that.

During a weekend drill with the Army Reserves, I got sick. I explained to Captain Friedman and the Company Commander about my terrible migraine headaches I described how my head and stomach hurt, and how I couldn't see as the result of the blurry vision.

I suffered immensely under Patty Jo's constant intimidation. I felt so powerless to cope with her attacks on my basic worth and dignity. As she pressured me more and more, the fear for my safety and wellbeing grew.

1984

Because the single theme of human existence is atrocity, it seems that whatever man can do that will irreparable harm his fellowman, he will certainly do if it will bring profit and gain. I have reached the point in my life when I am seized with an utter hopelessness about the human race. I like human beings a lot more than wart hogs or stingrays, but I assure you I would receive far more justice and mercy from a wart hog than from a human being who wears a black robe and sits in judgment against his fellowman.

Attorney Jim Gonzales told me not to get him involved in the criminal case unless I had $7500.00. I went to Attorney Linda S. Lombard. She presented a good battle plan in her office, but I couldn't afford her $5000.00 fee.

Pam stayed out late drinking. I followed her to her boyfriend's house.

On many occasions, Pam came home drunk around 3:00 A.M. and passed out on the couch. One morning, she couldn't find her checkbook and accused me of stealing it. I didn't have it. She looked behind the couch and found the tape recorder plugged into a spare phone jack. Pam gave me hell. She was worried I would use the tapes against her.

Pam did not support me in regard to my problems with Patty Jo. Pam created her own problems for me to deal with. Considering her drinking, the bars and the prostitution, was the good worth the tears I cried? I kept suppressing and denying my problems and hung on to a false hope that things were going to get better.

I went to the Courthouse again and spoke with Solicitor Condon and Mr. Frank Hunt. Solicitor Condon wanted me to accept a plea bargain. I didn't know what to do. Solicitor Condon told me it would be a misdemeanor charge. He said, "It won't hurt your government job or military career."

I connected the tape recorder to a phone line in the attic. I listened to her boyfriends, their destinations and love affairs. I told Attorney Jim Gonzales about the recorder.

Pam's boyfriends called, make rendezvous and visits while I am on weekend duty with the Army Reserve. It was hard for me to work on weekends knowing my wife was laying with another man. Captain Seymour asked me if Pam worked at a bar in Mount Pleasant. He saw her vehicle there almost everyday. I shared some of my problems with him and Captain Ritter.

They were making me a worried and exasperated man. They lied humiliated and exhausted me. They made me afraid, obedient, humble and made me cry. They made me sorry I was born.

Like the tide, the change came slowly, inexorably. I could no more have stopped it or altered it's course than I could have caused the sun or the moon to stand still in the heavens.

When I received phone calls from my attorneys, my stomach went inside out. I couldn't eat and would vomit. Whenever the phone rang, I feared there was going to be more bad news. I was being destroyed like a cancer patient being eaten away by a malignant disease.

I received a phone call from Baker Hospital. Patty Jo had left my phone number with them for her billing.

On April 22nd, my grandfather died. With all my problems, I had failed to visit him in a long time. It was too late now. Pam did not go to the funeral with me. Pam and I had made no friends in our years of marriage. She wanted no friends. She wanted her own private world, which included bars and one night stands. Pam was jealous of everyone I spoke with. She was jealous of Attorney Debbie Lewis, because I had opened the door for her at the Dock Restaurant during a trial recess. Pam started at least a hundred arguments over her sister, Sam. Pam told me I couldn't call over there looking for her, nor could I answer the phone if Sam were calling. She took the mailbox keys and wouldn't let me have one. I was weak from years of torment, and Pam controlled me as if I were a prisoner. Pam would go out and get drunk and whore around, but she knew I would be there. I was her safe harbor.

I parked outside a bar and watched Pam kiss and make out with a man in the parking lot. She would come home around 3:00 A. M. and want to fight. She wouldn't let me rest and would tear up things and call me terrible names. Pam was so jealous and envious of her sister, and she constantly accused me of her. There was no need for her to feel that way. Pam was younger and prettier than her sister, Sam.

On a half dozen occasions I had to call the Mt. Pleasant Police Department to produce some sort of peace in our apartment.

On one day, Pam would be drunk and curse and call me revolting names. She would be filled with jealousy and accuse me of no less than she was doing herself. On the following day, Pam tried to be the perfect wife and please me in every way to make up for her previous behavior.

I was committed to Pam. I wanted to love her, but I also knew my love wasn't enough. Two people had to work together at a marriage. When Pam was drunk, there were times when she didn't seem to recognize me. And when her mind was sober, sharp and frisky, we spent the day laughing and reminiscing, but when I prepared to leave, her eyes registered both goodbye and betrayal.

Pam admitted to having a drinking problem once. In a moment of sincerity, she said, "Freddy, you're the only person who has ever tried to help me stop drinking." I told her I would help her in every way, but she chose not to do anything about it.

Pam had a toll free number to call her boyfriend in Columbia. He worked for the Bell Telephone Company.

Pam started going out with a young teenage boy. She told me to find myself a girlfriend.

I dreaded the trips to Jim Gonzales' office. My nerves were a wreck, and I had to take more time off from work for my many trips to the Courthouse.

Several major parts of the drivetrain broke under my Jeep. I couldn't drive it anymore, so I bought a 1976 Ford F-150 pickup truck. The engine ran good, but I replaced the water pump, tires, windshield and exhaust system. It needed a paint job, but I was afraid to improve its appearance. I was afraid Patty Jo would want it too.

One of the mechanics in the AMSA Shop had "Van Fever" and wanted to sell his garage kept 1977 Corvette. He worked on the car for years and it was in mint condition. He had a burning desire to buy a van and he offered to sell me the Corvette for a reasonable price. I said, "No, I can't afford it." A few minutes later, he came back and offered it to me for $6400.00. The price was too good to pass up. It was a great deal and I knew it could be sold for a profit. I bought the car. In less than two months I was offered $8400.00 for it. I didn't sell it, for I knew one day the car would be worth even more. I parked the Corvette at my mother's house and didn't tell Pam. With her drunk driving she would have surely wrecked it.

When Pam got the desire to go out drinking, I couldn't stop her. I begged her not to go. I was lonely and the hurt wouldn't stop. Sometimes, I visited Joe and Karen Bennett to escape the solitude and loneliness of my apartment. My sadness was overwhelming.

I underestimated the dark part of mankind that is rarely seen in the light of day. I failed to reckon with the secret beasts that reside in the lightless forests of human souls.

Pam came home drunk and cut the tires on my truck. When I tried to stop her, she threw the knife at me with all her strength. I called the Mount

Pleasant Police Department. Pam was sarcastic with the two officers as she staggered and spoke with slurred speech. The officer's suggestion was familiar to me. They told me to find another place to stay for the night.

My mother was getting sick, and I didn't want her to get sick again. I took her to the doctor weekly.

Mr. Frank Hunt called me and said, "Bring a lawyer to court Monday!" I called Attorney Ben Peeples, but he was not in his office, I left a message for him.

The following day, Mr. Frank Hunt called me at work again. He wanted to know about the $10,000.00 deal. I told him that Patty Jo wanted $10,000.00 for her word; that she would not testify in court. Mr. Hunt said, "That is blackmail." I said, "I know and Solicitor Condon knows about it."

I went to Attorney Jim Gonzales' Office. He had spoken with Attorney Joe Runey about the $10,000.00 deal. He said, "I couldn't pin Joe down, they're dancing around the bush."

I spoke with Attorney Gonzales again. I asked him if Patty Jo got the ten thousand dollars, what would stop her from coming back for more?

He said, "Nothing." I asked him if he could get Patty Jo to sign a paper, so she couldn't come back for more and leave me alone.

Attorney Jim Gonzales got in touch with Patty Jo's attorney. He said, "They won't agree to sign any papers."

Attorney Ben Peeples called me and wanted $2500.00 for the trial that was to begin Monday. I told him about the call from Mr. Frank Hunt and Patty Jo's deal. I told him there may be no trial. Attorney Peeples demanded the money. I asked, " How much money will I get back if there is no trial?" Attorney Peeples said, "I'll give you $500.00 back."

I went to the Courthouse. Frank Hunt told me to hold on getting a lawyer. Court was postponed. Mr. Hunt told me he was going to check things out with Solicitor Condon. He also said, "I'm going to call Patty Jo about this $10,000.00 deal and see what she has to say about it."

If Mr. Hunt called Patty Jo, I never heard the outcome of the conversation.

Solicitor Condon asked me to come to the Courthouse. He told me, if I would plead to a lesser offense, it wouldn't affect my job. He said, "You will not have to serve any time in prison."

Court was set. Solicitor Condon said, "You won't need a lawyer." Solicitor would both represent and prosecute me. I was sentenced to either five or seven years in prison by Judge Fields. He suspended the sentence and put on my probation.

It had been three years since the incident in Dr. Sanders' office. Patty Jo agreed not to pursue the charges if I dropped the adultery charges on her. The charges were dropped. In the end, I was sentenced and had to attend probation meetings. Patty Jo had what she needed for her next course of action.

A deputy came to the AMSA Shop again to serve me papers. He knew where to find me without asking. He had served me court documents many times before. The Deputy shook his head and said, "Sorry, it's my job."

Patty Jo filed her lawsuit again. She got the criminal conviction out of her way. Now she wanted money. I read the court document. Patty Jo was suing me for $150,000.00.

Patty Jo knew she wouldn't be able to collect it all at once. She told me she would take everything I had for the next ten years.

I tried to stop Pam from going out drinking. She spent the weekend with her boyfriend in Columbia.

Reflections Upon A Sunny Day

My neighbor told me about other men being in my apartment, while I was at work.

I tried to bring Pam home from bars and stop her from DUI. Pam brought her drunk brothers and bar buddies to the apartment. I could barely tolerate the insanity of it all.

Pam got furious with me when I interfered with her drinking. In a fit of spite and rage, she called my job and tried to get me fired.

Pam often came home drunk and wouldn't let me rest. She dragged me out of the bed for 3:00 A.M. breakfasts.

I was often bone tired at work. It was difficult to decide or do simple tasks, and it took all day. I had to push myself to do things.

Pam told me it was my fault that she screwed around. She said, "You don't give me enough money."

My Supply Officer, Captain Ritter, informed me that Attorney Joe Runey and Solicitor Charles Condon were cousins.

I had to go to Attorney Joe Runey's Office to give a deposition concerning the $150,000.00 civil suit. Patty Jo gave a deposition to Attorney Joe Gonzales and lied about almost everything. I'd watched for years, and I've been absolutely astonished by her power to lie. Patty Jo was never daunted by something as inconvenient as truth, she made her lies a central part of our children's identities, too.

Attorney Gonzales caught her in some of her tearful lies. Later, while we were in the parking lot, Attorney Gonzales said, "She's a hell of an actor and will make a dangerous witness on the stand." Patty Jo's tears were simply weapons to be counted when calculating the order of battle, and her tongue was deadlier than any weapon.

I got into a fight with Pam's brother concerning her being in bars.

I spoke with Magistrate Leroy Linen about my problems in tears. I also spoke with CPT Brian Friedman, SSG Pat Alston, SGT. Charles Jones and SP4 Sandra Weston on occasion.

I visited Joe and Karen Bennett. I needed help and someone to talk to, but no one can feel or really know the pain or hurt a person is going through except the person who has the pain.

Reflections Upon A Sunny Day

My mother was getting sick. She was calling me on the phone about Patty Jo and it got on my nerves.

I had soaking sweats at night, and I had a bad odor.

Pam's car was stolen from the parking lot of the Citadel Mall. I bought her a 1982 Ford Pinto Wagon.

Pam got drunk and wrecked the car.

My children were seldom over to the apartment, but when they were they asked what everything cost and asked how much money I had. Pam said, "They're spying."

I got preoccupied with my burdens. I went to work and no one was there. It was a government holiday.

I became impotent as a result of all the pressure from Patty Jo and problems with Pam.

Pam came home drunk and violent. I couldn't stand it and slept in my truck.

My Labrador Retriever, which I had trained so well, was stolen.

Early on a Saturday morning, I got ready for a weekend drill. I showered, put on my fatigues and hurried to the Army Reserve Center. I found the parking lot empty, when I arrived. In my worry and confusion, I was alone. There was no drill.

Pam said, "I'm going to Florida and don't know when I'll be back." I figured she had a reason for going, but she wouldn't tell me why. I asked her not to go, but she wouldn't listen.

While Pam was in Florida, Robert Goodale called me and asked me if I'd like to attend a graduation party. His wife and her friends had graduated from nursing school. I went to a party and met Jan.

Jan and I went out a few times.

Pam returned from Florida and told me she met some old friends in bars there. I believe she went to the Bahamas, too, with her boyfriend.

Reflections Upon A Sunny Day

It was hard for me to do, but I moved out on Pam on the 19th of October in 1984. I asked for a divorce – no contest. I went to her attorney, Jan Kauser, and filed for a separation.

Pam begged me to come back. She said, "I didn't mean all the rotten things I said." Pam said, "I'll stop cheating on you." My recorder was still connected to the phone line in the attic. She was still communicating with her boyfriends. Pam and I talked and we cried together. I loved her, but I couldn't take her abuse anymore. Pam would not promise to stop drinking. I hurt deeply for her, but the problems were still there.

I had frequent and severe migraine headaches. My mind was always occupied with my problems.

Jan asked me how much money I made. I couldn't stand the thought of being alone. We rented an apartment on Dupont Road. Jan acted civilized. Her employer had been her boyfriend, but he was married. Jan acted like she had given him up. I didn't care. All I wanted was some peace of mind.

On several occasions, Pam visited me at work with alcohol on her breath and one of her boyfriends in her car. She always wanted money, and I gave it to her when I had it. I loved her for her good qualities, and she had a lot of potential if only she would utilize it. I was hurting deeply.

I often felt guilty when lying in the bed with Jan at night.

I missed Pam, but I knew I couldn't stand any more of her abuse. I felt myself sinking into a deeper depression. I had a constant sense of impending doom.

I was committed to Patty Jo as well as Pam. I tried to understand women, but this mystery only left me both enraged and wounded.

Jan Tweed had some problems, with her ex-husband, concerning the visitation hours with her son. Jan worked at the East Cooper Pharmacy. She got strong medication for her headaches and shared it with me. My migraines were coming more frequently.

My children visited more often. Jan's son lived about forty miles away. We picked him up every other weekend.

I tried to keep up a front and hold things inside. I swallowed my frustration and tried to make believe that my problems didn't exist.

Patty Jo and John pushed harder and harder. She flooded me with Dr. bills.

Reflections Upon A Sunny Day

I feared phone calls from lawyers and the thought of going to court. I just wanted to be left alone.

I came home from work and often sat on the couch and cried. Jan got off work later than me. I'd often fix a drink to calm my nerves.

My mind kept bouncing back and forth between my present and past problems. I tried to run from my problems and keep myself busy in a flurry of activity. I ran here and there in my truck to stay in motion. I browsed the stores, and roamed the rivers to escape the reality of my pain.

In December, I took my boys hunting and they shot their first deer. It was a large eight point buck.

When my boys were small, I taught them how to draw and color. They practiced until their skill was exceedingly good. Freddy promised to give me a painting for Christmas. I waited in anticipation for his work of art.

On Christmas afternoon, my children visited for a couple of hours and collected their gifts. The one thing I looked for was not found. There was no painting.

While shopping at Krogers, I saw Janice. She told me that she was sorry to hear about Joey's accident. I didn't know what she was talking about. She told me Joey and Freddy received motorcycles for Christmas. She said, "Joey wrecked his on the day after Christmas and had to be hospitalized." Janice said, "Patty Jo lets the kids go wild with no supervision."

1985

I struggled with my emotions. I had to hold things inside and all that was left of me was a shell. Everything else was eaten away. As a child, I was sensitive and afraid of my father and afraid for my mother. In grammar school, I could not pay attention or hold a thought. I felt a sense of alienation about my school and religion. I wanted to be liked and accepted as part of the group and activities, but I couldn't hold a conversation on one subject. Sometimes I could not keep up with my thoughts even though I talked rapidly. I rocked in my bed. I felt a need for love not punishment. I had no self-esteem. I thought I was dumb and ugly. I felt a deep unhappiness and asked myself why was I born? I became reckless and didn't care if I lived or died. I felt cursed for the things I did as a child and prayed for God to take my life. The free and clear mind feeling didn't occur often. I became concerned when I couldn't feel anything anymore. There was no joy and excitement in anything. I tried to deny and hide my problems. I brought to my adult life nostalgia for a lost childhood. With my children, I wanted to recreate my childhood as I dreamed it should have been. My marriage and family was most important to me. A part of me died when we were separated. If Patty Jo didn't love me, why did she want me back? It was only on a rare occasion that I was forceful with Patty

Reflections Upon A Sunny Day

Jo. Maybe I let too many things pass by like my mother did? Why did Patty Jo say, "Is it possible to love two men?" Why did she torment me with little pieces of information about Jon? Why did she scream and spit in my face, jab her finger in my chest and dare me to hit her? I needed Patty Jo's love. I held on to her just like my mother held on to my father.

My mother could see that I was coming apart and asked Patty Jo to leave me alone before she drove me crazy. Patty Jo said, "I don't care if I drive him crazy."

Patty Jo swamped me in doctor bills. I had $5000.00 worth of bills in less than three months. Patty Jo knew I had to pay all the medical bills, and she made a mess of them. I had to write letters to each office to straighten out the bills.

I received bills without knowing anything about the circumstances. I asked my children about the bills. They said, "Mama (Patty Jo) told us that you get rich every time we go to the doctor."

I didn't call my children on the phone, unless I had my mother call first. I tried to avoid all contact with Patty Jo; nevertheless she would get on the line and threaten me.

I spoke with Joey on the phone. He told me that he wanted to live with me. Jan was not happy with the idea of Joey living with us. I spoke with Attorney Jim Gonzales about the possibility and the legal steps it would take to have my son live with me.

Patty Jo dispatched her attorney, Joe Runey, on me about the doctor bills. Attorney Runey sent me a threatening letter and a file from Patty Jo concerning the bills.

Attorney Joe Runey called me on the telephone. I recorded the conversation. He was checking for Patty Jo to see how much life insurance I had, and if I had $50,000 payable to my children or their custodian. I pleaded, "Why won't Patty Jo leave me alone?"

Patty Jo told my children she was going to buy a yacht and a swimming pool after going to court.

Jack Willard told Jack Parker about my Corvette. Patty Jo found out and let me know she knew it was at my mother's house. I didn't paint my truck because Patty Jo wanted everything I owned.

Dr. Hill's Office claimed I had a year old bill that was not paid. The bill had been paid and I carried the year old canceled check to his office.

Reflections Upon A Sunny Day

I told the billing clerk that Patty Jo had a lawyer on my back and asked her to please give me her cooperation. I asked her to please apply payments to the balance of what my health insurance did not cover. She told me she would but didn't. Someone backed into my Corvette and wrecked it, while I was in Dr. Hill's Office.

Attorney Jan Kauser called me. He was confused. He saw my name on the court roster and wondered if it was concerning Pam. I explained to him that my first wife, Patty Jo, was suing me. He wished me luck.

The thought of court ate at me like a painful cancer. I was depressed, hurting and withdrawn. I couldn't sleep well and I was exhausted. My stomach stayed upset and hurt. I was taking strong medication for migraines, but they persisted to reoccur with frequency. My nerves were shot, and I was crying more. I felt like I could scream. I was coming apart.

Jan gave me pills for my headaches. I took Ornade for my sinus. My sinuses were never more ailing. With this problem and lack of sleep my eyes sank back into their dark colored sockets.

I had stopped making love to Jan. She thought I was rejecting her... possibly for another woman. Jan knew I was having problems with Patty Jo, but she didn't understand how seriously my problems were affecting me.

For weeks, I remained fixed to the kitchen table with the doctor's bills. I set up a file and put my affairs in order. I made my last will and testament. I didn't understand it at the time, but I was preparing myself for suicide.

My children told me that Patty Jo interrogated them after a visit with me. They told me Patty Jo bad-mouthed and put me down all the time. Patty Jo said, "When you visit your daddy, you don't really have a good time with him. It's all just a trick." I asked my children if they were happy with Patty Jo and Jon. The boys said, "No." I believe Lisa was satisfied.

I had no peace within myself. Patty Jo and her actions were constantly on my mind. I couldn't talk to anyone and really listen to what they were saying for my mind was spinning with thoughts about Patty Jo.

Patty Jo wanted me to send her cash. I flashed back on everything that had happened before.

I was taking my mother to the doctor weekly. She asked me about moving in with her. I was caught between taking care of my mother and my relationship with Jan.

My children were kicked out of Springfield Elementary School because of Jon's children. It was one of the reasons Joey asked to live with me.

Reflections Upon A Sunny Day

Things weren't going well for me at the AMSA Shop. My many problems were affecting my job. I couldn't get to work on time nor could I keep my mind on what I was doing.

I was absent minded. I would forget where I was going or why I was going some place. On one occasion, I even forgot Pam's name and couldn't remember no matter how hard I tried.

My eye jerked uncontrollably, and I couldn't make it stop. My bowels were upset. My mind was preoccupied. I almost got hurt at work. I stopped at green lights and sometimes ran red lights. I was at the limit of my endurance. I wouldn't admit to myself that I was losing it.

I was severely depressed, and what sleep I could manage to get during the night was restless.

My neck and back hurt with agonizing still tension. I took Rolaids for my stomach pain and my head hurt constantly. The headaches often rendered me temporarily blind with dark blurry vision, and bolts of light popped under my closed eyelids. I changed from hyper-virility to impotency. My nights were wracked with nightmares, until I cried out and hyperventilated. In my sleep Patty Jo would rise up from the dust of my terror and torment me. Her voice screamed curses in my head, and I argued with her in my sleep. I had violent dreams. Jan slept heavily and I didn't want to bother her.

On February 8th, I called my mother after work to see if my children were coming over for the weekend. Jan and I went to my mother's house. My children were there and I fed my dogs. Then we all went to Cottageville to pick up her son. Jan wasn't happy with my absent minded behavior. My problems were eating me apart, I tried to insure Jan that I cared for her.

When we arrived back to the apartment, I went back to the kitchen table with the bills. We ordered a pizza, and I played with the children for a little while. The kids watched TV, and I returned to the table again with the bills as I had been doing for weeks. I didn't know what was wrong with me.

Jan went to bed. The children went to bed after the movie. Lisa slept with Jan. I slept on the couch. The nightmares started again and Patty Jo's face came rushing at me out of nowhere. I thought I woke up. The next thing I remember was waking up in the cold woods. I felt something terrible had happened, but I couldn't remember. I felt a need to get away from Patty Jo, and I knew I was at her house. I wanted to get back home where it was safe.

Years of severe pain and torment drove me insane. Everything from my unhappy childhood to the out of control present took its toll. It happened to me gradually over the years, and I was not aware of how sick I had become until I had lost control of my actions. My mind had been reeling back and forth between my past and present problems. I had swallowed my frustrations for years trying to make believe they didn't exist; furthermore, I was ashamed to ask for professional help. I had grown up believing that a man required strength, and to seek help was an admission that I was weak or sick. I tried to hide my feelings and put on a pleasant face, so that no one would know that I was sinking into a severe state of depression. My self-denial did not work. With the increased intense pressures focused on me, I was taken beyond the limits of my endurance. I became sick and irresponsible.

No one has the patent on human suffering. People hurt in different ways and for different reasons. Each of us are individuals with different family backgrounds, religious training, education, experience and physical and mental capabilities. We each have acquired different levels of resilience or ways of responding to the distinct kinds of problems, losses or setbacks in life. And each of us as individuals has a breaking point. All it takes is enough pain, torment, stress and pressure and we can all go over the edge.

I was apprehended while walking down the highway in a daze, by a policewoman. I thought she looked like Jan. I was shuffled from one police car to another and taken to my former home on Yonges Island. I was shown blood and the officers asked me where Patty Jo, Mr. Wilkerson and Jason were. They drove me around and asked me questions. My mind was a blur.

I felt disoriented and alien to myself. I felt I had been in a nightmare that would not stop or end. I wanted to wake up in my bed at home and for the nightmare to end. The events did not seem real to me.

As I laid on the floor of a dirty jail cell, I felt lost and without hope. The turn of events reeled through my mind constantly.

I don't remember when but, piece by piece, like a slow motion projector film, I began recounting parts of what happened. It was like a nightmare. Even after I started remembering things it was difficult for me to accept that I was really doing the things I did in the nightmare. The world had transformed into a gauzy overcast fog and my eyes could not focus clearly.

I wanted to answer the questions asked of me but my mind would not focus on anything. There was a constant blur of thoughts going on in my mind and nothing would stay still long enough to make sense. I could not think or concentrate with any success.

I was depressed, confused and could not read a sentence and grasp its meaning. I felt a great deal of remorse about the things I was remembering, and I cried and cried for days.

Reflections Upon A Sunny Day

I did not feel capable of killing anyone, but my recall of the nightmare and the evidence shown to me convinced me that I had killed my first wife, her father, and her lover's son. Somehow I was not in control of myself and did it in a false state of mind. I had become something or someone else, but I was not myself.

I was locked in a hallway, at the Charleston County Jail, without a bed or toilet. I was lowered to begging for water to drink and the use of the bathroom. I laid on the floor, day and night, with the bright lights burning from the ceiling. I was a broken man. I felt like screaming and screaming, but I held my pain within. I felt a strong impulse to run and smash my head through the bars at the end of the hall. I laid on the floor in mental agony.

Attorney Edmond Robinson spoke with me at the County Jail about legal representation. I was confused and didn't know what to do. Attorney Robinson had a life sentence already arranged with Solicitor Charles Condon, but I had no knowledge of it at the time.

Magistrate Leroy Linen and Attorney Keith Kornahrens visited my cell. My cousin, Keith, advised me not to retain Attorney Edmond Robinson for legal council. Instead, Keith recommended me to seek Attorney William Runyon for legal representation.

My sister-in-law, Joan Murdaugh, visited me in the conference room with two detectives. Joan asked me for the bodies. I told her I would help.

After finances were secured, Attorney William Runyon agreed to give me legal representation.

I wasn't able to concentrate. The pressure was intense. I told Attorney Runyon I could remember some things. He told me to give up the bodies. I went with detectives to the gravesite. When I was taken back to jail I was charged with three counts of murder.

I was taken to the County Police Station to give a statement.

Jan visited me only once. She told me someone called her on the telephone and threatened her life.

Dr. Edward Schleimer spoke with me at the Charleston County Jail. He was very sick with the flu. He gave me a test, and I didn't see him again.

Pastor Thomas Duffy, a Catholic Priest, visited me at the jail.

Reflections Upon A Sunny Day

Attorney William Runyon was paid a handsome fee. He could have sent me to a private institution for psychological evaluation, but he didn't. Instead, he turned me over to the State Facilities.

I was taken to the Columbia State Hospital and put in a small cement cell. There were no facilities for water or a toilet in the compartment, only a bed. I wondered how many times my mother was put in such a place. The men defecated on the floor at night and cleaned it up in the morning, when it was time for shower.

I was transferred to the Stoney Building at CCI for further evaluation by the State. Several doctors and other individuals, who may have been employed by the Attorney General's Office, asked me questions. I answered their questions as best I could. My mind was still spinning with a blur of thoughts. I saw cruelty and filth. I felt helpless and less than human. Rats jumped into my bed at night and roaches were everywhere.

I could not sleep at night. I was given Vistaril as a sedative.

I needed help but found none. I wanted answers but none were given. I listened for a kind word but none were heard. I sought understanding but none was offered. I longed for some compassion but none was available. My personal wellbeing was in the hands of the State.

In February or March, I was returned to Charleston County Jail. I received one letter from Jan Tweed. She said, " My doctor said I should put you out of my life; that you are not the same person I knew; that the Freddy I knew is dead." Jan did not want to hear from me again.

My attorney, William Runyon, told me I had a lot of people supporting me. I asked, "Who?" He never told me. He told me I would most probably receive manslaughter and would be home in less than ten years. He told me that my children were living with Joyce Avant. The Avant's hid my children from my mother and sister. I didn't want my children to be with the Avant's. Attorney William Runyon said, "Let's not aggravate them right now, it could hurt our case."

I tore scraps of paper and pages from small notebooks on which to jot down pictures and words that exploded in my mind.

I was locked in (sick bay) a four-man cell. A number of men spent various amounts of time in this cell with me during the months preceding my trial. There were a few times when eight men were cramped into the small cell.

I couldn't concentrate on what I read. I had to read something several times to understand. My memory wasn't good, so I had to write things down.

Reflections Upon A Sunny Day

I felt lost and without hope. I was stripped of everything; my clothes, my freedom, my career, home and possessions, my things. I no longer had my material possessions and my good time friends abandoned me. I had thought of myself as a decent citizen; a family man, a government employee with a military career and even a registered voter. I used to go to church. I even had the feeling that I was as good or morally better than some of the people around me.

I came to realize that I had really lived my life for myself; not for God or according to His Will for mankind. I had never truly admitted to myself that I was a sinner. I was suffering; wracked with sin and grief. I felt a burning need in my heart for God. With everything stripped from me I finally realized that God is all that really matters. I picked up a Bible and studied it with sincerity for the first time. I prayed, cried and sought forgiveness. My heart was full of pain.

While reading my Bible one evening, a kind slender eighty five year old man approached my cell with a smile on his face and a Bible in his hand. Mr. Vachel T. Chears became my friend in the strange and hostile place. He visited me on Wednesday nights and Sunday mornings. We held hands through the steel bars. I cried and we prayed together to our LORD. He loaned me his much cherished Family Bible, and he sang me songs in his old sweet voice. I looked forward to his visits, and I wanted to know all I could about my God and Savior.

My attorney, William Runyon, told me Jon and Beverly were still married, but I found out later that they weren't. He spoke with me concerning which prison I would go to. He told me I would probably work at the State House. He assured me that he would take care of getting my children from the Avant's. He told me he would put all my witnesses on the stand including a guard from the jail, but he didn't. He said, "Patty Jo had a Will, but it wasn't worth the paper it was written on." He said, "My children will receive benefits from Patty Jo's social security."

I woke up early each morning and missed going to work. For thirty years, I lived on a straight line; school, work, marriage, children and a few hobbies.

Joan Murdaugh made a statement that she knew Patty Jo was putting too much pressure on me.

While in jail, I heard stories about the man who killed my father. I heard his name mentioned on seven different occasions. He was a drug dealer and most of the people in jail were addicted to marijuana, cocaine or whatever they could get.

The crippled "City People" were frequent occupants of Sick Bay. They were alcoholics, drinkers of cheap wine, and lived in cardboard boxes in the alleys of downtown Charleston. They didn't complain much about being in jail, but were always anxious to leave when it was time to go back to the streets. Mr. Driggers had only one leg. He wasn't permitted to wear his wooden leg when in the cell, so he hopped around on one foot. He would crawl on the floor and under the beds to collect tobacco crumbs. Mr. Rogers' jaundice colored skin was as greasy as a stick of butter, but he wouldn't shower. Mr. Hubbard was rolled to the cell and couldn't walk. I took his food to him and carried him to the toilet. Mr. Nagle was better known as "Nasty Nagle." He was sixty-five years old and wanted to run around in the cell naked. The cell temperature was about 100 degrees and humid. I observed him take his washcloth and wipe the sweat from his chest and arms, then he wiped his scrotum and anus. After that, he opened the cloth and wiped his face. He gobbled his food down like a starving pig and then rushed to the toilet before the rest of us had hardly begun eating. He would squirt and thunder his bowels into the toilet, while we ate our beans and cornbread. He would grunt and squirt and get up off the toilet to see the results of his efforts. It was a disgusting ritual.

While the crippled city drunks argued with one another, I laid on the hard prison bed and thought about my past. I had often thought about running away from Charleston and leaving my problems, but I was anchored to Charleston. I couldn't leave my sick mother, my job, my military career, my home and children, for they were most important to me.

Mr. Chears stuck by me as a brother, week after week and month after month. I was sincerely sorry for all the sins in my life and wanted God to love and forgive me. Like King David, I cried, O Lord have mercy on me in my anguish. My eyes are red from weeping; my health is broken from sorrow. I am pining away with grief; my years are shortened, drained away with great sadness. My sins have sapped my strength; I stoop with sorrow and with shame.

My heart was turned inside out; empty of my confessed life of sins. I was open for anything God would allow me. I continued to pray and study my Bible. I followed the chosen men of God through the Old Testament as if I were there with them. I saw that these chosen people were not perfect, but men like me who had fallen to sin and through prayer and sorrow found their way back into God's love.

God forgave the deception of Abraham, Isaac and Jacob; the murder committed by Moses; the recurring lust of Samson; King David's sin of adultery and murder; Rahab's prostitution; Mary's adultery; Peter's public denial; Thomas' cynical doubting; and Saul the persecutor and murderer of Christians was forgiven and changed to Paul an Apostle of Christ! These people and many others were changed by their faith in God.

Moses spoke of a man whom we must listen to and obey. King David was promised that one of his sons would sit on an eternal throne. Both God and man, Jesus was born David's descendant. I learned that man could not mend his broken relationship with God on his own. The relationship between God and man, broken by Adam and Eve, was restored. Jesus paid the penalty for our sins. He also removed all guilt produced by that sin. I began to understand things that I had taken for granted all my life. My need for God continued to grow, and I felt the changes taking place within my heart, mind and soul.

Early one morning, while it was still dark, I had a dream. I was never more conscious of reality than during this dream. I saw my wife, Patty Jo, and her father, Harry Lee Wilkerson. They were with a man, who was

Reflections Upon A Sunny Day

dressed in a brown robe with a cowl pulled over his head. The cowl was open, but I could not see his face. My wife and her father were dressed in their everyday clothes. I could not understand how I could be with them at my father-in-law's old home in Ravenel, for I was fully aware of my confinement in the county jail. The man standing with Patty Jo and Mr. Wilkerson appeared to be young, approximately twenty-five of thirty years of age, and he had clean smooth hands. I tried hard to see his face, without being disrespectful, but I couldn't see it. His face was as a shadow even though it was the middle of the day. I talked with my wife and she told me that everything was alright. I indicated to her that this must be a dream. I even pinched myself, because I could not believe that this was really happening. My wife assured me that our meeting was very real and not just my imagination. I did not speak to the man dressed in the brown robe, and I was too embarrassed to ask about Jason. My wife and father-in-law appeared exactly the way they looked before minus the cares, the hurts and other problems. Mr. Wilkerson was very friendly and Patty Jo laughed a lot. They, the three of them, were going somewhere. I joined them for a ways down the long dirt road where we saw three wild baby piglets. They were surviving on their own without a sow. The three piglets were symbolic of my three children. It was a warning. Then I found myself back in the jail cell.

I wrote this experience down on paper and sent a copy to Attorney William Runyon.

In June, Charles Brendle was put in the sickbay cell with Samuel Brown, Wendel Washington and myself. Brendle told us he was being held on a bad check charge and had papers indicating something about a bad check. He told us a story about what had happened at the bank, and he mentioned that he was being represented by Attorney Debbie Lewis. I told him that his attorney had assisted in a trial, concerning a DUI charge against my wife. Brendle told us he had written a check at the SCN Bank and the teller told him it wasn't any good. He said, "She tore it up and put it in the trash." He told us he was arrested in the parking lot beside the bank.

Brendle claimed to have been a wrestler for twelve and a half years. He told us that he recently had a heart attack. He said, "I should be in a hospital instead of this hot jail." He was given medication; however, I never saw him take any of it. I did see him flush some pills down the toilet. He asked me if I wanted any of them. He said, "They will give you a rush." I didn't want them. I said, "No."

Brendle was given a pillow for his bed. No one else in the jail had a pillow. He was given an extra fan to blow on him. He was given extra food; milk and sandwiches at night.

Brendle was hyperactive. He wanted to play cards all day, and he smoked a lot. He wanted the TV channel changed repeatedly, and he always wanted something. He let no one, who got near the sickbay cell, escape without calling them over and asking them a question. He asked for the Sergeant, Lieutenant and Captain everyday. He bragged about his privileges and what he could get and do. Jokingly, I called him a Privileged Character.

Brendle liked to get his way, and he used his size to intimidate people. He pestered me and Washington to play cards with him. He wanted service;

such as, his water brought to him. Brown and Washington moved to another cell. Wendell Rogers was in the cell for a few days. Mark Hammond was put in the cell on June 28. Hammond played cards with Brendle, while I read my Bible. I didn't play cards or exercise on Sundays. He pestered me to play cards, but when he finally realized I wasn't going to play, he began slandering the power of God. He said, "There is power in the devil."

Brendle had visits almost everyday in the conference room. He told me the visits were from the FBI and Attorney Debbie Lewis. He claimed that the bank teller had made an error in having him arrested and to cover herself she forged a counter check with his signature. He revealed to me that the FBI checked his and the bank teller's handwriting. He said, "The FBI told me the handwriting on the check belonged to the bank teller." Brendle asserted that the SCN Bank was willing to settle for $75,000 rather than go to court. He said, "The FBI told Debbie Lewis not to settle for that amount." Brendle explained that Debbie may have to have help, because she was somewhat new in law. Brendle said, "Debbie is considering several lawyers – Mr. Runyon being one of them. I told Brendle that Mr. Runyon was a very good lawyer. He asked me about other lawyers, but I had never heard of them.

On another trip to the conference room, Brendle revealed that the settlement had increased to $225,000.00.

I suppose I played about 20 games of rummy with Brendle and lost all but one game. He hated to be behind in score and would cheat to win. He had a lot of luck though; such as drawing all the aces one hand after the other. I told him, with all his luck with cards and the business with the bank, that he should go to Las Vegas. I told him I could use some of his luck.

Brendle mentioned SGT Nicholas' name a lot about one thing or another. Brendle asked me about my charges. I told him my charge was murder. I told him that I had a hard time for the last six years. He read my poems and a little summary of my life. Quite a few times he proclaimed that he wasn't as dumb as he looked. He insisted that he was smart. I didn't comment on it, for I figured he was looking for praise.

After he read my life summary and poem, Brendle acted like it didn't make any sense to him. He asked me question after question, and wanted me to explain details. I told him how rotten things had been. I never mentioned Jon's last name or hard feelings towards anyone. I told him that my ex-wife and her lover had driven me crazy, and I was sorry about what happened. Brendle liked to see me sad.

Usually, I went to sleep around 11:00 P.M., but Brendle often tried to keep me up later, as he did on June 30th. Brendle pestered me so much that night to stay awake past 11:00 P.M., until Hammond said, "Why don't you leave Fred alone and let him sleep." Brendle wanted to tell me stories about how mean and brutal he could be. Hammond went to sleep. He told me he had a friend that would skin a man alive with a razor. Brendle said, "I tied a woman up and put a stick of dynamite in her pussy and lit it." He mentioned that he pulled the fuse out before it exploded. He also explained how he held off a bunch of men with two hand grenades, while his friend broke a man apart with a baseball bat.

After his stories of blood and gore, he asked me if I wanted him to take care of Jon. I said, "No."

Brendle insisted that he would do something to Jon. I said, "No." I said, " Jon will have to pay for what he did in the end on Judgment Day." I was tired and wanted to go to sleep. The jail guard came towards the cell to punch the time clock and asked Brendle what he was talking about. I fell asleep and don't know if anything else was said.

Brendle made sly remarks about Jon a few times afterwards. I ignored him. He wouldn't leave people alone. If he was playing cards with someone, he would pester the other or me by saying, "Fred! Fred! Look at this!" Over and over he would say, "Come here; right here so I can tell you something." I would be deep in a book or trying to sleep when he did these.

Brendle made trouble. He said, "C.O., the guard, is up to something, and you better watch out for him." Brendle said, "C.O. asked me questions about you. He was digging for information." Brendle informed me that C.O. said, "Do you know you're in the cell with a dangerous man; a murderer?" Brendle told me he asked, "Who?" Then he informed me that C.O. said, "Fred." I did not believe everything that Brendle told me. I wondered how much truth he was telling. I did not like his constant trouble making in the cell. Brendle said," A seventeen year old boy got raped in the hall, Monday." He always had some story to tell, and he constantly called the guard to the cell for something.

When Brendle read my poem, about The Good Ole Days, he began spouting off trivia information. He proclaimed to be a trivia expert and insisted that he had won some prizes from the SX 97 radio station. He mentioned that LT Miller and SGT Nicholes had asked him about his prizes. Brendle told me he sold a big screen TV, a Curtis Mathis TV, a washer and dryer, a stove and a refrigerator for $2800.00. I asked him why he has sold all so cheap. Brendle said, "Money is not important to me." He had carried on earlier saying, "You don't know who I am, " like it was some sort of mystery. He said, "My brothers own Brendle's Department Store." He said, "There are thirty-nine of them and I have six percent ownership."

I asked Brendle about the scars on his legs. He told me he got hurt in a Chemical Company when he was a boy. He claimed he got a settlement check for his injuries every few years, and the next check was due in 1986.

He showed me a scar on his leg and claimed to have gotten it from the Georgia chain gang. Brendle told me he used to work in the Texas oil fields. He insisted that he found gold in the drill bits. He also claimed to have worked the California Post Office as GSA 15.

Brendle continued to have visits in the conference room. He told me Debbie wasn't going to need any help. Brendle informed me that he was waiting for a Judge to sign his release papers. He told me he was going to get out on Friday, when a judge got back in town. Brendle revealed the settlement with the bank would be $350,000.00. He said, "Debbie will get a $100,000.00. I'll get $200,000.00 and the state will get $50,000.00.

Reflections Upon A Sunny Day

Brendle said, "You have money don't you." I said, "I used to have nice things, but I don't have anything now." Brendle said, "That's not what I hear." I asked, "Where do you get your information?" Brendle said, "From the guards, they talk about you." I said, "I don't have anything anymore." I had been calling the clerk at the AMSA Shop to check on my retirement.

Brendle told me he had a list of goods he had won, along with his $13,000.00 Rolex watch, up front with his property. He told me he was on his way to Florida and had two Evinrude 165's that he would sell for $200.00. I said, "I've never heard of a 165 horsepower Evinrude." Brendle said, "It's a new model that came out in 1985." I asked, "Could it be a 175 or 185?" He said, "No." Brendle insisted it was a golden edition and showed me, in my magazine, a similar model but it wasn't a 165. I asked brindle if he had all the paperwork on them. I suspected they were stolen. Brendle said, "Yes. I have the paperwork. I won them. I didn't steal them." Brendle said, "What's the matter, the price is too high?" I said, "No. I can't argue about the price. I'd like to have them." I asked him why he was selling them so cheap. Again, Brendle told me that money didn't matter. Brendle told me he was going to call an Outboard Shop and see if they wanted them if I didn't. Brendle said, "I need to get rid of them by Friday." I asked him if he knew what the motors were worth, he said, " The motors retail for three or four thousand dollars a piece, and if you don't want them I'm sure I'll have no problem getting rid of them." Brendle also mentioned that he had a metal detector; that he would sell for fifty dollars. A moment later, he told me he would throw it in with the motors.

My mother came to visit on Tuesday. I told her about Charles Brendle; that he was rich and was going to sell me two new motors for $200.00 on

Friday. I asked my mother to pay him if he showed up with the motors and paperwork. Brendle told me his prizes were stored in the warehouse of the Brendle's Department Store.

When I got to use the telephone, I called Mrs. Mary Clark and told her the story about the motors. Joe Bennett arrived home, while I was speaking with Mrs. Clark. I shared the story with Joe. I said, "I don't know if Brendle is full of crap or not, but just in case he's not I might need your help with the motors."

I drew a map for Brendle, so he could find my mother's house. He agreed to put the motors on her carport. Brendle was released from jail on Tuesday morning. Before he left, he asked for my mother's phone number. I tore off an address label from my mail. I wrote my mother's phone number and Joe's beeper number down on it. I never mentioned Joe's last name. I informed Brendle, if he needed help unloading the motors, my friend would help.

I was sort of excited about the motors. I spoke with Hammond about it. I told him I didn't know whether to believe Brendle or not. I called my mother on Wednesday and asked her if she had heard anything about the motors. She mentioned that Joe had said something about them. I asked he if he had them. My mother told me that she didn't know. I didn't get another opportunity to use the phone again. SGT Gilliard took the phone. It appeared that SGT Gilliard did not want Hammond to use the phone. There had been one other person in sickbay. I believe his name was Anderson. He was in the cell for one day during the weekend.

Reflections Upon A Sunny Day

On Wednesday, July 3rd, at approximately 4:30 P.M., I was told to get dressed and get ready to go up front. I thought Attorney Runyon had come to see me. I carried my legal envelope and was escorted up front. When I was told to go beyond the conference rooms, towards the side entrance door, I thought maybe I was being taken to the courthouse again. To my surprise, I was handed paperwork and charged with two counts of soliciting murder for hire. Television news cameras were waiting for me outside. They asked me questions, as I tried to walk in chains and shackles. I told the newsmen I was being falsely charged. Later, Attorney William Runyon visited me. He said, "I saw you on the news." His first comment was: "Charlie Condon can't get away with this!"

Solicitor Charles Condon was on television, about a month earlier, announcing that he had received a death threat from someone on Death Row. He never announced that the allegations were unfounded. Attorney Runyon said, "Charlie is running for a political office, and he's seeking publicity anyway he can get it."

I suspected Brendle had rifled through my letters and papers, while I was asleep. I had written a letter to Pam and expressed my opinion of Brendle. He mentioned one morning; that he had screwed with my stuff during the night. I said, "I better not catch you screwing with my things." Brendle asked, "What you gonna do about it?" I was reading my book and he was playing cards. Jokingly I said, "I'll have to mop your ass all over this floor." Brendle was six foot six inches tall and weighed 295 pounds. Brendle said, "Well, come on then." I said, "Naw, I'm busy reading my book right now." Brendle had quoted some things I had written to Pam.

On July 3rd, I was charged with two counts of soliciting for murder. I was charged with the murder for hire on the life of Charles Condon and Jon Avant. Charles Brendle stated that he was hired for $20,000.00 to kill these two men.

I called Joe to tell him what Brendle had done. Joe told me that Brendle had gotten in touch with him. Brendle told him about the motors and offered to sell him one of them. He asked Joe about going out with some women from the Brendle's department store, and he asked Joe for $25.00 to hold him over until the next day and agreed to deduct it from the price of the motors.

Joe told me he received a phone call from Mr. Frank Hunt. Mr. Hunt worked in the Solicitor's Office. Mr. Hunt told Joe that Brendle had a wrap sheet as long as your arm. Mr. Hunt lied to Joe and told him I was in solitary confinement and wasn't allowed to use the phone. Mr. hunt told Joe that he was in serious trouble. Joe said, " If I'm in serious trouble why are we talking on the phone about it?" Mr. Hunt told Joe that he was involved in a planned hit; that a man from Walla Walla, Washington, was supposed to be flying in from Charleston. I asked Joe if there was such a place as Walla Walla. It sounded all too ridiculous to be true. Joe spoke with his attorney, Mr. William Ackerman, and he called Solicitor Condon.

Every time I asked Attorney Runyon about what Brendle had done and what was going on, he would tell me not to worry about it.

Reflections Upon A Sunny Day

I did not have a prior criminal record; therefore the state was building a case. They were using the public media; the newspaper, TV and radio to spread the false accusations and present me as a notorious criminal.

At a pretrial hearing, it was decided that Solicitor Condon would not be the prosecutor in my trial. Attorney Runyon stated that Solicitor Condon would not give me a fair trial.

Shortly thereafter, Solicitor Condon officially made my case a Capital Case and it was turned over to the Fifth Judicial Circuit. Solicitor James Anders would be prosecuting me. I learned that he is a ruthless man, and he loves publicity.

On August 19th, my son, Freddy, was in the hospital. The jailers would not let me talk to him on the phone. I was told that a message was sent to the jail with instructions that I could not talk to my son.

On August 27th, the Avant's called the AMSA Shop asking about my health insurance.

February 9, 1985 – Arrested.

Fred H. Kornahrens III et al.

June 10, 1985 – Indicted

July 3, 1985 – Charged for two counts of Solicitation for Murder; murder for hire on the life of Charles Condon and Jon Avant.

August 26, 1985 – Hearing at Courthouse to stop Solicitor Condon and his staff from proceeding with prosecution.

September 5, 1985 – Solicitor Condon advised Attorney Runyon that the State intended to seek the Death Penalty.

September 20, 1985 – Judge Lawrence E. Richter Jr. ordered Solicitor Condon and his staff off the case.

October 4, 1985 – Solicitor James C. Anders, 5th Judicial Circuit, was made Special Prosecutor by Attorney General to assist Assistant Attorney General G. Wells Dickson Jr., to prosecute my case. (TR-I, Statement of Case, 1)

October 7, 1985 – Intent to seek the Death Penalty was confirmed by the Attorney General. (TR-I, Statement of Case, 2)

Reflections Upon A Sunny Day

October 8, 1985 – Notice to seek the Death Penalty was delivered to me by jailer. (It was Patty Jo's birthday)

October 23, 1985 – Arraigned for murder on all three indictments.

October 31, 1985 – Judge Lawrence E. Richter Jr. found that the Appellant was competent to stand trial and was not mentally insane at the time of the killing of the three victims.

November 11, 1985 – Trial began: THE STATE vs. FRED KORNAHRENS, in Charleston, South Carolina, before Judge Lawrence E. Richter. Appearing for the State: G. Wells Dickson Jr., Esq. Assistant Attorney General and James Anders, Esq. Solicitor, Fifth Judicial Circuit as Special Prosecutors. Appearing for the Defendant: William L. Runyon, Esq. and W. Robert Kinard, Esq.

During my nine months of incarceration in the Charleston County Jail, I lost forty-five pounds of body weight. Much of my physical strength was drained, and I fell down a few times.

Names of the witnesses, announced by the Court, for the defense that did not appear to testify: Charles Jones, Sandra Weston, William Seymour, Henry Seigling, Leroy Linen, Charles Long, George Ridgell, Janet Baldwin, Debbie Chaplain, Mack McGrady, Joey Kornahrens, Lisa Kornahrens, Captain Ellie Ritter, Benjamin Peeples, James Gonzales, Pam Kornahrens, and Glenn Fee. Attorney Runyon did not subpoena these witnesses for the defense.

There is no such thing as a perfect trial or harmless errors when the sentence requires taking human life. In a capital punishment trial the odds for obtaining the death sentence are stacked in favor of the State. All members of the jury must be death qualified; meaning that every juror is in favor of the death penalty and is willing to sign their name on an indictment sending a man to the electric chair. Any potential juror, who has doubts about capital punishment, is sent home. The death-qualified jury both convicts and sentences the person on trial to life or death.

Being prone towards death from the start; renders the chance of getting a life sentence unbalanced. Moreover, hardly any regular citizen understands the principles of law or the legal garb of language used in courts. The laws are explained so that only a lawyer can understand it's meaning. Many jurors are intimidated by the Court and they are strongly influenced by the theatrical performances of expert prosecutors. They seek the sentence of death no matter what the situation and problems of the defendant. The objective is not about seeking the truth, but to win a conviction. Most jurors do not understand the law and assume that a life sentence means that a prisoner is paroled in less than ten years. This is an incorrect assumption, and the judge will not explain this to the jury during trial. In 1986, the Omnibus Crime Bill was passed. There remains a twenty-year life sentence for murder trials, but the sentence is different in a capital punishment trial; for if the jury decided against the death penalty, the defendant automatically receives a thirty-year life sentence without the possibility of early release.

A murder trial has one phase – the guilt phase. The defendant will be found either innocent or guilty by the jury. The judge does the sentencing. If the jury becomes deadlocked and cannot give a unanimous decision, a mistrial may be declared and the case can be retried if the judge wishes to do so.

A capital punishment trial has two phases – the guilt phase and the sentencing phase. The guilt phase is the same as above except that the jury is death qualified. If the jury's decision finds the defendant guilty of murder, they proceed into the second phase. In the sentencing phase they hear any additional evidence if there is any and then they deliberate on the sentence of death or life in prison. – The jury does the sentencing!

In South Carolina, if any juror refuses to agree with the other eleven jurors, on the sentence of death, the defendant automatically receives a life sentence. However, these instructions are **not** given to the jurors. In my trial, Judge Lawrence Richter, instructed the jury that all decisions must be unanimous. He told them that their decision for life or death must be unanimous. The jury was given misleading instructions, and the fact is just about any intimidated juror would change their vote to match the majority.

November 11, 1985 – Veteran's Day (TR-I, 70: 1-8).

THE COURT: Also appearing for the State will be Mr. Wells Dickson who is a Deputy Attorney General and who appears here because of certain **Special Orders** that I have issued in this matter. (TR-I, 77:19-21)

JUROR: Orelia M. Heyward (TR-I, 101:6). Q. And to continue on with the Judge's questions, could you yourself sign your name to an indictment imposing death by electrocution in an appropriate case? A. Yes. (TR-I, 104:5-8)

JUROR: Arthur L. Hanton (TR-I, 107:1). Q. Mr. Hanton, in an appropriate case could you sign your name to an indictment sending a person to the electric chair to be electrocuted? Yes. (TR-I, 109:12-15)

JUROR: James R. Switzer (TR-I, 153:20). Q. Could you, assuming the facts were present, sign your name with eleven other jurors to send a person to the electric chair? A. Yes, I could. (TR-I, 156;11-14)

JUROR: Joann Brown (TR-I, 170:1-2). Q. Okay? Now, could you sit in this jury box and sign your name to an indictment sending a man to the electric chair? Can you do that or not? A. Yes, I could. (TR-I,173:4-7)

JUROR: Thomas P. Taylor Jr. (TR-I, 204:12) Q. And could you sign your name to the indictment with eleven other jurors, which in essence would send a person to the electric chair? Could you do that? A. Yes. (TR-I, 208:1-4)

JUROR: Benjamin E. Anderson – Foreman of the Jury (TR-I, 223:17). Q. And could you, if the facts were such, join with the other eleven jurors in signing your name to an indictment sending person to the electric chair? A. Yes, sir. (TR-I, 226: 24-25, 227:1-2)

JUROR: John M. Wright (TR-I, 234:15). Q. Well, I want to know whether or not if in fact the second stage, there are aggravating circumstances—given those facts, could you sign your name to an indictment sending a person to the electric chair? A. Yes, sir. (TR-I, 238: 16-20)

November 12, 1985 – Tuesday (TR-I, 255:21)

JUROR: Pamela Deveaux (TR-I, 273:2). Q. I mean from the witness stand, and if the facts were aggravated, could you sign your name along with eleven other jurors to send a person to die in the electric chair? A. Yeah, it depends on the facts. (TR-I, 276:18-22)

JUROR: Wilma I. Venters (TR-I, 298:21). Q. All right. Could you, if you were on the jury, sign your name to the indictment, which would in essence send a person to die in the electric chair, if the circumstances were aggravated? A. Yes, sir. (TR-I, 302:6-10)

MR. RUNYON: Your Honor, for the record, we would repeat our objection to excusing the juror based on her beliefs on capital punishment, and one other factor, Your Honor. We are now well into the jury pool. There have been several jurors excused for various causes, and I would point out the fact that of the six jurors who have been excused because of their views on capital punishment or opposition thereto, they have in fact been black, and we would at this time insert into the record a further ground that the exclusion of those who have a deep and abiding opposition to the capital punishment in fact operates de facto in this demographic setup in Charleston County to exclude minority citizens from participation in the jury process in a capital punishment case.

JUROR: Joe L. Youngblood (TR-I, 316:23). Q. So, Mr. Youngblood, could you sign your name to an indictment sending a man to Columbia to be put to death in the electric chair, if the facts were appropriate? A. Yes, sir. (TR-I, 320:10-13)

JUROR: James W. Ballard (TR-I, 343:11). Q. And could you, Mr. Ballard, if the circumstances were appropriate, sign your name to an indictment along with the other eleven jurors, which would—which could send a person to Columbia to die in the electric chair? A. Yes, sir. (TR_I, 346:9-13)

JUROR: Barbara C. Early (TR-I, 377:15). Q. If it were aggravated and terrible, could you sign your name to an indictment sending a person to die in the electric chair? A. Yes, I could, if it was proven to me. (TR-I, 381:4-7)

ALT JUROR: Kandee Flynn (TR-I, 412:24). Q. Yes, ma'am. Let me see if I understand your answer. Let me specifically ask you, if the situation warranted could you sign your name to the indictment. A. Oh, yes, sir. Q ... recommending the death penalty? A. Yes, sir.

ALT JUROR: William E. Bissette Jr. (TR-I, 428:7). THE COURT—could you find a verdict of death by electrocution? JUROR: Yes, sir. (TR-I, 430:19-21)

November 13, 1985 – Wednesday (TR-I, 470:20-21).

MR. ANDERS: This is a motion in limine to restrict counsel from making reference to the nol prossed indictments concerning burglary, housebreaking—other charges. I just don't think that be a part of this trial. We're going to present our aggravating circumstances based upon the law. We can prove those without having to indict on them. (TR-I, 491:23-25, 492:1-4)

Following State's Exhibit entered in evidence without objection; State's Exhibit 39 and 40, autopsy photos of Patricia Kornahrens; State's Exhibit 41 and 42, autopsy photos of Harry Wilkerson; State's exhibits 43-50, autopsy photos of Jason Avant; (TR-II, 582:5-9). State's Exhibit 38, autopsy photograph of Patricia Kornahrens, entered over objection in evidence. (TR-II, 582:12-13) Autopsy photos were given to jury to view.

GLYNDA J. PIERSOL – (TR-II, 610:5). From the description, I stopped and told him we had a problem in the area and I needed to see some identification. (TR-II, 621:2-4) At the time of arrest, County Policewoman Glynda J. Piersol looked like Jan Tweed to me. At trial, I was surprised and realized she looked nothing at all like Jan Tweed.

November 14, 1985 – Thursday (TR-II, 645:4).

THE COURT: Gentlemen, as I understand it, the State has moved for a view of the scene. That is your motion, is it not, for a view of the scene. That is your motion, is it not, for a view of the scene. That is your motion, is it not, for a view of the scene. That your motion, is it not, for a view of the scene. That is your motion, is it not, for a view of scene. That is your motion, is it not, Solicitor?

MR. ANDERS: That's correct, Your Honor.

THE COURT: And the defense has not objected to that.

MR. RUNYON: We concur in that, Your Honor.

THE COURT: You concur and are acting jointly?

MR. RUNYON: Yes, Your Honor. (TR-II, 734:1-7)

I was permitted to participate in this part of my trail…to view the scene, to witness the actions, statements, conditions or anything relevant to my trial being a capital case. The jury viewed the site of the crime and the gravesite without my presence, and Mr. Runyon didn't go to the scenes with the jury either.

ESMOND CARROLL SMOAK (TR-II, 777:12) – A false witness for the State. I had heard of Carroll Smoak, but I had never met him.

JON WHILDEN AVANT (TR-II, 793:25) – Q. Patti had a pistol, didn't she? A. … Q. She carried in the glove compartment and in her purse from time to time? A. She sometimes carried her daddy's pistol. (TR-II, 815:17-21) Q. Now, you indicated that you and Patti Jo and Fred had had trouble for over five years, right? A. We have lived in fear from Mr. Kornahrens for five years, yes sir. That's why we carried a gun all the time. (TR-II, 824: 16-20)

JON WHILDEN AVANT (CONTINUED) – Q. Now, when you arrived home—let's go back a minute. Frankly, Mr. Avant, you and Mrs. Kornahrens never formulated a marriage, did you, sir? A. Patti Jo was extremely afraid to get married. Like I say, we went to Mr. Hans Paul one time I was doing a job in Mississippi and she was handling some legal matters for me, and I was going to get her to have a power of attorney. When I introduced Patti as my wife, Mr. Paul said there's no need to; she can handle all the affairs as your wife then. (Jon was being sued for faulty work. He put things in Patti Jo's name "Kornahrens" then they blackmailed me with threats of court and lawsuits to cover Jon's legal matters.) Q. And that to you was your marriage? A. Well, we were married in heart, Mr. Runyon. Q. You were married in heart? As a matter of fact, you were married in heart a good time before you and—before Patti and Fred were divorced? A. ...

MR. ANDERS: Your Honor, I fail to see any relevance to the prior relationship.

THE COURT: I'm going to allow it. Go ahead.

Q. Isn't that correct? A. You have to repeat that question, sir.

Q. You and Mrs. Kornahrens had a very personal relationship prior to her divorce from Mr. Fred Kornahrens, did you not, sir?

A. Patti and Fred were getting a divorce—before that time, we dated on her first separation. Q. And you continued to date even after their reconciliation, did you not, sir? A. No, sir, that is not correct. Q. And in fact you knew Fred Kornahrens for a long time, did you, sir? Since about 1977 or '78? A. No, sir. I didn't move down here from Ohio until—it might have been that time, yes sir. Q. So is that a fair statement about '77 or '78'? A. Yes sir, that's correct. Q. Okay. Now, did you know Patti Jo when she worked at the private school? A. She worked for St. Paul Academy. Yes, sir, I knew her then. Q. And you sent her flowers there on many occasion, did you not, sir? A. No, sir. I sent her flowers one time. Q. Sent her flowers one time? That was when she was still married to Mr.

Kornahrens and was living with him? A. They were still living together, yes sir. Q. You visit with Mrs. Kornahrens at their home there on Toogoodoo Road where she lived with Mr. Kornahrens? A. No, sir, I did not. Q. You never went and visited over there? A. No, sir. You mean to visit? Q. Yes. Sir. A. Prior to that my wife—my first wife and I were acquaintances with Fred and his wife. We did visit there. Q. Well, I'm talking about visiting over there without your first wife. A. I was on the way to Metal Trade one time and I stopped by. You know, I stopped by there for a few minutes. (Jon paid my son, Freddy, money to go outside and play so he could be alone with my wife.) (TR-II, 825: 12-25, 826:1-25, 827:1-22)

JON WHILDEN AVANT (CONTINUED) – Q. And you met with Patti Jo after hours at her place of employment at Dr. Sanders' office, didn't you, sir? A. Patti Jo called me one night in particular and said Freddie was abusing her and she wanted to talk to me, and at this time it was about five o'clock in the afternoon and I stopped by and talked to her, and that's when—this particular time when he assaulted us. (TR-II, 828:16-22) (Patti Jo told Solicitor Charles Condon that Jon had come to Dr. Sanders' Office, after working hours, to loan her some money.) (AB, 77)

Q. Now, these documents were sent to Mrs. Kornahrens in a period of time when she was married and living with Fred Kornahrens, were they not? A. I wrote Patti—like I said, Patti Jo and I dated—we dated when they were separated and after he threatened us I got—well, I was scared of him and I quit. I don't know when those were written. They might have been written—they were written sometime when I knew her, yes, sir. Q. They were written sometime when I knew her? A. Yes, sir. Q. Before she was divorced? A. I believe they were when she was separated and when they weren't living together. Q. You believe that? A. Yes, sir.

MR. ANDERS: We have no objection to them.

THE COURT: Let me see them. (Examining notes.) Without objection, they're admitted. (Handwritten notes entered in evidence without objection, as Defendant's Exhibits 8, 9, 10.)

Q. Mr. Avant, you did not sign your name to any of those documents, did you, sir? A. I'd have to look at them. I don't know whether I did or not.

THE COURT: Hand them back to him, please. He needs to look at them.

Q. ... A. No sir. Q. In fact, these were sent to Mrs. Kornahrens ostensibly, were they not, sir? A. I gave Patti a lot of notes, on occasion and I gave her—you know, I gave her letters and talked to her and things like that? Q. Matter of fact, you sent her cards and books? A. Yeah, I sent Patti Jo a lot of cards. Q. Without signing them? A. Pardon? Q. Without signing them? A. I gave Patti Jo a lot of cards and a lot of little gifts while we were dating.

THE COURT: I didn't understand you.

WITNESS: I gave Patti Jo a lot of cards and a lot of little gifts while we were seeing each other.

THE COURT: Go ahead. What's your question?

Q. In point of fact, you did not sign any of those items nor did you sign this correspondence because you did not want Mr. Kornahrens to know who was sending her the letters and the cards, did you, sir? A. I gave them to Patti Jo while we were dating. Every time we'd be together I gave her a card or something. (TR-II, 861:1-25, 863:1-2)

November 15, 1985 – Wedding Anniversary (TR-II, 870:14).

Reflections Upon A Sunny Day

There was gossip in the Jail cell about Charles Brendle and some of the guards were making bets I'd get the death penalty. Today would have been my 16th Wedding Anniversary with Patty Jo.

My children, whom I wanted to share perfect love seemed unrelated to me, and I wanted so much to make them unlike me in certain ways, because I wanted to make sure they would never have a childhood like mine; that they would never be beaten senseless by me and that they would never fear the approach of their father.

THE COURT: Well, there's nothing more important than what goes on in this Court in a capital case. It's just the most important thing we do. All of the work is important, but this is the most important work that we handle, and it can be ignored or overlooked. It's extremely significant. (TR-II, 871:15-20)

JAN KAY TEAL TWEED (TR-II, 896:25) – Q. During the time that you and Fred lived together, did Fred ever manifest any violence towards you or anyone else? A. No. Q. You think Fred was a violent person? A. No. Q. Did he ever talk with you about his situation and his ex-wife and John Avant? A. Sometimes. Q. Did he seem angry about that situation? A. No. Upset, not angry. Q. Did he seem like he was under pressure? A. He seemed tense, distant at times. (TR-II, 897: 15-25, 898:1-4)

MR. RUNYON: Your Honor, there's no real difficulty, I've been dealing with the real power of the prosecution team, Mr. Dickson, and through him he made some arrangements with regard to these children which we had placed under subpoena but which had been in the care, custody and control of the Avant Family. (TR-II, 908:16-21)

FRED HERMAN KORNAHRENS IV (TR-II, 911:17) – Q. Are you living with your aunt? A. No, sir. Q. Who are you living with? Dad — John. Q. You live with John Avant? A. Yes, sir. (TR-II, 911:25, 912:1-5)

DR. EDWARD J. SCHLEIMER (TR-II, 925;15) – Q. And when you saw him, did you—what did you do? A. Well, I saw Mr. Kornahrens on Saturday Morning at the Charleston County Jail for a period of about three and a half hours, and conducted some brief examination with psychological testing, perhaps thirty minutes worth or forty minutes, and then three hours of interview. (TR-II, 928:24-25, 929:1-4) Q. All right. Now, can you tell us what your diagnosis or impression was with reasonable medical certainty as regards that mental status exam—which regard to the mental status of Fred Kornahrens in February of this year? (TR-II, 932:10-13)

DR. EDWARD J. SCHLEIMER (CONTINUED) A. May I refer to my summary with regard to that? Q. You may refer to your summary. A. Well, of course, my major concern during the examination was whether there was any evidence of schizophrenia at that time or psychosis, and I did not see any evidence for that. I felt there were a number of personality problems and that in the sense of his being able to be perhaps diagnosed in a psychiatric sense that there would be a general consensus, I felt, among people in my field, to perhaps say there was a mental disorder of some sort based on his degree of anxiety and the stress that he was under, his marital difficulties in the past which were fairly consistent and his somewhat dependent style? A. Well, it seemed to me that he would repetitively find himself in a situation where he would in a sense be dependent upon other people's needs or desires. He would attempt to behave so as to please them or care for them, rather than initiating self-caring kinds of behavior, and, because of some characteristic behavior or style from a person who was likely to be somewhat dependent, I felt he was dependent in the sense of having to be in a marital or love relationship situation, perhaps more than an average person would have to be. Q. What about Mr. Kornahrens' stress situation? A. I felt that he was under a rather prolonged or severe stress from relationship problems with is ex-wife. (TR-II, 932:14-25, 933:1-17) Q. Did you note any obsessions? A. Well, yes, I felt that he was—in a sense obsessions are uncontrollable thoughts that reoccur and are experienced by the person as being not wanted or being alien to himself, and he reported experiencing things that I would call obsessions a number of times, and primarily I think in the last—in the last week itself when he was having to anticipate having to deal with another legal suit which was a Hundred and Fifty Thousand Dollars, I believe. (TR-II, 934:22-25, 935:1-5) Q. Now, Doctor, did you note any symptoms that were reported to you; that is, physical symptoms that would be significant in your evaluation as to his mental status? A. He reported having nightmares, sleep disturbance, tension headaches and anxiety associated with those obsessions or ruminations. He had reported over some time before the event—I'm not clear on whether it was a year or two but some period of time after the divorce while they were still—while he was still experiencing problems with his ex-wife over financial matters, he reported stomach disorders and anxiety problems for which he consulted his physician, a Dr. Reynolds I believe. Also, he consulted a psychologist, Dr. Diane Hamrick, and I believe this was after the altercation in 1981. (TR-II, 935:18-25, 936:1-6) Q. Doctor, I take it then that your testimony is that there was some psychological difficulties at the time but certainly no psychotic or schizophrenic episodes? A. There were some, I think, severe psychological and adjustment difficulties with him continuing, but they did not reach the level of psychosis. (TR-II, 938:23-25, 939:1-3)

DR. EDWARD J. SCHLEIMER (CONTINUED) – CROSS EXAMINATION BY MR. ANDERS: Q. And at the time of the offense, the time of the crime, you're not clairvoyant? You can't go back and determine what a person was thinking or what was in their mind at that time, can you? A. Well, I cannot determine their mental state, but I can make some—render an opinion about—you know, based on what the person tells me. Q. Yes, sir. A. About what possibly was going on in his mind. Q. That would be if the person told you the truth in every respect, wouldn't it? A. That's correct. Q. Matter of fact, he told you on this occasion he was married a second time, didn't he/ A. He had said he was married to a lady named Pam, yes, sir. Q. If I told you in fact that he had not been married for the second time, would that indicate to you that he represented something incorrect to you? A. Yes, sir.

MR. RUNYON: Objection, Your Honor. I'd like to approach the bench.

THE COURT: No point in your approaching the bench. Put it on the record. Take the jury out. (Jury excused from Courtroom at 12:23 P.M.) All right, sir what do you have?

MR. RUNYON: Your Honor, the Solicitor is now getting a lot closer to the Pee Dee News. He asked this witness if he in fact reported to him that he was married to one Pam Kornahrens, and then he said but if he was not in fact married to her—now, our—everything we have is that there was a legal, statutory marriage between those two people. He's making a –an absolute false statement that they weren't married. He's leading the jury to believe that this Defendant lied to this psychologist during the course of the evaluation about his marital status, when if fact that's not the case. (TR-II, 939:22-25, 940:1-25, 941:1-8) (Solicitor Anders did not clarify his question nor take back the accusation that I had lied to the psychologist.)

MR. ANDERS: Q. Were you paid for that examination? A. Yes, sir. Q. Who paid you? A. Mr. Runyon. Q. Mr. Runyon paid you? And I don't guess you have any idea who paid Mr. Runyon? A… (TR-II, 950: 9-15) Q. And you cannot tell the jury whether or not this man was insane the night of the offense? A. Right. I cannot say that he was insane. That's correct. Q. In fact, you wouldn't say that he was insane at any time, would you? A. That's correct. Q. He had his sanity throughout the entire time, did he not? A. I'm not sure. (TR-II, 951:11-20)

MR. RUNYON: Q. Now, do you have an opinion that you can state as to whether or not at the time of the occurrence Mr. Kornahrens had a recognizable mental disorder that would affect his judgment? A. I would say yes. Q. And that's the distress disorder you're making reference to? A. Yes, anxiety, tension and stress disorder. Yes, sir. Q. Would that have impaired his judgment? A. That's difficult. That's difficult to answer. It depends upon the exigencies of the moment; depends upon exactly what is happening whether or not the person will lose control. (TR-II, 959:6-18)

DR. EDWARD J. SCHLEIMER (CONTINUED) – Q. You say whether or not the person will lose control? What are you making reference to, losing control. A. Really and simply not being in charge of what you do at the moment physically or in charge of his thinking. Q. Even though you may know right from wrong? Yes. Q. Would a lay term be . . .

MR. ANDERS: Object to leading.

THE COURT: It's leading.

Q. What would a lay term be for not being in charge of your faculties? A. Losing it. It's the most common one I've heard lately. Q. So colloquially it would be losing it, and he had an identifiable mental disorder at the time of this occurrence? A. In my opinion, yes, sir. (TR-II, 959:19-25, 960:1-9)

RECROSS EXAMINATION BY MR. ANDERS: Q. The mental disorder on that night, are you able to identify the particular mental disorder? A. I think you might get different diagnosis if you get different psychiatrist up here. Q. Yes, sir. A. I would say it was a combination of identifiable disorders. One would be called an anxiety reaction. Another would be called—probably be called a gross stress reaction. Q. Could you use diminished capacity? A. I don't use that term. How do you mean that? Q. Well, diminished capacity—you really don't know what was wrong with him on that night, do you, Doctor? A. I know what he told me led up to the events and what happened from his standpoint, and you are asking me do I know what went wrong with him? Q. Of course you don't know that, do you, Doctor? A. Only in the sense of the interview findings and rendering an opinion. (TR-II, 960:18-25, 961:1-10)

(Jury excused for lunch period 1:02 P.M. Court stood in recess until 2:45 P.M.)

THE COURT: Mr. Runyon, are you ready to proceed?

MR. RUNYON: Yes, Your Honor. Your Honor, I don't mean to be picky but my friend over here, would it be possible for him not to sit right next to the witness box?

THE COURT: He's been sitting there for a portion of the trial.

MR. RUNYON: Except for the fact that there hasn't been a Sherriff's deputy seated between the Court and the witness chair for the entire week of this trial.

THE COURT: He's been there most of the morning and he's only going back there for the afternoon session. I don't remember when he sat there or for what portion of the trial but my law clerk sits there and . . .

MR. RUNYON: Your Honor, your law clerk is not wearing a badge and gun.

THE COURT: You think it's prejudicial somehow?

MR. RUNYON: I think it is, Your Honor.

THE COURT: I require that you sit there, Sheriff. In the exercise of my discretion I find there's nothing prejudicial about it. (TR-II, 969:8-25,

970:1-21) (Judge Richter seated the armed deputy beside the witness chair just before I was to testify. This action could only lead the jury to believe I was exceptionally dangerous.)

FRED H. KORNAHRENS III (TR-II, 971:5) – CROSS EXAMINATION BY MR. ANDERS: Q. Why were you going over there? Why were you going to the location? A. I wanted them to leave me alone. I just wanted to plead with them to leave me alone. (TR-III, 1037:15-18) Q. Now, what were you doing out there when you saw Mr. Smoak? A. Mr. Smoak has got me mixed up with someone else. Q. That wasn't even you? A. No, sir. Q. He was your neighbor, wasn't he? A. I know Mr. Smoak by name. I don't know Mr. Smoak personally. I never rode in his vehicle. I don't know why he would say that. I've got my own vehicle to ride in. I bought a Christmas tree during that time at Kroger on Highway 17, and the last time I got a Christmas tree in that area was I think 1981. Q. So he is wrong to say that you were out there? A. Yes, sir, he is wrong. Q. Had you ever met him on a prior occasion? A. If I did, I can't remember. I was not friends with Mr. Smoak. I just heard some people from that area mention his name. Quite frankly, I don't know exactly where he lives out there. (TR-III, 1052:21-25, 1053:1-14) Q. Do you remember talking with this officer? A. . . . Q. This officer right here. A. Not really, sir. Q. Do you remember riding with him out to the gravesite? A. The only officer I remember riding with was Lieutenant Perry and detective Hawkins Detective Chevy. Q. You don't remember being in this man's presence at any time? A. No, sir, not really. Q. You remember him advising—you remember Chevy here with you advising you about your constitutional rights on the time you went out there, didn't he? A. ... Q. Chevy is the black officer. A. . . Q. You remember talking to him, don't you? A. Yes, sir, I remember talking to him but I don't remember him reading rights. No, sir, I don't. Q. You don't remember that? A. No, sir. Q. Do you remember making any statements to this officer or to this officer? A. I remember talking to Detective Chevy, yeah. Not the other—I can't recall the other officer. No sir. (TR-III, 1057:21-25, 1058:1-20) Q. You can remember very well digging that grave? Your mind came back to about that time? A. No, sir. It may sound that way, but I can remember the action of digging the hole. I dug hard. I remember getting hot. I remember taking my jacket off but fine details, no, sir, I can't remember. Q. Matter of fact, you already had the grave dug, didn't you? A. No, sir. Q. You just had to dig it a little bit deeper because you had an extra body with you, didn't you? A. No, sir, that's not true. Q. You only really planned to have two people in that grave, John Avant and Patti? Right? A. No, sir. I didn't plan for anybody. (TR-III, 1063:2-16) Q. You talked about Patti Jo, going back to your domestic difficulties, and, of course, she's not here. Did you ever do anything wrong? A. Have I? Q. Yes. A. Yes, sir, we all do things wrong. Q. Matter of fact, you were having affairs with Dee Ann about that time, weren't you? A. I had one affair. Q. It was sort of a continuing affair, wasn't it? A. No, sir. Q. So this domestic deal wasn't all one-sided, was it? A. No, sir.

THE COURT: I'm sorry, I didn't hear. Go back and ask the question again. (Repeated again to the jury) (TR-III, 1065:24-25, 1066:1-13)

MR. RUNYON: . . The defense of self-defense is not available but it can operate to reduce the homicide from murder to manslaughter. It's part of the fact situation that the jury could consider to reach a decision as to what actually happened. In addition to that, Your Honor, we have the question about mental capacity, and . . .

THE COURT: Well, if all of this is so, why can't you give me some authority for some of this?

MR. RUNYON: Well, Your Honor, if you'll let me get to it. We've got some books here, some South Carolina cases. In addition to that, Your Honor, with regards to the question of mental capacity, diminished mental capacity, I refer the Court to the case of State vs. Hernandez which was on an insanity question, but when that question of sanity is put into the evidence it says the State has certain obligations. Here what we're saying is the question of his ability or his capacity to be able to formulate the malice is put into question, and therefore . . .

THE COURT: But you specifically represented to this Court before the Defendant and your opposing counsel that sanity was not an issue in this case.

MR. RUNYON: I'm not suggesting it is, your Honor. Insanity under the M'Naghten test is not an issue in this case, and I'm not suggesting it is. What I'm saying is, Your Honor, that using the same theory of Judge Chandler, he says that when you put the question of sanity in issue then the State has to show something or you're entitled to a reversal as under Hernandez. What we're saying is that spring boarding from that if in fact you put into question the capacity of the person, the mental capacity of the person to formulate the requisite malice, then you're entitled to—they either have to rebut that or we can argue that the jury can conclude that he didn't have the requisite mental capacity or ability to formulate the malice which is an absolute requirement for murder, which in fact if there is no malice but it is unlawful it would at least be voluntary manslaughter.

THE COURT: I'll be glad to read whatever authorities you have if you have a photocopy of it.

MR. RUNYON: All right, sir.

THE COURT: Frankly, I don't understand how this case can be ten months old and I not have a single case authority from the defense before if those issues are so significant. (TR-III, 1085:14-25, 1087:1-10)

November 16, 1985 – Saturday (TR-III, 1088:8).

THE COURT: What is the sudden heat and passion to which the Defendant can be entitled from the record made before me in this case?

MR. RUNYON: Your Honor, the jury can conclude that the killing occurred in the sudden heat and passion as a result of long standing difficulty just as in State v. Martin. That's why they reversed that conviction and sent it back, because there was in fact no sudden heat and passion in the certain sense of the word. What they said was that the jury can conclude that the man after all this period of indignities over this period could suddenly in seeing a man have such sudden heat and passion that he would shoot him from ambush, and it's a jury question.

THE COURT: Tell me what act by the victim or the witness John Avant as testified to in this record this Defendant could rely upon as constituting sufficient legal provocation?

MR. RUNYON: Long standing domestic history, the discord between this man, his wife, and John Avant. The circumstances of the –one of the victims, Mrs. Kornahrens, and Mr. Avant attempting to extract money through misprision of a felony . . .

MR. RUNYON: Yes, sir.

THE COURT: . . .do you realize the import of what you're saying?

MR. RUNYON: Yes, sir. They in fact stated that, and it was testified to, that they asked this man for money and they would drop criminal charges, which is compounding a felony.

THE COURT: I want to make sure you understand who all you're implicating in that.

MR. RUNYON: I understand, Your Honor.

THE COURT: In making such a statement on this record.

MR. RUNYON: I understand, Your Honor. There's no question about that. That was testified to.

THE COURT: The record should also be clear that Mr. Anders and Mr. Dickson had no involvement with this case whatsoever prior to— when did I appoint the Attorney General?

MR. ANDERS: I don't remember the exact date. The end of September.

MR. RUNYON: There's absolutely no question about that, Your Honor.

THE COURT: Well, I think that's an extraordinarily serious matter you're alleging. (TR-III, 1095:15-25, 1096: 1-25, 1097:1-21)

THE COURT: All right, let me hear from the State. What's the position of the State?

MR. ANDERS: Your Honor, we handed up State versus Clements, Your Honor.

MR. ANDERS: Hitting right on manslaughter, and that's what we're talking about. We believe that the burden in that case sets forth, and, of course, manslaughter is the unlawful killing of a human being in sudden heat and passion upon a sufficient legal provocation. That case clearly set out, Your Honor, that heat of passion alone will not suffice to reduce murder to voluntary manslaughter. When death is caused by a deadly weapon, words alone are insufficient to constitute legal provocation. That's in essence our position. This was handed down June 3rd, 1985. (TR-III, 1101:1-17)

THE COURT: I don't think that there can reasonably be made an argument that under the facts presented in this proceeding there can be a lesser included offense of manslaughter. I want the record to be clear in that regard, and for that reason I decline to charge manslaughter. This is either—Solicitor, you have either proved murder or you have not. I'm not going to make a mockery or what I think is a mockery of this process by injecting matters that can not clearly be considered in this proceeding. So manslaughter is out.

MR. ANDERS: Thank you, Your Honor. (TR-III, 1102: 11-22)

THE COURT: Now, is there anything else before I bring the jury in?

MR. RUNYON: No, Your Honor.

THE COURT: Bring the jury in, please. Sheriff, please seal the Courtroom during arguments and charge. Anybody wants to leave they can leave now. Let me further state there can be no emotional display by anybody watching the proceedings. If you can't handle this—I realize it's an emotionally fraught situation, but if you can't handle that, I urge you to leave now. (TR-III, 1110: 13-18)

THE COURT: Very well, you may proceed.

MR. KINARD: Thank you, Your Honor, may it please the Court.,

THE COURT: Yes, sir.

MR. KINARD: Mr. Foreman and ladies and gentleman of the jury, we've all been sitting here for a long time this week, and as you heard Mr. Runyon say when we started this thing I'm Bobby Kinard, and Mr. Runyon is my partner. You haven't heard very much out of me in the last five days because I'm the quiet one of the law firm. (TR-III, 1111: 16-25)

MR. KINARD: Speaking of advocacy, I suppose you have all wondered from the time this trial started why the Solicitor of the Fifth Circuit and the Attorney General are prosecuting this case, as opposed to your Solicitor and his staff from the Ninth Judicial Circuit, in Charleston. Solicitors stay where they belong to prosecute cases. Maybe there's not enough work in Richland for Mr. Anders to do.

MR. ANDERS: Your Honor, I hate to object but I can't see how these matters could possibly...

THE COURT: Let me say that they are entirely improper for the jury. Ladies and gentleman of the jury, because of certain legal rulings I made which are not for your consideration anyway I appointed the Attorney General or his designee to proceed with prosecution of this matter. Do not transgress in that area further. Go ahead.

MR. KINARD: Your Honor . . .

THE COURT: Take the jury out. (TR-III, 1112:19-25, 1113: 1-13)

MR. KINARD: I had no intention of saying anything about your ordering or anything like that. I was making a comment that . . .

THE COURT: If there's nothing further to be considered, I'm not going to allow it. Let the record reflect my instruction to the jury stands. I'm not going to allow you to pursue that. I told the jury it can't consider it. If that's error, then so be it. That's in the record, and I'm not going to change that. There's no need to pursue it any further. You've got the benefit of that ruling in the record. Okay, bring then in, please.

MR. KINARD: I accept the ruling.

THE COURT: I understand. Bring them back in. (Jury returned to Courtroom at 11:15 A. M.) Very well, you may continue.

MR. KINARD: Thank you, Your Honor. Mr. Foreman and ladies and gentleman, what we'll ask you to do today, and as you have done all week, is pay particular attention to everything. There has been a voluminous amount of evidence introduced to you, in excess of a hundred and fifty exhibits. (TR-III, 1114:15-25, 1151: 1-12) (There were over a hundred color photographs presented to the jury, including those taken in the autopsy room of the naked bodies.) As Mr. Runyon told you at first, this is not a matter of who it is. It's a matter of what it is. What happened? Now, subsequent to that altercation down at the doctor's office, some charges were brought against Freddie they never did come up for whatever reason. They just never came up, and before this even began they were divorced and he was paying child support, and you heard the testimony that several times he would be back in Court. They said he owed Seventeen Thousand Dollars after they had reconciled one time. Now, how do you get to owing Family Court Seventeen Thousand Dollars when you've never come to Court? Does that make any sense? (TR-III, 1120: 11-23)

MR. KINARD: No, it doesn't make any sense to me because that's not the way things go. A lot of it depends on who your lawyer is. Appearing for the Plaintiff, Patricia Kornahrens, Rawl and Runey by Joseph P. Runey, Esquire. Rawl is a member of the House of Representatives. Runey is the . . .

MR. ANDERS: Your Honor . . .

THE COURT: Is that in the record, counselor?

MR. KINARD: It's a matter of public record, Your Honor.

MR. ANDERS: Your Honor . . .

THE COURT: Take the jury out. (TR-III, 1120:23-25, 1121:1-9)

MR. KINARD: Your Honor, I wasn't . . .

THE COURT: Don't worry about that. The second part of it I'm not ruling on. There's evidence in the record about the second half of that. All right, let's bring the jury back in, please. (Jury returned to courtroom at 11:31 A. M.) Okay, you can proceed.

MR. KINARD: Thank you, Your Honor, Mr. Foreman and ladies and gentleman, I apologize for that. (TR-III, 1123:19-25, 1124:1-2) After the charges—the initial charges were dropped or not brought or whatever they do, he gets a call from the Solicitor who unbeknownst to him at that time was a first cousin or cousin to his wife's attorney. He says come down to the Courthouse; I've got some bad news. The charges had been brought up again. Who was your lawyer, Freddie, at that time? Mr. Condon was my lawyer. He comes down to the Courthouse, not one time but many times. He was dissuaded from bringing his own lawyer down to the Courthouse, and instead he had the Ninth Circuit Solicitor representing him in a guilty plea. So he pleads guilty to get this thing over with. He pleads guilty. He struck a deal. He's not going to go to jail. He gets probation. And what happens? The Solicitor's cousin files a lawsuit for some Hundred or Hundred and Fifty Thousand Dollars, because Patti Kornahrens and John Avant had been trying to get him to pay them Ten Thousand Dollars to drop the charges. John Avant said, well, that's true, but Seventy-five Hundred Dollars was for doctor bills and Twenty-five Hundred Dollars of that was for attorney fees for the cutting incident, when he cut them several years ago. What attorney's fees? They had been divorced for some time and the lawsuit hadn't been filed yet. The lawsuit hadn't been filed until after he pled guilty when the charges were brought up because he wouldn't pay them Ten Thousand Dollars. There weren't any attorney fees. If it was, it was in anticipation of the lawsuit. What kind of doctor bills did they have? At the time the cutting occurred, Patti was living with him, as his wife. It was covered by insurance through the National Guard, the best insurance you could have. Freddie's insurance. What doctor bills? What attorney's fees? Maybe John had some attorney fees—I mean doctor bills. Patti certainly didn't. I submit to you that John himself didn't have Seventy-five Hundred Dollars in doctor bills. He had his hands cut up. (TR-III, 1124:17-25, 1125:1-25, 1126:1-5)

MR. KINARD: It's kind of hard to fight the Broad Street ring. That's what it is. That is exactly what it is. If you've ever tried to fight them, you know exactly what I'm talking about. They get on you and they don't get off. The Ninth Circuit Solicitor's hands were on that knife just like.

MR. ANDERS: Your Honor, I hate to object again, but I don't believe a reasonable inference can be drawn.

THE COURT: I'm going to let him argue. Go ahead.

MR. KINARD: There are times in my life in the past ten years when I have been ashamed. This is one of them. This is one case where they ganged up on this defenseless man, didn't let him have a lawyer, took everything he had. Then when things blew up in their face, they don't have the nerve to come in here and prosecute the case. They call in the hired guns.

MR. ANDERS: I'm reluctant to object once again, but Your Honor has ruled on that point.

THE COURT: The objection is sustained. On Defendant's motion, I disqualified the office of the Ninth Judicial Solicitor.

MR. KINARD: I understand, Your Honor.

THE COURT: Then don't—take the jury out for just a minute. (Jury excused from Courthouse at 11:37 A. M.) So the record will be clear about my ruling, you are clearly arguing inference or just did a moment ago that the Solicitor had gotten together with his lawyer-cousin and did whatever you claim the jury can infer he did. (TR-III, 1126:6-25, 1127:1-11)

MR. KINARD: I apologize, Your Honor.

THE COURT: That's fine. It's over now. I'll tell the jury they can't regard that. Bring the jury in. (TR-III, 1127: 23-25)

MR. ANDERS: I simply want to in behalf of the State of South Carolina thank each one of you for your close attention to the facts which came to your knowledge from the witnesses and the exhibits. I am new here, and I want to thank the Court for being so nice to me, and I want to thank the Charleston County Police for the fine job that they did in this case. I want to remind you that Fred Kornahens is the Defendant in this case. That is who is on trial here today, Fred Kornahrens. I want to get that straight with you right away. I want to go through some of the facts with you in this case, and I want to tell you as I told you the first day I talked to you and I submitted to you that it was a planned execution. Last night I sat down and jotted down a number of reasons that I submitted that you could consider at arriving at this being a planned execution. (TR-III, 1130: 2-19) I submit to you the testimony will sustain this—Mr. Smoak testified he knew this Defendant, Fred Kornahrens. He testified he knew him. He picked him up, and he testified he told him he was looking for a Christmas tree. A reasonable inference to be drawn from that testimony, I submit to you, is that he was out there looking for the gravesite even then, planning. (TR-III, 1132:20-25)

MR. ANDERS: I want you to look at this boy's—look at his face. He weighed ninety pounds according to the evidence. This is his back. This is his back. See the holes in this? (TR-III, 1135:18-20) I submit to you that remember the testimony of Dr. Conradi. Even one of those wounds to this child's chest was post-mortem. (TR-III, 1136: 1-3) And his memory, does it fade and come back conveniently for us? You know, he couldn't remember but just swinging back to a person he thought was John Avant when he killed the child. Now, do you believe that? Do you believe that? (TR-III, 1136: 10-14) And the lie of lies. How much he loved children. Do you believe this man loves children? If he was as good as a person he presented to you, and if Patti Avant was as bad as he said she is, do you think she would have those children in the first place? Do you think she would have custody of them? Of course not. He would have had custody of the children if he were the angel that he presents to you. And, if course, he blames her for everything. She was running around. She was spending money. She was taking care of the doctor's bills for the children. Never mind his Corvette and never mind his girlfriend. It was all her fault. All some lawyer's fault. All somebody else's fault, and none of his own. None of his own. (TR-III, 1136: 19-25, 19-25, 1137:1-7) He knows it's damning to him, the fact that he pre-dug that grave. He knows it. That's his reason for denying it. You know, we use to call that the gentle art—the gentle art of confessing error. The gentle art of confessing error. Tell the jury the truth, tell them some truth, and then get by with a big lie, but tell them a little truth along. They refer to this mass murder as an unfortunate incident, something that's unfortunate. Well, I submit to you it's just what it is. It's a hard and cruel murder. That's what it is. Let's talk about the grave that you viewed. I made a few notes on that last night too. Use your own mind, use your common sense and experience. Your Honor, Judge Richter, is going to tell you what circumstantial evidence is. It's simply where you take bits of information and put it together to come out with a result. You can use direct evidence, you can use circumstantial evidence. You can use all the facts in the case, everything, to make your final determination. (TR-III, 1138:3-24) I submit to you it's very difficult dealing with these types of people, but you know, every murderer comes in the Courtroom and something went loose in every darn one of them.

Something went loose in their minds. That doesn't relieve them of the responsibility. Can you imagine that night at one thirty or sometime about that time, one forty, one forty-five, being out under those trees in that thick area that you went to, and being able to take that shovel and digging a grave like that? He may have dug it a little deeper because he had a bigger man to throw into the grave. He may have dug it a little deeper, but this grave was there. It was there. (TR-III, 1141:5-17)

MR. ANDERS: I told you if you can remember my opening remarks—I told you that you would remember February 9th and February 11th even after this case. I'm sure you will. This was a planned execution as I told you. I told you why. I told you about the F.B.I. Agent. I told you about the pre-dug grave, told you you'd be going to the scene, and I submit to you I hope that everything I indicated to you that first day we've been able to comply with. If not, there is certainly ample evidence in this record, and the Defendant admits it himself, that he killed these three people. I submit to you he's guilty of murder, nothing less, and I submit to you that you should consider nothing other than murder for this individual. When you go to the jury room, talk among yourselves, but join hands and find this person guilty of murdering each of these three people. It doesn't matter if he had some problems with his prior wife. That doesn't give him the right to murder Jason Avant. It doesn't give him the right to kill Harry Wilkerson. What has Harry Wilkerson ever done to him? You know he wanted to talk about his wife, Rambling Rose as he said from the stand. Of course, she's dead at his hands and she's not able to be here to defend herself. But I submit to you the one thing that I hope you can observe about this individual and what he has done. He's mean. He's mean. Can you imagine a meaner person anywhere than this person? Did you ever read about anyone that was as mean as this person? That's the way he was. You don't see any blisters down there, do you? He didn't tell you about any blisters on his hands from digging that grave that night. That's because he didn't dig the grave that night. On behalf of the State of South Carolina, I ask you to find Fred Kornahrens guilty of murder. Thank you. (TR-III, 1141:18-25, 1142:1-25, 1143:1-2)

MR. RUNYON: Mr. Foreman and ladies and gentleman of the jury, you know, when you're weighing evidence you have to look at it and some people are going to be right and some people are going to be wrong. Some people are maybe not going to tell the truth, and one way you can test things is by what evidence there is. (TR-III, 1143:3-8) Mr. Wilkerson was stabbed and he died in the trailer where the blood was and he was dragged out, and you were there under the carport. Two spots where Jason died and Patti died. Those are facts. You can't change that around. Jason wasn't dragged behind that trailer. You can't change the geography. That's where the evidence is. That's where that happened. And in what conjunction? Just as Mr. Kornahrens said. He was struggling with Patti. She was stabbed. She died. No question about that, and he hears a noise behind him and this person is trained—he's spent fifteen or sixteen years now with his division and as a civilian employee, and he's trained for certain skills and he reacts. No one is asking you or no one is suggesting to you that somehow, you know, excuses what he did. But the point of it is that there was a melee that night, a fight, argument, tussle, rumble, whatever you want to call it. (TR-III, 1144:2-19)

MR. RUNYON: And the question is how did it all come about? Well, you've heard the evidence. Longstanding hostility between these folks, longstanding hostility. I would suggest to you that it's not unusual in our society, that longstanding hostility between folks. I'm not going to suggest to those difficulties should be settled by going out and killing people. No one is suggesting that to you. But, you see, the problem we have is, the State does not ask you for anything but a verdict of guilty of murder. That's all the State is asking. And in order to find someone guilty of murder, you have to find that there was a homicide and you have to find that the Defendant brought about the death of that person which he did, and you have to find the intent and malice—the malice. It's a one issue case. To a large extent, when Fred Kornahrens went there that night did he have the malice? Now, the Court will instruct you that it doesn't have to be there for a long period of time. Malice doesn't have to be there for a long period of time. It can be there for a short period of time. But the simple fact of the matter is that you can listen to all of the facts and derive from them that this man went out there that night to kill those three people. (TR-III, 1144:20-25) He knew these people had guns. In Mr. Wilkerson's truck there was a gun in the glove compartment. Why was that gun there? Let's face facts, folks. Mr. Wilkerson, John Avant and Patti Kornahrens all were afraid of Fred Kornahrens. Crazy Freddie. Crazy Freddie was afraid of them. (I never thought of Mr. Wilkerson being afraid of me, but if Patty Jo and Jon were so afraid of me why didn't they leave me alone?) Were they right or wrong? We don't know. We don't know who had the right to be afraid of whom but at the same time they were all armed. It was a feud. Now, feuds are not something that should go on in a community. I was born in Kentucky. My grandmother's maiden name was Polly Hatfield. I am a Hatfield. I know something about feuds or the history of feuds. If anybody is a McCoy around here, well, we settled all that back in 1910. (TR-III, 1147:20-25, 1148:1-8)

The simple fact of the matter is that he'd been all around the area and that countryside and he was a strong fellow, and he knows what he's doing when it comes to a shovel. He testified to that. There is no evidence that grave was pre-dug. None whatsoever. Remember Mr. Anders asked about these roots, they found one root. Did that extend into the grave? No, sir, no evidence of that. There is no evidence that what happened did not happen as Mr. Kornahrens said it did except Mr. Avant's statement. Now, what you have to do is you have to determine, number one, whether or not he's guilty of murder or guilty but mentally ill. (Sentence of guilty of murder but mentally ill was not explained to the jury.) You have the evidence. (TR-III, 1153:24-25, 1154:1-11)

MR. RUNYON: Did he lose it as Dr. Schleimer said, or did he go out there with evil in his heart? That's it. That simple, and that complicated. I'm going to wrap it up at this point. There have been some allegations in this case which are not pretty. One of those allegations is that—amounts to an allegation that there was an abuse of this Courthouse. That is a serious allegation, and I would ask you—I understand the seriousness of that, but there's a man on this trial for his life and I'm not going to shirk from calling to your attention something that might be relevant. The abuse of this Courthouse is an issue, and you know what I'm talking about. The arranged conferences between the victims and the Defendant. Don't get a lawyer. Just do what I say. That's in evidence in this case. Once again, what can a man like Mr. Kornahrens do if he goes time after time after time through the system and time after time after time the system uses and abuses him? What can he do? Have nightmares? He can drive his old truck to lawyers time after time after time. He can drive his old Corvette to lawyers time after time after time. And then when the system uses and abuses him, it's not responsive, what would you do? What would any person do? You try. You use self-help. You go out there and say leave me alone, and that's what he did. That's what he did. That doesn't make these deaths excusable. It doesn't make these justifiable in that sense, but the question is whether these deaths are murder. That's the difficult thing because you simply can't be asked to find someone not guilty of doing something that Mr. Kornahrens said he did, you know, except one thing. No one has asked you to find him guilty of anything but murder. If it's not murder then there's really no other choice. It's that simple. (TR-III, 1154:16-25, 1155:16-25, 1156:1-2) I would remind you that your decision on this issue leads us on another path, depending upon your decision. I would ask you to return a verdict that speaks the truth. I can't ask you to find Mr. Kornahrens not guilty of homicide because he did in fact kill these people, but I can ask you to find Mr. Kornahrens not guilty of murder because they haven't shown the requisite malice and I can ask you to find a verdict alternatively of guilty but mentally ill because of the circumstances you have in this case. Thank you. Perhaps after your verdict we may have additional proceedings. I would hope not, but that is entirely up to you. Thank you. (TR-III, 1156:19-25, 1157:1-6) [I was not allowed to give a closing statement to the jury. I was not informed by Judge Richtor or Mr. Runyon that it was permissible.]

THE COURT: Mr. Foreman and ladies and gentleman of the jury it now becomes my responsibility to charge you, which means to instruct you, as to the law that applies in this case. By this indictment, the State of South Carolina charges the Defendant, Fred Kornahrens, Third, with three counts of murder. The allegations of this indictment have been explained to you and read to you, and I will not read to you now in detail. You will have it with you in the jury room during your deliberations. (TR-III, 1157:7-16)

THE COURT: If upon the whole case you may have reasonable doubt as to the guilt of the Defendant, he is entitled to that doubt and would be entitled to an acquittal. Likewise, if you have a reasonable doubt as to whether or not the Defendant has made out any defense he may have put forth, then he would also be entitled to that reasonable doubt and would be entitled to an acquittal. Now, I do not mean by the term reasonable doubt some whimsical or fanciful or imaginary doubt. It is not a **slight** doubt. It is a **substantial** doubt for which a person is honestly seeking to find the truth can give reason. It has been defined as a **substantial** doubt arising out of the testimony or **lack** of testimony in the case for which a person honestly seeking the truth can give reason. (TR-III, 1159:9-23) It is your duty to weigh and consider the evidence and so determine what the facts are from the testimony as you heard it from the witnesses on the stand. I cannot intimate any opinion that I may or may not have about the facts, and any interferences you may have gathered from any action or saying on my part as to the facts of this case you must disregard. As I have previously said, you are the sole judges of the facts. Hence, you must necessarily pass upon the credibility of the witnesses. You have the right to believe one witness and disbelieve another. You may believe one against many or many against one. You may accept part of a witness' testimony and reject some other part. (TR-III, 1160:8-21) Having thus determined what the facts are, it is your duty to apply the law so as charged by the Court to the facts as found by you, and so arrive at a true verdict. You must take the law as I instruct you, not as you wish it were or how you think it ought to be. Just as you are the sole judges of the facts of the case, I'm the sole judge of the law of the case, and you must take the law as I instruct you. In this case, ladies and gentleman, as I have indicated to you, the Defendant is charged with three counts of murder. The sole issue before you in this case is what is the appropriate verdict as to each of the three counts. You have no other issue to adjudicate in this matter. (TR-III, 1161:8-21) During this trial, ladies and gentleman, you heard reference to a certain guilty plea or certain prior record—criminal record. (Incident at Dr. Sanders' office with Jon and Patty Jo.) I instruct you concerning evidence or testimony present or an alleged prior conviction by the Defendant as follows: This evidence was admitted for a limited purpose. I instruct you that you must not consider the evidence for any purpose except the purpose for which it was admitted. This evidence was admitted and may be considered by you only for the purpose of evaluating the credibility or believability of the testimony presented by the Defendant himself, and for no other purpose. You cannot and you must not consider any prior record, if any, of the Defendant as evidence of his guilt or the charged for which he is now being tried. (TR-III, 1164:4-18)

THE COURT: I also want to define for you motive. Motive is that which leads or tempts the mind to indulge in a criminal act, or it is the cause or reason that induces a person to commit a criminal act. Although motive is not an essential element of the crime charged need not be shown, the presence or absence of a motive may be considered in determining criminal intent which is an essential element of a crime. In deciding the question of the Defendant's guilt, the jury may consider motive, to commit the crime charged. (TR-III, 1165:25, 1166:1-10)

Reflections Upon A Sunny Day

Malice is a word that suggests a wickedness or a hatred or determination to do what one knows to be wrong without just cause or legal provocation. Malice need not be in the mind of the one doing the killing any particular length of time before the act of killing in order to render the killing murder. If it is present in the mind of the one doing the killing any length of time before the act, then it's presence would be sufficient to render the killing murder. Malice is said to be express malice where there is manifested a violent, deliberate intention to unlawfully take away the life of another human being. Malice is **implied** where one intentionally and deliberately does an unlawful act that he or she knows to be wrong in violation of his duty to another, and where no excuse or legal provocation appears, and when the circumstances attending the killing show an abandoned heart or malignant heart, fatally bent upon mischief. Malice is defined in the law of homicide as a term of art; that is, a technical term importing, as I say, wickedness and excluding just cause or excuse. It is something that springs from wickedness or depravity, from a depraved spirit, from a heart devoid of social duty and fatally bent on mischief. The words I've expressed just referred to, expressed an implied, do not mean different kinds of malice, but merely the manner in which the only kind known to law may be shown to exist; that is, either by direct evidence or by inference. As I say, malice may be expressed as where previous threats of vengeance or lying in wait or other circumstances show directly that an intent to kill was really entertained. Malice may also be **implied** as where though no express intent to kill is proven by the direct evidence it is indirectly but necessarily inferred from facts and circumstances which are proved. The law says if someone intentionally kills another with a deadly weapon, the **implication** of malice may arise. If facts are proved beyond a reasonable doubt sufficient to raise an inference of malice to your satisfaction, this inference will be simply an evidentiary fact to be taken into consideration in the case by you the jury along with other evidence in the case, and you may give such weight as you determine it should receive. In considering malice, I tell you that you may take into consideration whether or not the Defendant was mentally capable of having malice. (TR-III, 1166:24-25, 1167:1-25, 1169:1-20)

THE COURT: Now, in this case, ladies and gentleman, certain reference was made to a certain statement by the Defendant. If there be an alleged statement placed in evidence in the case unless the State has satisfied you beyond a reasonable doubt that such statement was freely and voluntarily made, without any threats or inducements addressed to fear or hope of reward. (TR-III, 1169:20-25, 1170:1-3) [I was told: 1. Give us the bodies and it will go lighter on you. 2. Tell us where the bodies are or you will be on death row facing the electric chair 3.Tell us or we will put a foot in your ass.] Our Legislature in South Carolina has enacted a Statute which provides as follows: A Defendant is guilty but mentally ill if at the time of the commission of the act constituting the offense he had the capacity to distinguish right from wrong and to recognize his act as being wrong, but because of mental disease or defect he lacked sufficient capacity to conform his conduct to the requirements of law (TR-III, 1171:5-12) [The sentence, for guilty but mentally ill, was not explained. Could it mean life in prison or six months in a mental hospital? The jury had no way of knowing.] Now, the burden of the proof is on the State to prove guilt beyond a reasonable doubt, as I have already charged you. However, the burden of the proof as to the existence of the mental defect or disease is on the Defendant, and he must prove that at the times the crimes were committed, that he suffered from mental defect of disease that rendered of the law. The burden of the proof required of the Defendant, however is not the burden of proof beyond a reasonable doubt, but rather only by the preponderance of the evidence. Preponderance simply means that if you weighed the evidence on this point for the State and the defense, the Defendant has the burden of tipping the scales in his favor; that is, the Defendant's burden as to proof of the entitlement to the verdict of guilty but mentally ill, or not guilty. Now, in this case your verdict must be unanimous, all twelve of you must agree. (TR-III, 1172:7-25, 1173:1-5) In our daily lives we are all accustomed to doing favors for one another and taking sides and really the world is a better place because we all do that and help each other get along. That's in your daily lives. Here, however, you cannot be partial. You must be absolutely impartial. You have no friends to reward and no enemies to punish. Your verdict here must speak the truth. Nothing more or nothing less will suffice. Both the State and the Defendant are entitled to a fair, impartial trial at our hour hands, nothing more or less. (TR-111, 1175:9-19)

When I arrived on Death Row in 1985, all I had was my Bible. At Christmas, I was allowed to have a thirteen-inch TV sent to me by my family. A radio/cassette player was sent to me, too, but D/W Claypoole refused to let me have it. I spent most of my time reading and writing. For over a year I was locked in cell 22 on F tier. I had two visits in 1985 and four from my mother in 1986. I wrote letters to my attorney, Bill Runyon, about the welfare of my children.

There were tiers of cells below me. These prisoners on B and D tiers were the worst prisoners in South Carolina. They were the men that no other prison wanted. Everyday, the screaming and banging continued throughout the day and night. State TV's were bolted outside the cells against the wall, and in order to see the screen you would have to look through the bars and a wire cage at approximately a twenty-foot distance.

The guards turned the volume on the televisions to full blast to combat the noise. It was total insanity. Fights, riots, fires, cursing, stabbings, and flooding were the commonplace events happening on the tiers below. – These men were not death row prisoners

Tear gas and burning powders were used almost daily as punishment. These burning gases made their way into my cell on each occasion. There was no way to get away from it in a five by nine foot cell.

D/W Claypoole would not let me have my cassette player because I was a Christian. He let another man [Butler] have one because the prisoner was so violent.

I bought an old broken radio/cassette player from a prisoner [Gleaton] for fifty dollars and repaired it. When D/W Claypoole saw it in my cell, he expressed his displeasure.

The D/W would not allow me to move into an empty cell on the opposite side of CB-2 where the majority of the death row prisoners were housed on two tiers. He had some sort of strange system set up in his head that he was lining up the death row prisoners by cell in military formation to be executed.

There were several occasions when I was not fed. The officers said they forgot. When I got sick, I could not get medical attention for a week a time if at all. When I requested to speak with a counselor or social worker, I was ignored.

I spent two Christmas' in cell 22. When D/W Claypoole took another job within the prison, D/W Areheart took over CB-2 and moved all the death row prisoners on the west side of cell block two.

The entire judicial government in this country, from the Supreme Court to the lowly jail, isn't what you think it is. It's not about justice; it's about factional scheming for power and status within a group at the expense of others = politics.

The government cultivates criminal behavior, for it promotes sin, i.e., laws supporting abortion, homosexuality, greed, pornography, ban on prayer, Satanism, etc. And, I believe the increasingly violent and immoral TV programs that reach 99% of the homes in America, have and continue to fill and corrupt the minds of our youth.

The government wants the people to believe they have the answer for crime: more prisons, longer sentences, and more executions.

The Bible is often mentioned in debates about the death penalty. Supporters quote the Exodus passage, eye for eye, while opponents appeal to Ezekiel (33:11): "As I live, says the Lord God, I swear I take no pleasure in the death of the wicked man, but rather in the wicked man's conversion, that he may live." In fact, such use of the Bible (finding a "proof text" to affirm one's point of view) is inappropriate.

Scripture scholars teach us to understand the Bible (and it's individual books) in historical context: when it was written and why. Thus considered, there is an ambivalence about capital punishment in the Scriptures.

Clearly, the Hebrew Scriptures allowed the death penalty (for a much longer list of offenses than our society would be comfortable with – for example, striking or cursing a parent, adultery, idolatry). Yet, as we see Ezekiel and many other passages, there is also an attempt to limit violence and to stress mercy. In the Christian Scriptures, Jesus' life and teachings (see the Sermon on the Mount, Matthew 5:1 – 7:29) focus on mercy, reconciliation and redemption. (It may also be instructive to recall that Jesus' death itself was itself an application of the death penalty.) The basic thrust of the Gospels supports opposition to the death penalty.

It is said that this nation is a country of laws – not men. But, men make laws. They are the result of human effort subject to human error. There was a time in this nation when men and women were sold into slavery. Legally! And little children labored in factories and mines. Legally! And think how many legal wrongs exist today. Laws made by humans are chaff in the wind. Doomed to perish unless they are created with total faith in God. Only God's laws are infallible and forever. And, His law is LOVE!

As the 7:00 o'clock news said, there are presently 44 men on death row. Since 1912, two hundred forty one men and two women have been killed in South Carolina's electric chair. The youngest person in this country was killed in South Carolina's electric chair. He was a 14-year old boy. The boy was so small the straps had to be altered to secure him in the chair for electrocution.

For a few years, the death penalty was abolished by Congress. However, in 1976 Congress reenacted Capital Punishment and stated that the use of the electric chair to kill prisoners was not cruel and unusual punishment.

Four young men were sentenced to death row in 1977. One of them was 17 years old. Terry Roach was that young man and he was executed less than two months after my death sentence on 19 November 1985.

It is common knowledge to the men on death row that everyone will be moved to the Broad River Road Facility after Christmas 1988. The electric chair has already been moved and this relocation is in conjunction with a planned execution. Rusty Woomer is aware that his execution is coming up in the next month or two. This fact was confirmed by an aid to Governor Campbell.

It is sad the largest industry in South Carolina is the prison and jail system. We rank second in the nation in the lockup rate. Our sentences are among the most harsh and lengthy with little chance for parole considering the conservative members who serve on the board.

One member who serves on the parole, Mr. Ray Rossi, was instrumental in getting the Omnibus Crime Bill enacted. You may be aware that his daughter was raped and killed. Additionally, he was a founder of "CAVE", a group concerned with seeing all criminals getting their just desserts apparently no matter what their circumstances.

Being the father of a daughter I can empathize with him; there is no way he or I could serve on a parole board without being prejudicial. An analogy would be going before a jury of 12 SLED agents and my being charged with murdering a fellow agent.

Generally education is poor in South Carolina; it's even worse in prison. No more than 12% of the prisoners are enrolled in school at CCI and 70% of the prisoners are considered functionally illiterate.

This is not rehabilitation. We have a situation that is simply put a "human warehouse". The taxpayers' tab for each individual in the prison system is approximately $12,000 per year, which are mostly administrative costs.

Our Warden, Kenneth McKellar, stated in the News and Courier newspaper last November that he does not believe in rehabilitation. Since the word rehabilitation has left the vocabulary of prison officials, the only recourse is to build more prisons under the pretenses of locking up dangerous criminals and protecting an innocent society. What they don't tell the public is that they don't really try to rehabilitate prisoners and they keep them locked up as long as they can. All the system allows for is more squander and jobs at the prisons.

I have been here for three years and my requests for help have gone without any assistance from the so-called counselors, caseworkers, and social workers. What are they here for except 4:00 o'clock and payday? The alleged programs are a farce, in reality they don't exist, at least in any meaningful degree. Seldom are the innocent families of the prisoners taken into consideration. Psychologically and financially they suffer tremendously. Besides having to foot the bill for prisoners, many families become destitute and must become a burden to the taxpayers by applying for welfare, food stamps and housing to name a few. Children become resentful of law enforcement officers and often quit school and become prisoners as well.

The Nelson Decree, which apparently is not worth the paper it is written on is being violated at CCI and other institutions. For example, the mess hall at CCI is infested with vermin of all descriptions. Mr. Todd, the mess hall supervisor, knows it is filthy but can't do anything about it. The mess hall is inspected by "Headquarters" personnel only; NO OUTSIDE INTERVENTION. Meanwhile, we must eat food unfit for human consumption.

Reflections Upon a Sunny Day
1988 – Liars

"What a man desires is unfailing love; better to be poor than a liar" (Proverbs 19:22)

Lies have rocked the foundation of the earth, from having brought mankind to it's fallen nature... to the shedding of the precious blood of Jesus. "Woe to the earth and the sea because the devil [the father of lies who deceives the whole world] has gone down to you! He is filled with fury, because he knows that his time is short" (Revelation 12:12).

A lie will sprint around the world while the truth is lacing up it's shoes. – There were so many lies told at home and they drove me up the wall. I never knew what to expect next and they were so damn destructive. The ability to lie is a human achievement; one of those abilities that tends to set man apart from all other species.

Psychiatrists see lying as pathological when it is so persistent as to be destructive to the liar's life or to those to whom they lie. They are also grappling with lies that typify certain emotional disorders and are told by people who know they are lying.

Each variety of lies come more naturally to those who suffer from one or another personality problem.

Manipulative lies are the hallmark of the sociopath, or "antisocial personality," who is driven by utterly selfish motives. Such people are not necessarily criminals; they may gravitate toward the fringes of trades like sales, where their bent toward lying may serve them well. Since sociopaths feel no remorse or empathy for their victims, they are capable of the most cold-hearted of lies.

I remember my wife saying, you must tell me the truth about everything so that all will be forgiven; that if you tell the truth it will be a sign of good faith and all will be well. In desperation I believed her, and she took my truth and set out to destroy me with it.

My experience with lawyers and prosecutors tells me they are either born liars or they go to school to refine the skill. Many lawyers become judges and their aim is to end up somewhere high on the hill of politics. Do they lie for the self-serving motives or what?

Melodramatic lies make one the center of attention and are natural to the hysteric and histrionic personality. Such people are searching desperately for love. They are also more taken with the emotional truths than the facts of the situation.

When I think of a melodramatic liar I think of a person who is an actor. They cry and put on a performance to be convincing. Imagine yourself in front of a judge and a pretty woman [the plaintiff] is there in the courtroom crying, heaving, and sobbing. The judge looks at her with sympathy and cuts his eyes hard towards you with contempt. You are a hardworking man trying to make ends meet and you're innocent of the charge, but the woman tells a dramatic story to incriminate you for personal gain. Does the judge believe you or does he believe the pretty woman choking on tears?

I picture a melodramatic liar as one who is not only looking for love but for sympathy. Let's say you are married to a woman who has five sisters. You've been married for six years and your wife becomes restless and unfaithful. You complain about the late hours she spends away from home. She resents you telling her what to do and becomes spiteful, so she goes to her sisters and tells them you are being cruel to her. They believe every word she says and picture you as being the evil villain. What can you do?

Grandiose lies typify the narcissist, whose deep need to win the constant approval of other impels him to present himself in the most favorable light. They are prone to exaggerate their abilities or accomplishments in order to seem more impressive. Because narcissists feel entitled to special treatment, for instance believing that ordinary rules do not apply to them, they can be reckless in their lies.

Speaking of grandiose lies, take a look at this situation. Say you are a happily employed computer programmer, and then a job opening for a clerk becomes available in your department. Your boss asks you if you know someone who would be interested in that position. You call someone you went to school with and she takes the job. This new employee exaggerates her abilities in order to be more impressive to your boss. As you teach your friend the duties in the department, she takes an interest in the computer and goes to your boss to present herself in the most favorable light. Before you know it you are fired and your friend has your job.

Evasive lies are typical of the borderline personality whose wildly vacillating moods and impulsive actions constantly get them into trouble. Many of the borderline person's lies are told to avoid blame or shift responsibility for his problems to others.

I realize that children will sometimes try to shift responsibility on others to avoid punishment. If it becomes a regular practice a problem is developing.

If you were married and found that your wife was telling so many evasive lies that she couldn't keep her stories straight, what would you do?

Guilty secrets account for many lies of the compulsive person, a type who generally is scrupulously honest. Compulsives pride themselves on following the rule and attention to facts and details. But they also suffer from a fear of being shamed, and so lie to prevent other people from finding out about things they would meet with disapproval. Their lies are often mild, about things most others would find no cause for lying.

How do you feel about liars? Lawrence E. Richter was the judge in my trial. He is a professional liar. Professionals are paid to use their talents. His lies and dishonesty finally backed him in a corner, and he had to step down off his bench. He committed crimes but the law doesn't apply to him. And he sent people to prison for the very same things he did himself.

Lies can destroy lives. Solicitor Charles Condon, Frank Hunt, and the convict, Charles Brendle, certainly got their pound of flesh with lies. Jon Avant lied, and Carol Smoak lied for reasons unknown to me. – And God commanded man not to give false testimony against their neighbor.

Reflections Upon a Sunny Day
1988 — Judge Lawrence E. Richter

At a party in Charleston last summer, Circuit Judge Lawrence E. Richter tried to coerce, Miss Tara Anderson, a law student into the bathroom to snort cocaine, the young woman testified before the committee that determines whether judicial candidates are qualified to serve on the bench. Richter denied the young woman's allegation.

On Monday, March 21, 1988, Miss Anderson told the committee that Richter beckoned to her from a back bedroom while the party was under way and then tried to maneuver her into the bathroom with himself and the Charleston attorney Bobby Howe. She said she never saw cocaine, but they were both pointing to their noses and making sniffing sounds.

"From the totality of circumstances, I knew that's what he wanted me to do, and I was scared to death," Miss Anderson said. Richter later called her to his chambers "to intimidate me into shutting up about what happened" she said, "He said that Charleston was a small town and I had to keep his confidence."

She also claimed that Richter supporters tried to scare her out of testifying. Among those allegations, Miss Anderson said that the Colombia defense lawyers Jack Swerling and Dick Harpootlian spoke to her at the law school, where they teach a class. "You'd better be careful." She said she took that comment as a warning not to testify against Richter.

Two witnesses, who like Richter's style and discount claims that he's abrasive and abusive in the courtroom, were defense lawyers whose clients were sentenced to death by Richter but who found him fair. [Runyon]

Among the claims in Richter's screening is one involving a $55,000 cash transaction for land sold to Roy Riley who was charged with masterminding smuggling operations.

A young prosecutor scheduled to testify against the re-election of Circuit Judge Lawrence E. Richter told a screening committee that he was told his "blood will be on the carpet" if he speaks against the judge. Ralph Hoisington, an assistant solicitor in Charleston County, said the threat "gave me pause for thought" but that he was not intimidated by it. Hoisington made a brief appearance before the panel to vouch for the credibility of the law student.

Hoisington's allegations about the judge – apparently complaints about Richter's courtroom demeanor – were expected to come when the screening resumed. But the following day, the lawyer told the committee that his boss, 9th Circuit Solicitor Charles Condon, had told him that a prominent Charleston attorney "was saying that if I testified before the committee my blood would be on the carpet of the committee room floor." Hoisington also said the "threat was conveyed to me from Robert Rosen."

Rosen is one of several Charleston lawyers who are helping Richter rebut his critics during the hearings, which have turned into a bloodbath of words over Richter's conduct in and out of court.

Circuit Judge Lawrence E. Richter "double-crossed" federal agents when he failed to tell them a targeted drug trafficker paid off a mortgage for land the judge had sold him, a former U.S. attorney testified.

Reflections Upon A Sunny Day

Bart Daniel, a Charleston attorney, told a legislative panel that the judge did not cooperate with the agents in the Operation Jackpot drug investigation five years ago. Daniel said Richter sold two lots on the inter-coastal waterway in Charleston to Roy Riley, who was charged with masterminding drug smuggling operations. Riley was convicted of laundering money and drug trafficking. – A deposition from Richter on file in federal court shows he accepted the money in cash and deposited it in five separate accounts, but he said he didn't know it was illicit profit. Richter said he thought Riley was a wealthy tennis pro. Daniel said, "I think there's a whole bunch improper here for a judge. You just don't take cash like that and deposit it like that."

Daniel said Riley paid Richter $20,000 in cash in July 1981 and paid off the $35,000 balance on the property the following November in the front seat of a car. Richter, however, did not file notice in court that the mortgage had been satisfied until December 1982, Daniel said, "The government knew only about the $20,000 down-payment. They didn't know additional money had been satisfied with the $35,000 cash payment," Daniel testified.

Daniel said he was in Washington in December 1982 when he got an urgent telephone call from agents in South Carolina. They told him they routinely had checked courthouse records to make sure the property had not been sold, he said. "They told me they had been double-crossed by Larry Richter. If these agents hadn't checked, we wouldn't have known he had sold the property to Riley."

The drug agents later seized the property as a transaction executed with drug money, Daniel said. Earlier the same day, Richter had filed papers that he planned to sell the property to a family friend, he said.

In testimony, Gedney M. Howe III, a former friend of Richter's and member of one of Charleston's most politically powerful families, denied he mounted a campaign to unseat Richter, whom he called a liar, thief, and bully. Howe accused the judge of bullying attorneys, particularly young ones, and taking sides in court. Other witnesses called the judge a racist and a showoff.

Charleston Deputy Solicitor Ralph Hoisington dropped a bombshell on the hearings when he resigned so he could contradict his supervisor, Solicitor Charles Condon, about an alleged threat. Hoisington said Condon had not told the truth to the committee. He said Condon told him a Charleston attorney had said if Hoisington testified against Richter, Hoisington's "blood would be on the carpet." Hoisington said Condon told him Richter's friends would expose a drug arrest record against the deputy solicitor, which later was dropped. Condon, however, testified there was no threat to keep Hoisington from testifying but that he wanted him to know the allegations against Richter would be challenged with "dirty laundry" against Hoisington.

On the fifth day of tense testimony about his fitness to serve, Judge Richter said defiantly to the legislators, "I am in the race to the bitter end." He testified that his real estate transaction with an acquaintance convicted of smuggling drugs was not unusual. He also didn't think it odd that Riley could come up with so much cash in a matter of days. And, he told the committee that he never tried to entice a young law student to snort cocaine.

After six days of testimony, Senator Thomas E. Smith, D-Florence, said in a fiery speech on the Senate floor that Circuit Judge Lawrence E. Richter "disgraced the bar" and would have been rejected by a legislative screening committee if he hadn't dropped his re-election bid.

Richter shocked supporters and opponents by announcing his decision to retire from the bench. – His race had in fact come to the bitter end.

Reflections Upon A Sunny Day

In a fiery speech and in a scathing written report, Senator Smith said he and five others on the eight-member screening panel would have voted against Richter. No straw vote was ever taken, Smith said, but the screening panel appeared ready to vote 6-2 against qualifying Richter.

Richter said Smith's comments were "politically motivated" because his own re-election bid is in trouble. "He is making political hay at my expense," the judge said.

Charleston attorney Robert Rosen said that Smith promised him, as one of Richter's legal advisers, that the committee's conclusions would be no report of any kind. "I relied on his word," Rosen said. "We had a gentleman's agreement, and I passed that on to the judge. Judge Richter made his decision to retire on that basis." Rosen said Smith's conduct should be reported to the commission that discipline lawyers, because he probably broke the law.

Smith said Richter had proved himself unfit to remain on the bench through three land transactions: 1.) One involving a "secret partner" in the Charleston bar. 2.) One involving a $55,000 cash deal with a drug smuggler. 3.) One that resulted in Richter using the power of his office "to influence a personal business relationship."

The law student who testified against Circuit Judge Lawrence E. Richter Jr. in his aborted re-election, told police Sunday she found the body of a dead cat in her car.

Columbia police were called to Tara Anderson's Wheat Street home about 10:30 A.M. Police reports state that someone had used an unknown object to enter her 1984 Chevrolet Cavalier between 5:30 P.M. Saturday and 10:00 A.M. Sunday. Nothing was taken. Police said the body of a dead cat was on the driver's seat, and that the animal may have been Miss Anderson's cat, which she keeps in Charleston at her parent's house.

Investigators would not comment on whether the incident was believed to be retaliation for the student's testimony.

Police categorized the incident as an auto break-in. "It's just an auto break-in," Sgt. Kevin Mooney said. "It is under investigation." Mooney said no arrests have been made.

Richter, who strongly refuted the student's allegations, announced his retirement Friday from the Ninth Circuit judgeship. The 41 year-old judge, who said his bid had created too much divisiveness, laid to rest predictions that the Legislature would not return him to the bench.

RE: The State Newspaper/Columbia, S.C. 1988

Through prayer and study, my faith continued to grow in God. I prayed for wisdom and the next level of spiritual growth in the gifts of the Holy Spirit. I asked God about my future. No one in their right mind longs to stay in prison or suffer a horrible death. I did not understand how, but I felt that I would be out of prison in three years.

On the tenth day of the third year, I was out of prison. I escaped on January 19, 1988, and I had no evil intentions in my heart.

God does work in mysterious ways. My freedom turned into a test of faith. God protected me from harm and gave me strength. I overpowered two officers and took their weapons without hurting them. I went without food for over two weeks and endured the freezing winter weather in the woods without a coat or fire.

I had unarmed the officers of two loaded SOT .357 magnum pistols and could have taken whatever I wanted, but my heart told me to put the guns away. I could not break into anyone's home and demand food even though I was starving. And though my life had been sentenced to death in a barbaric way by people, I could not force anyone to help me. I was fully prepared to die and not harm anyone.

I went to a childhood neighbor, but she refused to help and called the police. I left and encamped in the woods.

My desire was to leave this country and start a new Christian life in Canada. Everyone I met or observed appeared to be very afraid of me. I was disappointed and deeply hurt by their behavior. And though the neighbors reported me, the intense police search failed. I am sure that I was being protected by my Lord and His angels.

Prior to my escape, I had made plans to pray outside, under the open sky and stars, during my freedom. The air was crisp and very cold. The sky was clear, without a cloud anywhere, and the stars were shining so beautifully bright. I was alone praying in the wilderness. It felt good to pray in the open away from the darkness of evil that is concentrated within the steel and cement walls of prison.

During a cold night, I had a dream. I dreamed that I was caught up in spirit and quickly swept through a lighted tunnel. The walls of the tunnel rendered its own light. The tunnel led to a corridor. I went to a room and stood in a large doorway. The room was spacious and symmetrical. The walls and everything in the room put forth light. As best I can describe the light, it was a pleasing soft blue glow like the color of the sky on a summer day. In this room were angels, sitting and standing, at a large table. The angels were pure, radiant, and dazzling white. They were beautiful. I paid particular attention to the face of a tall angel who was standing nearby. His face and beard was radiant as was His body and white robe. They did not appear to be young but they looked mighty. The angels were conversing over a book that was open on the table. It was very peaceful there. I did not approach the table. I felt that I should not venture far from the doorway, for they were glorified, and I was only to observe.

After I observed the angels from the doorway, I left the corridor and entered the tunnel of light and swiftly arrived in another place. I found myself, high in the sky, looking down at the Earth. The view was like from the window of an airplane. As I moved closer to the ground, I saw a pit. It was like an empty well, and from every direction there were countless numbers of large worms entering this pit. I was hovering over this scene not fully understanding the signification of the worms, so I went a little closer. I wanted to see the faces of the worms; however, I did not want to get too close to the pit. I had a bad feeling about the pit. As I got closer, one of the worms looked up at me. In its face I saw suffering and the torment of pain.

I woke up at daylight that cold winter morning with ice on my body and Jesus in my heart. I gave praise and thanks to God for all his blessings upon my life.

On Sunday morning, January 31, 1988, I left the cover of the woods before sunrise. I went to the home of a couple I had been corresponding with. He shook my hand at the courthouse on January 19th, and they knew me when I was a boy in their neighborhood.

I waited until they were preparing to leave for church before revealing my presence. When he came outside, I meekly handed a note to him. The note said, "I am a true Christian and I humbly ask that you share some food with a Christian brother. If you decide not to help me, please do not bring me any harm. Please do not call the police and I will leave."

He did not have the friendly face, as he did at the courthouse, when I was shackled in chains. He took my note, got into his car, and sped off spinning the tires. My old neighbor immediately called the police.

I left his property, but I did not have enough time to reach the woods. I had to walk down the neighborhood street in broad daylight.

Reflections Upon A Sunny Day

I felt a sense of protection, and my heart received a warning to step off the street. I hid near a mailbox on an empty lot and camouflaged myself under a few small pine saplings with straw.

Within moments a police cruiser stopped beside me. The officers looked straight at me and the driver said to his partner, "I wonder where he could have gone so fast?" The cruiser pulled off and within minutes an unmarked police car stopped beside me.

Officers, searching from their cars, stopped beside me several times and looked at the pine saplings where I was camouflaged in the straw. As police surrounded the block, I watched them get out of their cars and pump shells into 12 gauge shotguns. I remained perfectly still and prayed, "Lord protect me." I waited and thought this might be my last moment of physical life. The police were going to blow me away with shotguns and pistols, but I had no intentions of hurting anyone.

The pistols were packed away in an old school bag I had found in the woods. The bag was filled with things I had found in the woods to help me survive. The blue and red bag was beside me covered with the sparse straw I could find under the small trees. I waited and wondered if I had the bag properly camouflaged. I was not afraid. I was prepared for death. I waited.

My Lord protected me from their searching eyes. The officers got back into their cars and continued to circle the neighborhood. Police on foot, and those with bloodhounds, passed within a few feet of me many times. The search plane flew at tree—top level and directly over me all day.

During the search, the neighbors became interested in the police activity. They stood on the road right beside me for most of the afternoon.

As some of the neighbors left, others came and gathered to discuss what the police were doing. The officers stopped many times to speak with the people standing on the road beside me. A lady asked an officer about me. He told her that I was a desperate criminal. The lady replied, "At least he isn't hurting anyone." Her words brought tears to my eyes.

I remained still all day, while the police continued to search. I heard their plans of searching all night, and the moon was going through its brightest phase. I low-crawled, from the empty lot, in search of a darker place to cross the streets.

I didn't find a satisfactory place to cross. The moon was too bright between the streetlights, so I stopped in a neighbor's yard and buried myself in leaves.

On the following day, Monday, Mr. Graham spent his day off from work piddling around in the yard and splitting firewood. He spent most of the day right beside me and touched me on one occasion, but he didn't see me in the pile of leaves. I spent nearly twenty-four hours motionless eventhough there were fire ant attacks.

When it was dark and late at night again, I uncovered myself. I considered crossing the street but decided to let things simmer down a little more. I hid myself under a small fishing boat and trailer, which was covered and protected by a blue tarpaulin.

On Tuesday, I observed everything that was going on from under the boat. The Graham Family left early for school and work. About midday, as activities were calming down, the police responded to a false alarm and stormed the neighborhood. I watched the bloodhound pass nearby and directly across my previous path. The dog did not pick up my scent. Then two elderly ladies, from next door, walked over to get a better look at the activity and stopped beside me to discuss the current events.

Reflections Upon A Sunny Day

This was my fifteenth day without food and my third day without water. I asked God about my situation. I was ready to die, rather than return to prison, but my heart received the message that I was going back. I asked, "Why?" I did not understand my Lord's plans for me. I had not given up my hope of living a new Christian life in Canada. My need for food was great, but I would rather have had a telephone call for transportation. I needed a little help from a friend.

When I asked Mrs. Puckhaber for help, on January 19th, I was still wet from swimming Church Creek to evade a swarm of police. I had played at her house, with her son, when I was a boy. On January 31st, I asked Mr. Murray for help. Both of them knew me, refused to help, and called the police. Their rejection pierced my heart like a rusty sword.

I was looking for someone who would say, "Freddy we still love you. Come into our home and let us help you." - It didn't happen.

Where the helicopter, airplanes, bloodhounds, and hundreds of police had failed, a little yellow cat named Pumpkin gave me away. The little yellow cat led its seventeen year old master John Graham, to my hiding place and the young boy saw me. I did not want to scare him, so I acted like I was asleep. As the day ended, the young boy apparently kept his discovery to himself for the night.

The false alarm, which had caused additional search activity that day, carried over into the night. I had become weak from the lack of food and water. I was also having some physical problems. I considered moving but decided to wait one more day. My Lord had protected me when the police were practically stepping on me, and it appeared that the young boy was going to keep my location to himself.

I had observed the Graham Family and the neighbors for a few days and knew them all by name. They seemed like nice people, and I would have liked to have been their friend.

On Wednesday morning, February 3, 1988, the Graham Family prepared themselves for another day of school and work. When the young boy came outside, he came directly to the boat and looked at me. I laid still as if asleep. He and the rest of the family soon left the house. I planned to spend the day quietly under the boat as I did the day before, but I was regretting I had not made a move while it was dark.

When the young boy left for school, he reported my location and collected a three thousand dollar reward for information leading to my arrest.

A police cruiser pulled into the yard. The officers searched the property and utility rooms of the garage. When the search failed, the officers returned to their car and left. I could not safely move from my hiding place in daylight.

About an hour later, the police cruiser pulled into the yard again. I watched the officers as they came within three feet of me. They removed the tarpaulin and looked inside the boat. For a moment, they acted as if they were going to leave again, but one of the officers decided to look under the trailer. He was very surprised, and I was arrested without incident. I went back to Death Row without hurting anyone. And as far as I knew, my old neighbors and just about everybody in the world wanted me dead.

My following days were spent adjusting again to being confined in a small cement cell. I wasn't aware that my brief freedom had stirred up anyone's heart, but I received dozens of letters from people who expressed concern and compassion for me. After reading a few letters, I cried. My Lord was with me throughout my brief freedom. I was given an opportunity to show everyone that I am not an indiscriminate killer but rather a true Christian.

Reflections Upon A Sunny Day

Though in prison, God blessed me daily. He filled my heart with love, and I put my trust entirely in Him. And just as Job said, "Even if He slay me, yet will I trust Him."

Many people asked me why I didn't use the weapons to force someone into helping me out of the area. I didn't use the weapons, because I had no violence in my heart.

'No Violence In My Heart,' Kornahrens Says Of Escape

By CHRIS SOSNOWSKI
Post-Courier Reporter

"It's pretty apparent I'm not violent, because I didn't hurt anybody, I didn't hurt the neighbors, the police officers," condemned triple-murderer Fred H. Kornahrens III said Thursday.

Kornahrens spoke to The News and Courier by telephone Thursday afternoon from the Central Correctional Institution in Columbia.

He is being held on Death Row for the February 1985 bayonet murders of his ex-wife Patricia Josephine Avant, her father, Harry Lee Wilkerson, 69, and 19-year-old Jason Avant. After his arrest, he led police to a shallow grave on Yonge's Island where he had buried the bodies.

Kornahrens said he stayed in the same area where dozens of police searched for him for 15 days following his Jan. 19 escape. "They were close. I was just hoping I wouldn't be seen. I had no violence in my heart at the time."

Charleston County Police Chief William J. Sidoran said Kornahrens stated that the massive police presence kept him pinned in the Pierpont area.

Kornahrens revealed that Johnny Graham, father of 16-year-old John Graham whose sighting of Kornahrens led to his capture early Wednesday, actually made physical contact with him as he was hiding. "But they couldn't see me at the residence where I was caught," Kornahrens said.

The elder Graham "bumped into me Monday morning when he was

Fred H. Kornahrens III
...Back In Prison

splitting wood, when I was covered up in leaves in the yard," Kornahrens said. He said that at the time he was not under the tarpaulin-covered boat where he was eventually discovered.

"Nobody was in any danger from me," Kornahrens said. "I'm not a criminal type, never had trouble before. I had a career (as a mechanic) with the government and the military. I was a federal employee for the U.S. Army Reserve for 16 years." He said he also served with the Army Reserve during that time.

"I was a family man, overwhelmed by stress and the pressure of a bad marriage and an unfaithful wife.

There was a relentless pursuit for money, to make my life as miserable as possible."

In 1981, Kornahrens was charged with two counts of assault and battery with intent to kill his wife Patricia Josephine Kornahrens and Jon Avant. The charges were later dropped by the solicitor's office with her consent, according to court records.

After they were divorced, his ex-wife again sought prosecution of Kornahrens on the assault charges and filed a $150,000 damage suit. He pleaded guilty to one count of aggravated assault and was given a suspended six-year sentence with two years probation, according to court records.

He also filed a countersuit claiming she had an affair with Jon Avant, causing Kornahrens "to become temporarily insane." Kornahrens wanted her claims dismissed and $200,000 in damages. Mrs. Avant, as police later referred to her, denied an adulterous relationship with Avant and attributed Kornahrens' damages to his own actions.

The murders were committed a few days before the Kornahrens suit was scheduled to be heard in court.

"I wrote a long story about the whole thing that happened, about what led up to me doing a crazy and bizarre thing," Kornahrens said. He wrote his story from Death Row, "adding bits and pieces together, jotting notes last year," for his post-conviction relief hearing.

See Kornahrens, Page 16-A

...Kornahrens

Continued From Page 1-A

"I'd like people to know I'm not a mad-dog killer .. just a victim of circumstances, something I could not handle ...

"I wouldn't intentionally kill anyone. I'm sorry for what I did do," Kornahrens said tearfully on Thursday. "I loved those people, they were all family. Her (Patti Jo's) father — I loved that man dearly. I'm just not a killer by nature or instinct. It just happened that I lost my mind."

Asked where he got the handcuff key he used to free himself while riding with two Charleston County sheriff's deputies, Kornahrens said he found it. The key was found with several articles in his possession when he was captured. He said authorities had talked to him about where he got it, and that "I don't think I should really go into it" with a reporter.

"I'm very sorry those two officers lost their jobs on my account. It wasn't their fault. I wish the sheriff would give them their jobs back."

Kornahrens was asked if he'd planned his escape.

"I think anytime anyone is in this situation, somebody in prison, they think about freedom. I had no desire to live a criminal life (at CCI). I just wanted to start a new life." If his escape had been successful, "I'd have gone to Canada," Kornahrens said.

Authorities said that a knapsack found with Kornahrens contained the handcuff key, bobby pins and the two deputies' .357-caliber Magnum revolvers. There were also a pencil, paper, a blue overshirt and a tablecloth.

"I found that stuff in the woods. I didn't go through anybody's trash," he said. "I wasn't going to break into anybody's house. I am a real Christian and my heart doesn't hold anger and revenge toward people.

"When I left the police station I was asked (by reporters) about Jon Avant. I don't like what he did to me, (but) I killed his son. I'm sorry for that. I found it in my heart to forgive him. He has my children. I hope to God he's doing them right."

He said he's worried that his children have the impression "your daddy is an animal'... and I'm not. I'd like for my children to know I'm not a mean, vicious person. I can't express how sorry I am for the things I've done wrong."

Police have said that during a two-hour interrogation following his recapture, Kornahrens said he'd had nothing to eat since he escaped, and nothing to drink since Sunday when he handed a handwritten note to a Magnolia Ranch resident.

Kornahrens said Thursday that "I could have (eaten), I decided not to. I had those weapons, and I could have shot (small animals). If I could have gotten out of the neighborhood, I would've started hunting. I decided not to hunt at the time, to let things cool down. I could bear people shooting, probably (at) squirrels. I don't believe I would have drawed any attention.

"No one helped me. I've never gone that long without food. (But) after a week without food, it didn't bother me that bad.

"The last three days, I couldn't get enough water. Before, I would go to different people's houses and to their (outdoor) faucets." He said that on some of those occasions, he could see the people were at home.

"I think ... rybody was in a panic that I was .. dangerous person, but I'm not. I wasn't going to hurt those officers (deputies) — I was prepared to die, but I wasn't going to hurt them."

During the struggle in the deputies' cruiser, "I fired a round in the ground — the door was open — to make them stop. They still wanted to fight, that (shot) was to make them know that I had the weapon." He said the cruiser was slowing to a stop at the time. Police said one of the deputies, Terry Hoffman, tried to escape from the cruiser during the struggle.

"I told them (the deputies) I'd rather be shot, that way, than sit up here (CCI) and die in a barbaric, medieval way. they've got designed here." Kornahrens said that after leaving the deputies with the cruiser and walking into the woods, "for the first first few hours, I just made distance between me and where I left the car."

During the telephone interview, Kornahrens said he hadn't heard from his lawyer, Ray McClain, and asked that he be called. A secretary at McClain's law firm said he was involved in a deposition in Myrtle Beach Thursday afternoon, but was expected back today.

The News & Courier February 5, 1988

Kornahrens' Great Escape

Lowcountry Diary
By JOHN BURBAGE

I talked to fired Charleston County sheriff's deputy Sandra Schaber the other day about her role in the Fred Kornahrens ordeal. Mrs. Schaber was driving when Kornahrens somehow got out of his handcuffs, dove into the front seat, overpowered her and Deputy Terry Hoffman and escaped.

Mrs. Schaber — a husky-voiced, 49-year-old widow and mother of six children — offers a riveting account of what happened that day:

"Suddenly, Kornahrens was in the front seat with us. He went straight for Hoffman's gun and, with his feet, pinned me against the door. My right hand was wedged between his foot and the arm rest. I was trying to steer the car through rush-hour traffic with my left hand.

"While he wrestled for Terry's gun, I was trying to get the car over to the side of I-26. I managed to free my right hand, grabbed my baton and struck Kornahrens across his back several times. Then I thrust the stick between his legs. He grabbed the baton with one hand while his other was on Terry's gun. I released the baton and grabbed Kornahrens in the groin area. He kicked me hard in my chest and I let go."

By then Kornahrens had complete control of Hoffman's gun, she said. "That's when I turned the steering wheel loose and reached with my left hand for my gun, which was between me and the driver-side door. I tried to shoot him. Kornahrens grabbed the cylinder of the revolver — which prevented it from firing. Terry opened the door and tried to get out. The car was out of control."

"I grabbed the barrel of my gun with my right hand and pulled it to Kornahrens' side. With my left hand, I tried to shoot again but the cylinder wouldn't turn because he still had a strong grip on it."

Kornahrens fired Hoffman's gun out of the door and demanded that the deputy shut it, she said. "Then Kornahrens jerked my gun from me. He had both guns. He pointed one at my right temple and ordered me to drive fast while holding the other gun on Terry. It was like he had his eyes on both of us at the same time."

Mrs. Schaber said she refused to drive over 35 mph, hoping another deputy, who she believed was somewhere behind her, would see what was happening. She said she told Kornahrens to shoot her if he wanted to but they'd all die in a wreck if he did. "Kornahrens hollered that I was crazy and held both guns on Terry — one at his left temple and the other in his left shoulder," she said.

About that time, she eased her hand down and keyed the police radio microphone for about a minute, hoping another deputy would hear what was going on in the car, she said. Kornahrens grabbed the mike and ordered her to drive across the Ashley River bridge toward Highway 7.

"I stopped at a red light at Orange Grove Road. He told me to go but I refused. Then the deputy who I thought was somewhere behind us walked up to our car, looked in and saw Kornahrens in the front seat holding the weapons on Hoffman. He ran back to his car."

She said Kornahrens was obviously confused at that point, and had no escape plan. They drove down Highway 7 until a city policeman drove up head-on in front of them and stopped. "I stopped too," Mrs. Schaber said. "Kornahrens told Terry to radio the cop to get out of the way, and told me to turn right."

The deputies and Kornahrens were on Orleans Road then. They later turned onto Highway 61 and were headed toward Summerville. Kornahrens told her to turn into the St. Philip's AME churchyard.

"He knew a dirt road (Old Bee's Ferry Road) was there by the church. I stopped the car, and another police car turned into the parking lot." She said Kornahrens told Hoffman to use the radio to tell the other officers not to follow them. Mrs. Schaber then drove down the dirt road.

They came to a fork. "I saw a lot of rocks across the road to the left, blocking it, so I turned that way." She said she stopped at the rocks and asked Kornahrens what he wanted her to do.

"He ordered me to give him the keys. I told him no because my house keys were on the chain. He snatched them away and ordered Hoffman out of the car." Hoffman went to the back of the car while Kornahrens went into the woods in front of the car, she said.

"He disappeared into the fog and the dark. I got my spare keys out of my pocket, unlocked the glove box and grabbed my .25 automatic pistol." She turned on the car, waiting a few seconds for the radio to warm up (it operated on tubes) and reported that Kornahrens was in the woods. Several county police officers arrived and a perimeter was quickly set up. Mrs. Schaber waited at the scene for more than two hours, wanting to help with the search, but was told by Sheriff Michael O'Dowd to go home, she said.

Both Mrs. Schaber and Deputy Hoffman were cleared as accomplices in the escape by the State Law Enforcement Division. However, following an internal investigation by the Sheriff's Department, they were found to have been "grossly negligent" in carrying out their duties. They were fired by Sheriff O'Dowd. Mrs. Schaber believes that her dismissal was unjustified.

"In O'Dowd's apparent zeal to make himself look good in the voters' eyes by saving taxpayers' money, he cut the department's overtime hours so drastically that security and performance were seriously compromised," she said. "Under (the late) Sheriff Dawley, at least three deputies — two in the front seat and one in the back — were assigned to transport people like Kornahrens. Only two of us were assigned under O'Dowd. Why wasn't a third officer assigned? Deputy Hoffman and I did not assign duties; we carried out orders.

"Under Sheriff Dawley, even routine General Sessions court cases required at least four deputies and two to three court security personnel. However, only two of us were assigned to the Kornahrens hearing (on Monday and on Tuesday, the day of the escape) and no other deputies were assigned to the prisoner holding area to keep it secured while we were in the courtroom. Kornahrens surely noticed that security had been cut drastically from that provided at his trial and previous hearings."

Under Sheriff Dawley, when killers such as Kornahrens were taken anywhere, at least one "chase car" was assigned to follow the transport vehicle, she said. "No chase car was assigned to follow us on the day Kornahrens escaped. The deputy who happened to be behind us was on his way home from the courthouse."

She said she was fired because "policies and procedures" were not followed by her. "Policies and procedures were never spelled out," she said. "I have never seen a policy and procedure manual in the Sheriff's Department. Common sense would indicate that the sheriff or a supervisor should have assigned sufficient personnel to safely carry out the mission."

(John Burbage is a Post-Courier Assistant Metropolitan editor.)

The unique experiences God has blessed me with are so unbelievable from our human viewpoint, that I was very hesitant to share them. It is a known fact that people all over the world have spiritual experiences. There has also been scientific study investigating the astonishing journeys described by people who have had a near death experience. God speaks to us in many ways; through dreams, visions, and gifts of the Holy Spirit.

On Friday the 17th of June 1988, my son Joseph Wilkerson Kornahrens visited me in the CCI Death Row visiting room. This is the first time I have seen him since January 1985. I have not been able to talk with my son Joey for over three and a half years. As I write these words I already know that I cannot properly express my present feelings. My emotions are numerous.

Today is Sunday; Fathers Day, and my thoughts have been on my son day and night. Our visit together was good; better than I expected. Tears flowed from my son's eyes for two hours. He vented his anger by expressing his feelings. We talked about his present situation and how he deals with life. My son feels responsible for what happened and I assured him there were no reasons for him to feel guilt. We shared things from our past and even laughed at some of our experiences. My son said he loves me even though what I did and wishes I could come home so we could be a family again. My son needs me and how I wish I could be there for him. My son's emotions are like my own. He has many different feelings and they are overwhelming. My son said that he loves me but doesn't want to feel the pain that love brings. He does not want to bear that pain again when I am killed in the electric chair. These are his words and he expressed himself honestly. He has my admiration.

Although our visit was productive; it was not alone. Our visit was in the presence of my brother in law; Carol Murdaugh, and a Counselor from the Medical University. My son may have felt somewhat intimidated but did not express it openly. Joey still has his respect and love for me. He was embarrassed to talk about some of his personal faults. When he called me "Dad" my heart skipped beats. It has been ages since I had heard that name. My eyes were floating in front of a flood of tears and it hurt to hold them back. My heart felt like it had formed a fist reaching up putting a burning chokehold in my throat. I have cried in front of my son before but this time he needed my support. He didn't need to see me have an emotional breakdown. Carol sat with us at the table and joined the conversation. The Counselor sat to the side and only observed. Fortunately, the mental picture of my son is frozen in my memory of 1985. My three and a half years in prison seem like an eternity. My son has changed very much in these past years. It is difficult for my mind to suddenly catch up to his older appearance. My mind is torn between the past and present Joey. He has changed but his smile and laugh are the same. It was so good to see him smile. His smile and tears have my heart on an emotional roller coaster.

I believe Joey and I share the same feelings. He could not sleep the prior night because of his anxiety. He felt relief when I expressed love. He felt pain and emptiness because we cannot live as a family. He was surprised to see how similar our childhood years compare. I feel sure Joey discovered some answers that will be helpful to him.

We hugged several times and I told Joey I love him and that I was sorry for everything. He is going to remain in the Medical University for a while longer at his own request. He truly wants help and my heart burns with love for him. He said that he would visit me again.

Joey is my son and I can help him in ways not understood by others. With my love and understanding I can help him understand his present emotional problems.

My prayers have been answered. Praise our Lord.

On March 2, 1989, Jim Anders brought another tour group to death row. I was reading my Bible when I heard them announce that Jim Anders and his tour group were in the building. I looked over my shoulder as I was reading and saw Joan's husband, Carol Murdaugh, standing on the (rock) ground floor. The group did not come on my tier. They were taken on the third tier. I don't know if Carol was alone. He may have had the whole family with him.

Solicitor James Anders was identified as a "Special Prosecutor" in my trial. He and Deputy Attorney General Wells Dickson were assigned to my case after Solicitor Charles Condon falsely charged me with two counts of Soliciting Murder for Hire. Solicitor Anders prosecuted, used false witnesses, and was successful in obtaining the death penalty for the state. Solicitor Anders' love for power and the limelight led him to appear on the trashy Morton Downey Show.

On March 4, 1989, Bob McAlister visited death row and spoke with me at my cell door. Bob works as Chief of Staff to Governor Campbell. He told me that their Church organized "Half-way House" was closed down by Solicitor James Anders, the community, and the sheriff's department. It was a Christian home, located on 37 acres of land, to help paroled prisoners adjust back into public society.

It was difficult to get weekend visits, but another memo from DM Rodgers stated: "As of March 6, 1989, weekend visits as a matter of routine are discontinued. Weekend visits will be granted upon meeting either of the two criteria: 1. Verified emergencies (must be initiated by Chaplin). 2. Bonafide out-of-state visitor with a picture ID and one other form of ID. Any other reason must be in the form of a written request to Warden McKellar for the visitor. This request must be made for each visiting occasion and the visitor must be on the prisoner's visiting list."

Reflections Upon A Sunny Day

On March 16, 1989, D/W Rodgers cursed me. He had a habit of unloading curses on prisoners who played his game of exchanging obscenities. He wasn't playing a game with me. He was showing his contempt for me. I believe the man had a psychological problem.

On March 20, 1989, a prisoner in the CCI kitchen defecated in a pot of grits and it was served for breakfast. I rarely eat breakfast and I didn't eat that morning.

My mother and Joey visited on the 20th and 31st of March. It was good to see them. I encouraged Joey to be a responsible person, to use good judgment and seek the righteousness of God.

On April 8, 1989, we had another shakedown. My cell was searched and my fan was taken apart.

On April 9, 1989, Bob McAlister visited the row. His visit was mainly with Rusty Woomer, but he usually visited the other men before leaving.

On April 13, 1989, we had a major shakedown. During the shakedown a .25 caliber semi-automatic pistol was found. The guards knew it was in the building before the search began. I heard from a reliable source that Inmate Lucas was responsible for the weapon and for leaking out the information to its discovery. It was hidden in the little room we use as a chapel. Lucas is the drug kingpin in CB-2, and he has about half a dozen or so men who run drugs for him. His actions have brought a lot of misery to the men on death row. One of his runners was caught with five hundred dollars and a bag of marijuana. There were several men caught with drugs and too much money, but in some cases I feel that the confiscation of money was not justified. One man had fifty-two dollars, and all his money was taken. We are allowed to have fifty dollars and anything over that is contraband. They should have taken only the two dollars and left the rest. I am certain that the guards knew the weapon was here and where to find it.

On the following morning, a couple of men and myself began moving the weights around to the exercise area, but we were stopped. We had been keeping the weights in an area separated by a fence to keep that away from the SSR prisoners, for in the past they always tore everything up just for spite. They would crash the weights down on the bench, destroying the bench and bending the weight bar. They often tore down the basketball goal, too.

About twenty minutes later, all the weights, bars, bench, etc., were completely removed from the exercise yard. I asked why they were taken and a guard told me that a shank was found in the weight bench during the shakedown inspection. I had used the weights the prior day and helped put them away when our exercise period was over, and I didn't see a shank. The building work-outs used the weights in the afternoon, when they had their exercise period. Unless the work-outs put one in the equipment, I believe the story about the shank to be false. I believe they took the equipment just because they didn't want us to have it. It's just more of their Gestapo get—tough policy. They've been taking everything else, so we suspected that the weights would be taken, too.

On April 14, 1989, my mother and Joey visited. They arrived late and our visit was only fifty minutes long. They weren't getting along well. My mother was being demanding and protective. Joey was being disrespectful and irresponsible.

Dear Joey,

3 July 1989

Reflections Upon A Sunny Day

I hope all is well with you at home. I wrote a letter to your cousin, Christina, and the contents are worth sharing with you. Besides, I told you in a letter a couple of months ago that I was going to explain the same subject.

In response to my last letter, Christina told me that she had never thought of herself as being deceived. She also answered my question about Christian Holy Days. She said the first one that came to mind was Christmas then Easter, Ash Wednesday and Good Friday.

Since she mentioned Christmas first, I began there. And this is the subject I mentioned to you two months ago "When you were a small child you were told a story about a fat man dressed in a red suit that would bring you toys if you were good. Your family celebrated Christmas with a tree and decorations. You were deceived as a child into believing in a Santa Claus and later you found out the truth. Why were you deceived in the first place? Why did you put up a tree in your house each year? If you think about it don't you find it strange to cut a tree down, drag it into your house, stand it up and decorate it with lights, ornaments and tinsel? What about the fat man in the red suit; does it make any sense? What does all this have to do with Christmas?"

The word Christmas means "Mass of Christ" or as it came to be shortened, Christ-Mass. To properly explain all the material concerning Christmas would take many pages of writing but I'm going to try and make this as short as possible. The exact date of Jesus' birth is entirely unknown, as all authorities acknowledge. But the Christmas celebration originated in ancient Egypt in the days of King Osiris and Queen Isis and their son Horus, about 3000 BC. After the untimely death of King Osiris, his wife, Isis, propagated the doctrine of the survival of Osiris as a spirit being. She claimed a full-grown evergreen tree sprang overnight from a dead tree stump, which symbolized the springing forth unto new life of the dead Osiris. On each anniversary of his birth, she claimed, Osiris would visit the evergreen tree and leave gifts upon it. December 25th was the birthday of King Osiris reborn as the son Horus. This is the real origin of the Christmas tree.

Now skipping through a whole lot of history, the early Church of Christ beginning with the Apostles, were a minority in a pagan world. The majority of mankind believed in false gods and practiced pagan traditions handed down over the eons. During the human life of Christ, Rome was the world power and continued to rule until 476 AD, when it fell apart. During this period and for years afterward, the Christians were persecuted severely. But, in 312 AD Emperor Constantine made a big change. After three hundred years of persecution, Constantine said Christians could have religious freedom. Does this sound good? Remember the Christians were the minority. Constantine had been a pagan all his life and suddenly claims to be a Christian. What does he do? Besides formally establishing Christianity as the official religion of the Empire, he makes changes to the original Church of Christ started with the Apostles. He adopts pagan customs into the Church so that the majority will join the Church. The Church becomes a mixture of Christian and pagan beliefs; a False Church.

What sort of changes took place? There are many but to keep this brief, I'll discuss mainly the Christian Holidays that were mentioned. However, let me add something very important. The Bible is the Word of God, who is Truth. We believe the Bible but I tell you people are often misled by false teaching (false prophets). God gave the Ten Commandments to His people. We are His people! Are all the Commandments good? Are there any that we shouldn't keep? Is there even one out of the ten that we can ignore? If your answer is "no", then why do you ignore the fourth Commandment?

Reflections Upon A Sunny Day

The fourth Commandment is a very special Covenant to last forever. If you have any doubt, I can show you the proof in the Old and New Testament. It is the many, not the few that have been deceived:

In 321 AD, Constantine issued an edict forbidding work on "the venerable day of the sun" Sunday. You see, the majority of the pagans worshipped the sun. It was a religious custom of theirs to gather on Sunday and worship towards the east at sunrise. There is a reference in the Bible stating this fact. Now what happened? Sunday became the substitute for the seventh-day Sabbath (sunset Friday to sunset Saturday). Then in 365 AD, the Council of Laodicea formally prohibited the keeping of the "Sabbath" by Christians. The Christians were forced to work on the Sabbath and rest on Sunday. The laws then or present cannot replace God's requirements!

So what about Christmas? Is it Christian? Is it in the Bible? The pagan festival with its riot and merrymaking was so popular that the people didn't want to give it up, so it was adopted into the Church. The date of the festival depended upon the pagan Brumalia (Dec. 25) following the Saturnalia (Dec. 17-24), and celebrating the shortest day of the year and the new sun. The pagans were worshipping the sun and they were reluctant to give up the festival. The Christians (the Pagan Christian church) adopted the festival and encouraged the worship of baby Jesus instead of the sun. Do you think Christmas honors our Lord Jesus?

The pagan custom of kissing under the mistletoe was an early step in the night of revelry and drunken debauchery celebrating the death of the old sun and the birth of the new at the winter solstice. Mistletoe, sacred in pagan festivals, is a parasite. Holly berries were also considered sacred to the sun-god. Round shiny ornaments represented the sun and the yule log is in reality the "sun log". Yule means wheel, a pagan symbol of the sun. Yet today professing Christians speak of the sacred yuletide season!

Who is the Santa Claus of whom we hear so much about that can drive a sleigh pulled by reindeer through the clouds to every place in the country at the same hour? Santa Claus is a corruption of the name St. Nicholas, a Roman Catholic bishop who lived in the fourth century. The original St. Nicholas, of Myra, did not go down people's chimneys or wear a red nose, or drive reindeer, or leave presents in children's stockings, and he had nothing to do with Christmas. But he did on one occasion throw three purses of gold through an open window into the room of a trio of Lycian virgins who were in great distress for a little ready cash.

Moreover, it is said that he did on one occasion raise three little boys to life who had been killed and salted down in a tub for food, in a time of famine, by a wicked innkeeper who, it's said, was a son of Satan - and thereby the Saint became the special friend and patron of young children. Accordingly, he soon came into great repute in the countries of Europe, and had more churches built in his honor than almost any other saint in the calendar.

St. Nicholas of Myra, clearly the prototype of Santa Claus, developed new characteristics by natural evolution in the nursery and in the storybooks. His chief object became to give things to children, and these gifts consisted largely of toys; wooden playthings.

Who is this Santa Claus of whom we hear so much today? He is still a source of materialism to children, but not only to children. Grownups are on his list now. At tens of thousands of department stores all over the Western World he cheerfully touts everything from solid gold wristwatches to full-length fur coats to expensive perfumes for both men and women. And of course you can still get carved wooden toys, but Santa's prices will knock your socks off. The Bavarians who whittle them are peasants no more. They drive Mercedes to work, just like doctors. Some people say, "The true spirit of Christmas is as much in evidence today as it has ever been."

Reflections Upon A Sunny Day

Christmas may seem right to some people, and be justified by human reason, but God says, "There is a way that seemeth right to a man, but the end thereof are the ways of death!" Old Nick, also is a term for the devil. Is there a connection? Satan appears as an "angel of light," to deceive! (II Cor. 11:14 and Rev. 12:9). Do you have any questions?

Now about Easter, it was mentioned to be an important Christian Holiday. Is Easter mentioned in the Bible?

Here we go again...when you were a child you were told that a big bunny rabbit was going to bring you a basket full of dyed eggs on Easter morning. What has a big rabbit with dyed eggs got to do with Easter? What is the meaning of the name Easter? Have you been led to suppose the word means "resurrection of Christ?" Look up the word Easter in your dictionary. You will find it reveals the pagan origin of the name. (Easter - Eastre, dawn goddess.) Easter was originally a pagan festival honoring Eastre, a Teutonic (Germanic) goddess of light and spring. At the time of the vernal equinox (the day in the spring when the sun crosses the equator and day and night are of equal length), sacrifices were offered in her honor. As early as the eighth century, the name was used to designate the annual Christian celebration of the resurrection of Christ.

The only appearance of the word Easter in the Bible is found in the King James Version. The word Easter is a mistranslation of "Pasha", the ordinary Greek word for "Passover" (Acts 12:14).

Easter is but a more modern name of Eastre, Eostre, Ostera, Astarte, or Ishtar. The ancient goddesses of the pagans had many different names.

I asked what a rabbit and dyed eggs had to do with Easter? Since rabbits are so prolific they became a symbol of fertility and the reason eggs have become closely associated with Easter is that they are regarded as a symbol of resurrection, for they hold the seeds of life.

The Encyclopedia Britannica states: "The egg as a symbol of fertility and renewed life goes back to the ancient Egyptians and Persians, who also had the custom of coloring and eating eggs during their spring festival."

Eggs were sacred to many ancient civilizations and formed an integral part of the religious ceremonies in Egypt and in the Orient. In Egyptian temples, walls are painted with an egg - the emblem of generative life, proceeding from the mouth of the sun god of Egypt. The egg was also a sacred symbol among the Babylonians who believed an old fable about an egg of wonderous size, which fell from heaven into the Euphrates River. From this marvelous egg, according to the ancient myth, the goddess Astarte (Easter) was hatched.

Pope Paul V (1605-1621) appointed a prayer Christianizing the egg by suggesting that the chick comes out of the egg, so Christ came out of the tomb. His prayer: "Bless, 0 Lord, we beseech thee, this thy creature of eggs, that it may become wholesome substance unto thy servants of our Lord Jesus Christ."

What is the connection between prolific breeding and fertility, and the celebration of Easter? Well listen to this: The ancient Babylonian and Assyrian goddess Ishtar symbolized Mother Earth in the natural cycles of fertility on earth. Many myths grew up around this Female deity. She was the goddess of Love, so the practice of ritual prostitution became widespread in the fertility cult dedicated to her name. Temples to Ishtar had many priestesses, or sacred prostitutes, who symbolically acted out the fertility rites of the cycle of nature. Ishtar has been identified with the Phoenician Astarte, the Semitic Ashtoreth, and the Sumerian Inanna.

Strong similarities also exist between Ishtar and the Egyptian Isis, the Greek Aphrodite, and the Roman Venus.

What about the Easter Sunrise Service? Look at the similarity of the vision God gave Ezekiel. "Again, He said, You will see them doing things that are even more detestable. Then He brought me to the entrance to the north gate of the house of the Lord, and I saw women sitting there, weeping for Tammuz. He said to me, Do you see this, son of man? You will see things that are even more detestable than this. He then brought me into the inner court of the house of the Lord, and there at the entrance to the temple, between the portico and the altar, were about twenty-five men. With their backs toward the temple of the Lord and their faces toward the east, they were bowing down to the sun in the east." See Ezekiel 8:14-18. Remember what I said about the pagans facing the east on Sunday and worshipping the sun as it would rise in the morning.

Do you see how Easter came into the Church? Can you Christianize a pagan custom? After Constantine took virtual control of the professing church in the fourth century, the visible organization became almost wholly pagan and began excommunicating and persecuting all who held to the true Word of God.

Constantine summoned a council at Nicaea in 325 AD. The decision of the council was unanimous that Easter was to be kept on Sunday, and on the same Sunday throughout the world, and that "none hereafter should follow the blindness of the Jews."

As the false, paganized church grew in size and political power, decrees were passed in the fourth century A.D. imposing the death sentence upon Christians found keeping God's Sabbath or festivals. Finally, in order to keep the true way of God, many (true Christians) fled for their lives. (Little Flock - LK 12:32 and Rev. 12:17).

Will you teach the Christmas and Easter celebration to your children? Do you know what a true Christian should teach their children? Do you know the true Christian Holy Days?

Ash Wednesday was also mentioned. Is Ash Wednesday in the Bible? Did the Apostles observe this practice? My dictionary says, Ash Wednesday, the first day of Lent and seventh Wednesday before Easter: so called from the practice of putting ashes on the forehead as a sign of penitence.

Since Ash Wednesday is the first day of Lent, I ask is Lent in the Bible? Did the Apostles of the early Church observe Lent?

Associated with Ishtar was the young god Tammuz, considered both divine and mortal (Ezekiel 8:14). In Babylonian mythology Tammuz died annually and was reborn year after year, representing the yearly cycle of the seasons and the crops. This pagan belief was later identified with the pagan gods Baal and Anat in Canaan. (Anat is sometimes identified with the "queen of heaven", to whom the Jews offered incense in Jeremiah's day (Jer. 7:18; hh:17-19, 25). But some scholars identify the "queen of heaven" with the Assyrian-Babylonian goddess Ishtar.) (Anat was the patroness of sex and passion; lewd figurines of this nude goddess have been discovered at various archaeological sites in Israel.)

According to the old legends, after Tammuz was slain, he descended into the underworld. Legend has it that Tammuz was killed by a wild boar when he was forty years old. But through the weeping of his mother, Semiramis or Ishtar, he was mystically revived in spring. The resurrection of Tammuz through Ishtar's grief was dramatically represented annually in order to insure the success of the crops and the fertility of the people. Hislop, points out that forty days, a day for each year Tammuz had lived on earth, were set aside to "weep for Tammuz." Each year these forty days were observed with weeping, fasting, and self chastisement to grieve with Ishtar over the death of Tammuz and celebrate the god's return in order to win anew her favor and her benefits. When the vegetation began to come forth, those ancient people believed their "savior" had come from the underworld, had ended winter, and caused spring to begin. This observance was not only known at Babylon, but also among the Phoenicians, and Egyptians. Even the Israelites adopted the doctrines and rites of the annual pagan spring festival for Ezekiel spoke of it.

Among the pagans, this "Lent" seems to have been an indispensable preliminary to the great annual festival in commemoration of the death and resurrection of Tammuz.

Because Christ's resurrection was in the spring of the year, it was not too difficult for the church of the fourth century (having departed from the original faith in a number of ways) to merge the pagan spring festival into Christianity.

The Encyclopedia Britannica says, "Christianity...incorporated in its celebration of the great Christian feast day "many" of the heathen rites and customs of the spring festival."

The Catholic Encyclopedia very honestly points out that: "Writers in the fourth century were prone to describe many practices (the Lenten fast of forty days) as of Apostolic institution, which certainly had no claim to be so regarded."

It was not until the sixth century that the Pope officially ordered the observance of Lent, calling it a "sacred fast" during which people were to abstain from meat and a few other foods.

The last Holy Day (Holiday) mentioned was, "Good Friday." Is Good Friday mentioned in the Bible? Did the Apostles observe it? Since the

Apostles were the first members of the Christian Church, shouldn't our Holy Days today be the same as theirs from the beginning of the Church?

My dictionary says, "Good Friday, the Friday before Easter Sunday, observed in commemoration of the crucifixion of Jesus."

Was Jesus crucified on Friday? Jesus said, "For as Jonah was three days and three nights in the belly of a huge fish, so the Son of Man will be three days and three nights in the heart of the earth" (Matt. 12:40).

What I am about to say is food for thought because we have faith in Jesus and know He died on the cross for our sins and did rise from the dead three days later to His beloved Apostles and friends.

Many theologians and scholars wonder about when Jesus did die on the cross. If it were on Friday, would He have been in the heart of the earth only one day and two nights? And just a reminder, the Jews day ended and began at sundown as ours today ends and begins at midnight.

Taking all of this into account, allowing for three days and nights, the death of Christ well may have been on Wednesday. But the question quickly brought up here is what about the Sabbath? Jesus was hurriedly buried before the Sabbath.

Placing the crucifixion on Wednesday, Thursday of that year may have been an annual Sabbath, the first annual Sabbath in the Days of unleavened bread?

So that we would know that the Sabbath that followed the crucifixion was not necessarily the weekly Sabbath, John the Apostle was insured to call it a "high day" or "Special Sabbath" (John 19:31), which according to Jewish usage, means an annual Sabbath that may occur any day during the week, not just on the weekly Sabbath.

Mark picks up John's account by adding that after that Sabbath, the women bought sweet spices to use in anointing the body of Jesus (MK 16:1). The purchasing of the spices could not have been on Thursday if it were the annual Sabbath. They would have made their purchase on Friday. Having made their purchase, the women prepared these ointments and "rested on the Sabbath according to the Commandment" (Luke 23:56).

Another point I'd like to make, Did Jesus rise from the dead at sunrise? "Early on the first day of the week, while it was "still dark", "Mary Magdalene went to the tomb and saw that the stone had been removed from the entrance" (John 20:1). Jesus rose from the dead and left the tomb before sunrise!

Having read this information, do you believe that Good Friday, Ash Wednesday, Lent, Easter, and Christmas are Holy Days? Do you feel that one Holiday is just as important as the next?

If Jesus had wanted us to celebrate His birthday it would have been done so by the Apostles in the early Church. There is no record of this practice in the Bible except for the celebration of Herod's birthday and he wasn't a Christian. He had John the Baptist's head cut off.

As I said before, "Can you Christianize a pagan custom? Can you take something unholy, revolting to God, and add it to something man makes up and call it "Holy"?

God has warned us in both Covenant's to stay away from pagan customs. By studying your Bible you will reach a deeper understanding of these things. These are a few Scriptures from the Bible:

"And after the nations have been destroyed before you, be careful not to be ensnared by inquiring about their gods, saying, 'How do these nations serve their gods?' We will do the same. You must not worship the Lord your God in their way, because in worshiping their gods they do all kinds of detestable things the Lord hates." (Deuteronomy 12:30)

"This is what the Lord says: 'Do not learn the ways of the nations or be terrified by signs in the sky, though the nations are terrified by them. For the customs of the peoples are worthless; they cut a tree out of the forest and a craftsman shapes it with his chisel. They adorn it with silver and gold; they fasten it with hammer and nails so it will not totter." (Jeremiah 10:2-4)

"Formerly, when you did not know God, you were slaves to those who by nature are not gods. But now that you know God, or rather are known by God, how is it that you are turning back to those weak and miserable principles? Do you wish to be enslaved by them all over again? You are observing special days and months and seasons and years! I fear for you, that somehow I have wasted my efforts on you." (Galatians 419-11)

"For certain men whose condemnation was written about long ago have secretly slipped in among you. They are godless men, who change the grace of our God into a license for immorality and deny Jesus Christ our only Sovereign and Lord." (Jude 1:4)

"The Spirit clearly says that in later times some will abandon the faith and follow deceiving spirits and things taught by demons. Such teachings come through hypocritical liars, whose consciences have been seared as with a hot iron. They forbid people to marry and order them to abstain from certain foods, which God created to be received with thanksgiving by those who believe and who know the truth." (I Timothy 4:1-3)

Can you take something unholy and add it to something holy and make it pleasing to God? I told you about the origin of Easter. Is the death and resurrection of Christ important? It is most important! Are we to celebrate this important event? How? The Bible tells us how!

The Council at Nicaea in 325 AD made Easter observance the law. God's requirements were made unlawful by man's political power. The observance of the Sabbath, the Passover, and God's festivals were punishable by the death sentence.

If you will look at Luke 22:7-32, it will tell you how and when to celebrate Jesus' death and resurrection. We are to observe the Passover. Jesus became the sacrificial "Lamb"!

The twenty-second chapter of the Gospel of Luke begins with Judas' agreement to betray Jesus. The seventh verse begins the details of "The Last Supper." This "Last Supper" was the celebration of the "Passover." What is the Passover? For the instructions of the Passover see: Exodus 12:1-17; Leviticus 23:4-8; or Deuteronomy 16:1-8. The Exodus as a result of the "Passover" was a supreme occasion when God acted to deliver His people from harsh captivity, binding them to Himself by a solemn Covenant. And to insure the future generations did not forget this event, the Passover meal was made an annual celebration. It is a festival to the Lord - a lasting ordinance.

Following the Exodus, the Law was given, an integral part of the divine plan to bring human beings back to God. The Law showed Israel (and the whole world) that, because of the broken relationship between God and man, it was impossible for people to please God or to meet His requirements. However, the Old Testament provided many references to a special individual who would provide salvation for His people.

If you have read the twelfth chapter of Exodus, you have seen that the sacrifice (the blood of the lamb) protected the people from death. Just so, God gave His begotten son, Jesus, the perfect sacrifice to deliver us from a harsh captivity, binding us to Himself by a solemn New Covenant. Jesus paid the penalty for our sin, He also removed all guilt produced by that sin. Further, He lives today and speaks continually to God on our behalf. "Jesus lives forever and continues to be a Priest, so that no one else is needed. He is able to save completely all who come to God through Him" (Hebrews 7:24-25).

When the time came, Jesus sent Peter and John, saying, "Go and make preparations for us to eat the Passover." When is the Passover? You may have noticed that in the first few Books of the Bible that days and months went by number rather than by name. Later on, God's people copied the names of months from their neighbors or captors. The Bible tells us: "These are the Lord's appointed feasts, the sacred assemblies you are to proclaim at their appointed times. The Lord's Passover begins at twilight on the fourteenth day of the first month" (Leviticus 23:4-5). In the Book of Deuteronomy the first month is identified as Abib. In my Bible Dictionary it says: "Abib - the first month of the Hebrew calendar (corresponding to our March-April). The Passover and the Feast of Unleavened Bread were celebrated during the month of Abib. After the Babylonian Captivity, the month was called "Nisan" (Neh. 2:1; Esth. 3:7). This year, the 14th of Nisan (the Passover) fell on Wednesday the 19th of April.

"When the 'hour came' Jesus and His Apostles reclined at the table. And He said to them, I have eagerly desired to eat this Passover with you before I suffer. For I tell you, I will not eat it again until it finds fulfillment in the Kingdom of God" (Luke 22:14-16). What did He mean by, "until it finds fulfillment in the Kingdom of God?" Turn to Zechariah 3. What does the name Joshua mean? What does Jesus' name mean? Both Joshua'a and Jesus' name mean the same thing; "The Lord is Salvation.

Successor to Moses

The relationship: As Joshua led the people to renew their covenant with God. Jesus completed the work the great leader began by restoring the relationship between God and man; a New Covenant sealed in "the blood of the Lamb - Jesus."

When Zechariah had this vision, Joshua had died hundreds of years earlier and Jesus was to come hundreds of years later. In verse two, The Lord reprimanded Satan and decreed mercy to Joshua. He was faithful and suffered to save his people from destruction. In the following verse the filthy clothes represent the sins of man. In verse five the turban is the headdress for a High Priest. In verse 7, what is meant by "you will govern my house?" See Revelation 4:4 - "Surrounding the throne were twenty four other thrones, and seated on them were twenty four elders. They were dressed in white and had crowns of gold on their heads." In the following verses, the Branch represents a future king in the line of David (Branch-Messiah). The stone represents Jesus. The "seven eyes" means the seven fold Spirit of God and "engrave an inscription on it" means, He will have the Word of God written in His heart. For the last verse concerning the "vine and fig tree," read John 15 and Revelation 5.

"And Jesus took bread, gave thanks and broke it, and gave it to them saying, This is my body given for you; do this in remembrance of me."

(Luke 22:19) Jesus made a change to the Passover feast. His body, not an animal; lamb, was being given for us. "In the same way, after the supper He took the cup, saying, This cup is the "New Covenant" in my blood, which is poured out for you." (Luke 22:20) I ask, does man have the authority to change our Lord's requirements?

Even though it is no longer illegal to celebrate the Passover when and how it should be observed, most professing Christians share communion at Easter. Why? Because it has been a custom or tradition handed down through the centuries from generation to generation; from parents to their children. Most people don't now the origin of Easter and most become hostile when you suggest a change in the practice of their religion. They become angry and defensive even though they don't thoroughly understand the significance of the Bible.

All of what I have been talking about concerns being deceived and who is responsible? Who is the master of lies and deceit? Satan is constantly at work trying to pull people away from God.

There is a lot more I can add to explain the Truth but as I said in the beginning of this letter, I wanted to make it as short as possible yet understandable. Even so, you must have a few questions?

Take care my son. Keep me in your prayers and remember to study your Bible. May our Lord's Peace be with you and may His Spirit fill you with understanding so that you may be able to teach your family the Truth.

> Love Always,
> Dad
> Fred H. Kornahrens

Reflections Upon A Sunny Day

Many people who visit death row are alarmed by the Gestapo type treatment here. It has been getting progressively worse. I was told that Zeb Osborne [Volunteer Chaplain] and Bob McAlister [Deputy Chief of Staff for the Governor] went to see the Commissioner Thursday, April 20, 1989. I don't know if they had any success, for several attorneys have spoken with the Commissioner and their appeals were denied.

The prison staff has been so offensive that I am convinced that they are trying to provoke a confrontation. They want an excuse for their harsh treatment, and they would like nothing better than something violent to happen so it could be spread all over the news. Some of the men here use little good judgment and talk about taking the cellblock over. We who have better judgment told them they are fools to do such a thing. That would be playing right into their hands.

We have been having numerous shakedown inspections. When this takes place the cells are torn apart as they search for contraband. Depending on how much stuff you have and how bad they mess up your cell, the cleanup and rearranging can be frustrating.

Things here at CCI are becoming increasingly difficult. The theory is: They are breaking us in for the new death row. We used to be treated with a little decency. We could go to the showers or use the phone without being chained and handcuffed, but no longer.

We are cuffed and chained before our cell doors are opened. We are locked in the shower stalls and phone cages. Both are like small animal cages. Changes are taking place daily. We can no longer use the phones in the building during our exercise period. To use the outside phone, the officer dials the number and passes the receiver with ten inches of cord to you through a hole in the steel wire. We can no longer call our children at night, who are in school during the day.

I received a memo stating that our attorneys must get permission to speak with us. The memo stated: "After hours telephone calls are for the express purpose of contacting attorneys. These after hours calls will be authorized only upon written request to Warden McKellar or Deputy Warden Rodgers from your attorney."

We used to be allowed out of our cell for a short period of time to exercise on weekdays. Now, they take all privileges on state holidays; moreover, additional days when prison staff declares them. We spent a week in our cells during Christmas without phone calls, showers, exercise, or visits.

Mr. Bruce Pierceson, the chairman for the Coalition Against the Death Penalty, visited death row each Thursday. They stopped him from this routine and required him to be separated from us by a steel wire fence. They, also, restricted the visits from the Broad Acres Baptist Church volunteers.

There are six fences and gun towers separating our exercise area from the outside. Never before have they posted armed guards with shotguns around our fence, but they do now.

Never before did we have to walk in cuffs and chains in front of our family and loved ones in the visiting room. They used to take them off in the adjacent room, but no longer. We even take a different route, and we must be locked in with our family and friends before the chains are removed.

The attitude of the prison staff has changed and many of the routine things that worked smoothly were changed too. Some of the attorneys, who are representing inmates, have written to Commissioner Evatt and plan to have a meeting with him.

Reflections Upon A Sunny Day

This is a typical example of the visiting procedure in CB-2: At approximately 1:30 P.M., April 14, 1989, Officer Shokes told me I had a visit. I got dressed and Shokes locked me in chains. Then we got to the cage [control room], Shokes asked who was going to take me up to the visiting room. The officer in the cage acted dumb like he didn't know what was going on. Then Officer Peterson spoke up and said he heard my name called for a visit. The officer in the cage is the one who takes the calls from up front, and he acts moronic as he often does. Peterson told him to call up front to check and see if I had a visit. Kiesler made a quick call and said nope no visit. The officers looked at each other and shrugged their shoulders. Shokes locked me back in my cell and took the chains off. I got undressed, folded my clothes, and put them away. I laid down and returned to reading a book, but a few minutes later Peterson came to my cell and said I had a visit. He walked away and I got dressed again. I had to yell for Shokes to unlock my cell. He chained me up again and let me out the cell. Then they had to find a couple of officers to walk me over the roof to the shakedown room. There I had to wait for the shakedown room to be cleared out. After a long wait at the shakedown room I finally arrived at the visiting room where my mother and son were waiting.

It is a shame that the prison staff is so cold hearted as to force us to wear chains and handcuffs in front of our family. A few weeks ago, a woman broke down and cried when she saw her son all chained up and surrounded by officers. The crimes of death row prisoners are not any different than those committed by over five hundred other prisoners at CCI, and they don't wear chains nor are they executed.

Many of our family members live in excess of a hundred miles from the prison and a lot of things can happen. Should a visitor be late or not arrive, the prisoner is not allowed to make a telephone call. The prisoner is forced to wait in his cell and wonder if his family had car trouble or worse yet a wreck, for the phone will not be available until the next recreation period.

It is not unusual for the temperature in the cells to be over 100° in the summer. So, when a prisoner anticipates a visit, he cannot remain fully dressed for long or he will become soaked in sweat.

Things are bad here and you can't imagine what it is like to spend every day and night in this terrible place, but I'll tell you something that comes from my heart. As bad as it is here in these horrid conditions, I was hurting worse in those years when my marriage was falling apart; with all the lies; with all the torment; the verbal abuse; the mind games; the threats; and the harassment. I could go on and on but that pain and suffering was so bad that it destroyed me. The wounds to my heart were not allowed to heal and year after year the stress and pressure increased until I broke. I did something that is wrong and totally against my nature. I had to do a lot of soul searching about what I had done. And, besides my children, no one has grieved more about their death than me. In this prison where men lose their humanity, I received Jesus.

It was April 28, 1989, and as I was getting dressed for the exercise period, a guard told me to get ready to go to Court, They waited until the last moment to tell me, and didn't even give me time for a shower. The CCI guards were scared. They chained me up with belly chains and leg irons to walk to the front building. After a wait and a changing of leg irons they were ready to transport me to the Courthouse.

There were five officers involved in the move. I've never had any personal dealings with the [white-shirt] supervisor who was in charge of the four [brown-shirt] officers, but I knew he had a bad attitude. He was nervous about the move. He and another officer went and got pistols. Then they escorted me to a prison van. Two officers drove the van and the rest followed in a personal car. Exhaust fumes were coming into the rear of the van and it made me feel sort of sick.

The Courthouse was less than two miles away. I believe the jail is connected to this building. Anyway, I was put in a holding cell and there I waited. They wouldn't take the chains off. I had left my cell at CCI around 8:00 A.M., and it was not a pleasant wait in that small empty cement cell.

I suppose it was near ten o'clock when they came to take me upstairs to the courtroom. The white-shirt was full of contempt and I ignored him. He was looking for trouble, and I behaved as though he wasn't even there. He did not realize it but I could have taken over an officer and his gun but it would have been a bloodbath. I try to avoid violence, and I am against killing.

When I arrived at the courtroom, I saw Joyce and all her family sitting there all puffed up on hate. They have heard me share my sorrow and compassion for the lives that were taken but there has been no forgiveness. Forgiveness is one of the greatest virtues of the Christian life. It clears the conscience, warms the heart, and heals the soul. It bridges the gap of reconciliation and scales the walls of bitterness and indifference. Perhaps more than any other factor, forgiveness is the key to Christian love and unity. Forgiveness is not an option. It is a command. Forgiveness is not something to consider when all else has failed. It is the first step in the reconciliation of Christian brothers and sisters who have offended each other. In fact, it is one of the evidences of the genuineness of our salvation. Saved people should be forgiving people. How can we not forgive, when we have been forgiven so much by God? Those who have received forgiveness need to learn how to give it.

I saw this family burning with vengeance and I can only feel compassion towards them. I know they were allowing themselves to be blinded with hate, and I know what hate can do to the heart. It eats away the heart and consumes the soul. Hate is evil.

As I approached the defense table, I noticed Carol Murdaugh [brother-in-law] sitting at the end of the bench with the rest of the family. He nodded his head and I returned a nod. The last time I spoke with him was on June 17, 1988, when I had my first visit with Joey. I saw him again on March 2, 1989, when he, Solicitor Anders, and what consisted of a tour group came in CB-2 to gawk at death row prisoners. I didn't notice who was with Carol. Other family members may have been with him, I don't know. Anyway, they were taken on E tier. I am on C tier so he didn't come to my cell.

I sat at the defense table and one of the officers removed the cuffs. Mr. McClain arrived and a few moments later Judge Mobley entered the courtroom. He is the judge that presided over my PCR hearing in Charleston. — I was told by the best appellant attorney in South Carolina, David Bruck, that Mobley has a history of not overturning cases when they should be.

The hearing began and Mr. McClain presented his argument; that my trial attorney, Bill Runyon, has been proven to be a liar in other hearings, and he lied in my PCR hearing. The judge appeared not to care and the state prosecutor denied everything Mr. McClain had to say. The hearing was over in about thirty minutes.

Mr. McClain asked that he be allowed some time with me. I was escorted downstairs to a holding cell. I waited there until Mr. McClain came down. When he did, we talked to each other in one of those prisoner-visiting booths.

Mr. McClain had heard about the increasing problems in C3-2. I told him about some of the things that have been happening; about the weapon that was found and how we are now denied chapel service. I told him about our being denied phone calls and visits on weekends, and about the hostility of the prison staff and that even visitors who have been coming to CCI for years are being harassed. Visitors have even referred to the officers as behaving like Nazi Gestapo. Mr. McClain told me that his father had some influence on Parker Evatt becoming Commissioner. He said that he would have his father speak with the Commissioner concerning these matters.

After our conversation, Mr. McClain left and I was escorted around to a room next to where the prison van was waiting. I sat in a chair and waited. The white-shirt changed his approach and acted like he wanted to be friendly. I recognized that he was only testing me. I answered his question but didn't pursue a conversation. I wasn't hostile but with all that I have been through I am able to discern when someone is not being sincere, honest, or truthful.

The short trip back to CCI was uneventful. I had to wait until twelve o'clock before someone escorted me back to CB-2.

Colonel Oliver North was recently big news. He was dishonest, but he was not totally in charge of all that mess. North was the fall guy for those who were. Our government did not want the embarrassment of having another President facing impeachment.

The politicians in the field of government are said to be in public service. They profess to be "public servants." They are installed in offices of authority and power. They execute the laws that regulate and govern the people. Theirs is the power to regulate society, guide it and make it what it is. They are the leaders of the people.

Today, too many of those who seek offices of power over people of cities, states, districts, or nations, promise great benefits, pose as public benefactors, while their inner motives are ambitions for personal power and wealth. Selfish, greedy individuals of excessive vanity, ambitions in their lust for rule, scheme to get their hands on the throttle of power for personal fame and monetary gain. Secret deals, graft, immorality, deception, and dishonesty run rampant in high places.

Politicians use dishonesty, lies, and treachery to put themselves forward in the most favorable light; defaming, denouncing, and discrediting their opponents to get a position in office.

Governments promise peace, but too often bring wars. They promise benefits for the people, and then extract from the people the cost of the benefits plus costs of government. We fail to find in human government knowledge of life's purpose, or dissemination of the true values.

As for humans being qualified to rule and administer government, God says of government officials today, "None calleth for justice, nor any pleadeth for truth, they trust in vanity and speak lies, they conceive mischief and bring forth iniquity. Their feet run to evil and they make haste to shed innocent blood, their thoughts are thoughts of iniquity, wasting and destruction are in their paths. The way of peace they know not and their is no judgment in their goings; they have made them crooked paths: whosoever goeth therein shall not know peace."

The highways of history are strewn with the wreckage of nations that forgot God.

When I returned from my escape last year, one of the guards said, "You should have snatched you some pussy before coming back here." He rubbed it in like I was stupid for not raping a woman while I was out on the loose. I say, "Who should be behind bars, me or him? Most of the men here said I should have shot the deputies, robbed people, broke into houses, taken hostages, and killed anyone who stood in my way of freedom. I wanted freedom, but I had no violence in my heart. I don't think the way criminals do. Even here in prison they think of the evil crimes they could do if they had the chance. I had two loaded pistols during my escape, but I didn't want to harm anyone.

A prisoner [Riddle] was beaten and gassed by the guards on Monday, June 5, 1989, while the rest of us were outside on the exercise yard. The man was in the building and his arms were handcuffed behind his back while the beating took place, and he was gassed inside his cell while still handcuffed. I noticed the gas when I entered the building. The guards beat the man because he wanted to speak with the Deputy Warden about their abuse.

On June 14, 1989, Rusty Woomer was escorted out of CB-2 by a mob of officers and taken to the execution facility.

On June 15, 1989, Attorney David Bruck and Prosecutor Jim Anders were on the "Today" television program. The host, Joe Pinner and Ms. Blackwell, were asking the questions. They didn't know of Woomer's stay of execution until David told them. Ms. Blackwell was so disappointed that she almost fell out of her chair. She was outraged.

Jim Anders told two outright lies concerning death penalty trials, and each of them had bearing on my trial. David's manner and speech was excellent. Anders was vicious and it seems he never misses an opportunity to get in a few crack remarks on Pee Wee Gaskins.

Here in Columbia, prison news is paramount on all the six o'clock TV News channels. There are quite a few prisons in this area, and for many who live in Columbia it's their bread and butter. The news concerning Woomer's execution was on media day and night over and over again. It was like the media was trying to work the public into a frenzy, and they were succeeding. And after Woomer received a stay, the media stirred up the public even more.

What Woomer did ten years ago was terrible. The families involved have not been able to heal because there is something about the death penalty that won't let them. The courts and prosecutors keep the family of victims boiling in hate and revenge; that justice will not be done until the execution has been carried out. Whereas the men who receive life sentences for the same crimes are not heard from or about. They serve time in prison and the victim's families seem to fair better.

The mail that was collected from the cells Monday morning, July 3, 1989, was found in the garbage can. The guard who collected the mail threw it in the trash. I wonder how often this happens and what about the incoming mail?

The demons of Satan are attempting to destroy our prison ministry. The harsh treatment continues from the prison staff. Volunteers from the Broad Acres Baptist Church are treated badly, rushed, and run out the building. The only thing that is missing is the whips and cattle prods.

Zeb Osborne complained to the warden about how our Chapel Service is delayed, interrupted, and cut short. The attitude of D/W Rogers and the officers in C3-2 became worse, and they sought revenge for the complaint. Last week the officers kept the men in their cells and caused them to be an hour late for chapel. The long delay left only minutes to hold a service. The Prison Chaplain does not visit death row. Zeb's ministry is needed in CB-2 and the prison staff is trying to run him off.

There are some crazy vicious men here and some of them wear uniforms. I've seen some men here whom I believe are possessed by evil demons. They go into fits and they don't behave human. I've seen men cut themselves open with razor blades and throw cups full of blood. I saw a man bite a mouth full of flesh out of his shoulder and bite other people like a dog. They growl like lions, bark like dogs, and curse God in a possessed chant. Their ambition is to plot evil; to take your money and your body. They are wicked and lust to sodomize. They will deceive you with charm, sweet words, like honey dripping off their lips, or they will rape you with the help of their perverted friends.

During the shower period some of the guards took an extreme interest in the naked bodies of prisoners. One guard used an extension ladder to sneak up to the second tier to watch men masturbate. And one of the supervisors had a prolonged homosexual relationship with the prisoner who was in the cell next to me.

Two of the guards, who were notorious for beating handcuffed prisoners with riot batons, were arrested for robbing banks. One guard was arrested for child molesting. And another guard shot two women, his wife and their neighbor, to death. — These guards worked in CB-2, and I'm sure there are things I don't know about.

Paul Harvey once said, "If you want to see the low-life of your Community, go sit outside a prison during shift change," ...and that's the rest of the story.

The heat and air system must have been designed by the Attorney General's Office. If it's not shifting back and forth from blowing dusty hot and cold air, it's inoperative all together. - It's perfectly designed for torture.

There's not one window in this building that will open, and they won't allow us to have a fan. And, the dust I mentioned is either coming from deteriorated air filters or the state is using us for an experiment with particle pollution. - I can wipe my little steel table off and within 24 hours I can work math problems in the dust. It keeps my sinuses on red alert.

On January 4, 1994, during the recreation period, everyone was ordered back to their cells. They told us that the maintenance crew was coming in the building. After everyone was locked up they brought in two drug-sniffing dogs. One was a German Shorthair Bird Dog. The other was a half-breed German Shepherd. They were using the Shepherd on my side of the building. The dog appeared to be scared and nervous. He went in and out of cells that were loaded with drugs and didn't do a thing. When the dog entered my cell, it sat down right beside my trashcan where I had some cookies and fruitcake. That was the signal that I had drugs in may cell, so I had to stand outside my cell with a few other men until the search was over.

Everybody, including the drug dealers, thought it was ridiculous that the dog had alerted in my cell. (I don't even allow a lit cigarette in my cell.) While I waited, I thought about that crazy dog and hoped that the guards weren't going to tear my cell apart. Either that dog had sniffed so much drugs that it was stoned, or it had something against clean cells. - The guard looked under my trashcan. Since nothing was there, he was satisfied. The dog looked hungry and may have alerted on the smell of cake and cookies.

On January 11, 1994, my dear friend, Jennifer Long, visited me. She visited me three times in January and it was so good to see her again. Jennifer had spent six months in Mexico City as a missionary with Latin American Missions.

On February 2, 1994, my friend, George Neese, a Christian volunteer, brought me a CBC Bible course, i.e., The New Testament Survey (Acts through Revelation). It was a tremendous amount of work, but I enjoyed the study.

On February 4, 1994, I called home and found out that my mother was sick. She was having difficulty breathing. The doctor told her that she had emphysema. She sounded terrible on the telephone and my heart just ached for her. My heart was terribly burdened over her suffering and I prayed for her. My prayers helped. My heart was lightened and mother got better.

Jennifer Long visited me twice in February and four times in March. I really appreciated the time she spent with me.

On March 3, 1994, everyone was required to take their medicine in liquid form because one man overdosed on pills.

On March 8, 1994, 1 called my aunt Virginia because I couldn't get in touch with my mother. She told me my mother was in Roper Hospital; that she had been on the floor and couldn't get up. EMS took her to the hospital. My aunt told me they were treating my mother for emphysema and giving her insulin for diabetes.

On April 6, 1994, I received a letter from my attorney, Ray P. McClain, and a copy of the Magistrate Judge's Report.

Well, his report didn't sound like a report from a fair and impartial judge. It sounded like a Prosecutor's Report. His facts were not accurate and his arguments were heavily slanted with a prosecuting mentality. Beside rejecting all my grounds for relief, his report has numerous remarks regarding Trial Counsel's ineffectiveness, e.g., he failed to raise it [issue] in his appeal, did not object; did not cross-examine the witness about that particular subject; bypassed state remedies; could have been raised at time of first appeal, so the specific claim is barred, etc.

At the PCR hearing [appeal] in 1988, there was overwhelming evidence of ineffective trial council, but Judge Mobley refused to grant relief. It was obvious that the judge had political ambitions.

My trial attorney William L. Runyon, failed to do many things in representing me. Among other things, he didn't have any witnesses appear in court! Besides his legal fee, he stole a large sum of money from me. He lied to me from the beginning about everything concerning my children and my case. He was well funded, but instead of admitting me into a reputable private institution for evaluation, he turned me over to state interrogators at the State Hospital. He failed to have my psychologist appear in court. There's a lot more. He even passed up an opportunity to avoid a death penalty trial.

Mr. Runyon denied all the evidence presented against his representation and turned to prosecuting me with lies rather than to admit to anything. Mr. McClain presented evidence, records and transcripts, to prove Runyon was lying. – Judge Mobley and transcripts, to prove Runyon was lying. Judge Mobley asserted that my trial counsel, William L. Runyon, rendered me effective counsel in spite of all the proof showing otherwise.

Judge McCrory's report contained information about trial counsel [Runyon] trial errors and bypassing state remedies that should have been raised at the first appeal. Now, these claims are barred at the federal level.

Mr. McClain was preparing exceptions to Judge McCrory's Report. He said there is a chance that there is still some vitality in the argument that the instruction on "reasonable doubt" given in your case was a constitutional error. The Death Penalty Resource Center is very hopeful that claims of error in these instructions will have to be heard on their merits, based on a recent Supreme Court case, which said an error in the definition of "reasonable doubt" could never be a "harmless error."

The high court's stringent standard of judging ineffectiveness of counsel now puts the burden of proof on a defendant's appellate attorney to demonstrate that defense counsel blunders directly affected the jury's verdict, and that minus those blunders directly affected the jury's verdict, and that minus those blunders the jury would have returned a different verdict. - But how are you going to demonstrate that, of all the variables in a case, a mistake of the defense counsel caused the jury to render a certain verdict? The Court just comes back and says that the attorney's mistakes were "harmless error" and the jury would have returned a guilty verdict anyway. Every person is supposed to have a constitutional right to effective assistance of counsel, but the courts, by imposing such impossible procedural structures, have reamed out that right to an empty shell.

It is said that this nation is a country of laws - not men - but men make laws. They are the result of human effort subject to human error. There was a time in this nation when men and women were sold into slavery. Legally! When little children labored in factories and mines, legally; and think how many legal wrongs exist today. Laws made by humans are chaff in the wind. Doomed to perish unless they are created with total faith in God. Only God's laws are infallible and forever. And, HislawisLOVE!

The attorneys from Washington, D.C., sent me a copy of the brief they filed to the U.S. Court of Appeals for the Fourth Circuit. The brief was well written; presenting facts that my trial lawyer did not represent me properly, new evidence, etc. However, the truth and facts aren't very relevant to the Courts these days. The get tough on crime policy doesn't separate the unrepentant from the repentant. Worthy evidence that used to overturn a death penalty case is often ignored now. Most judges do what is popular because they find it comfortable and advantageous to their political career.

Prisoners in SC can no longer receive radios, TV's, tennis shoes, and certain clothing items from friends, family, or charitable organizations. These items are now sold by the SCDC Canteen for a considerable profit. (A K-TV can be purchased on the outside for less than $150.00; whereas, the SCDC Canteen sells them to prisoners for $208.00).

Sometime in June or July of 1994, I requested to see Dr. Bradley. I was having serious problems with my ears, face, and scalp. He took a look in my ear canal, but his examination of my skin was less than satisfactory. Dr. Bradley said that I had a lot of hair in my ear canal; that I had a fungus on my face; that I had a barber rash. When I expressed my feeling that it was something other than a barber rash he seemed a little offended.

When I submit a medical request form, it should be returned to me with a reply. All too often this doesn't happen.

On August 17, 1994, I forwarded a request to see Dr. Bradley. I wrote, "Still having problems with ear infection, itching rash on chin [scalp]." Dr. Bradley wrote, "Change in Meds ordered." – His medicine wasn't working.

On September 22, 1994, I forwarded a request to see Dr. Bradley. I wrote, "My ears are swollen in places and raw. My ear is swollen and blood red." Nurse Robertson replied on the form, "You have an appt. with an ENT specialist this week." – I was allergic to the medicine.

On September 23, 1994, I saw an ENT Doctor. I received a prescription of Tolnaftate / Nystatin 1:1 on September 26, 1994.

On October 5, 1994, I forwarded a request to Dr. Bradley for a medication refill. Nurse Robertson wrote, "Mycalog ointment has been ordered for your ear canal." – I'd never had so many problems with my eyes, ears and skin. The water has a strong chemical smell and there are no windows in the building that will open for fresh air.

Reflections Upon A Sunny Day

On October 10, 1994, I forwarded a request to Dr. Bradley for a prescription of Benadryl so that I may get some relief and rest from the itching. My ear itch had increased; face and scalp itched terribly. Nurse Robertson wrote, "Benadryl has been prescribed."

On January 11, 1995, the local telephones were taken out. To call anyone local or long distance the call must be placed collect. We are permitted only twenty phone numbers, which must be approved and stored in their computer phone system. If a friend or relative sends you a letter and asks you to phone them, you cannot call them unless their number is approved and in the computer phone system. The SCUC staff say they did it to prevent inmates from committing telephone fraud. There's been no telephone fraud here on death row. The real reason for the change is about money. SCUC is going to get a tremendous kickback from Tele-Communications.

On January 13, 1995, there was a storm and the electricity went off at about 10:30 P.M. and didn't come back until about 1:00 A.M.

In the darkness, men can shine flashlights on a sundial and make it tell any time they want. But, only the sun tells the true time. The flashlights are the changing and fleeting options of men. The sun is the eternal Word of God. Only God makes truth. Men either discover it or fail to discover it. They either interpret it rightly or interpret it wrongly. But they have no power to make truth or change it. For truth is no man's servant. Ultimately, the truth must become each person's friend or his enemy, his master or his judge.

On January 14, 1995, death row was taken in groups of ten or so to the classification office. They took computer photos of us for their record and the I.D. cards we're now required to wear on our chest.

I called home Friday January 20, 1995. My mother told me that my daughter, Lisa, visited her. My mother, nor I have seen her in ten years.

Lisa asked if I had ever written to her. My mother said, "I believe he did." (I'd written letters and sent cards.) Lisa asked questions about the past and saw some pictures of me with Jennifer, Beverly, little Emily, and the Ritchie's. She asked for my address. My mother gave it to her. She said Freddy [my son] was kind of nervous and that Joan [sister-in-law] had something seriously wrong with her chest. Lisa asked about visiting me. When my mother suggested that they could visit together, Lisa said, "No." She said something about she may cry. My mother said, "That's alright, your dad might cry, too," or something like that. I got a little choked just thinking about it.

I pray for my children everyday; especially that they accept Christ as their personal Lord and Savior. For ten years, I have prayed for them and for reconciliation. I had a strong feeling; that one day my children would become curious and want to know about their father. I've also wondered if they would wait until the last minute… or too late.

Lisa was born in the beginning of my marriage problems with Jon and Patty Jo. My relationship with Lisa never developed the way I wanted it to. Lisa was so young and close to her mother, and Patty Jo was turning my children against me. I understand what was happening now. Patty Jo was denying her responsibility and shifting the blame to cover up what she was doing, and she was quite good at it.

I wrote a letter to Lisa and forwarded it to my mother's address. If she shows up again it will be there.

On January 24, 1995, inmates were no longer allowed to have/spend cash money. SCDC staff claim they did this to prevent drugs and gambling. This is ludicrous. The guards have never made a concerted effort to stop the drug action, and they participate in the gambling with the inmates. Besides, the gamblers and drug dealers will figure a way around all this. The real reason for taking the cash from (25,000) prisoners is about the {interest} profit that will be made from holding all the money in the Cooper Trust Fund.

I can no longer purchase typing cartridges from Office Warehouse and have them mailed to me. At OW it cost me $13.58 for a six-pack of cartridges including two spools of lift-off tape. SCDC is now forcing me to purchase the same cartridges from them for $20.95 and they come without the spools of lift-off tape. - Prison is the number one industry in SC and they're cornering every angle to make it profitable.

On January 30, 1995, Larry Hall got into a fight with the guards. Everyone was punished for Hall's actions. On February 1, 1995, our evening tier walk was taken. That was the end of evening Bible study, fellowship and showers.

On March 16, 1995, A/W Pris Mack conducted a clean cell inspection. She had Captain Reed crawling the floor and checking under my bed to inspect my cell. - In the past, my cell had been inspected by Mr. Rudisail, Mr. Duck, Captain Guyton, and A/W Miro. I have always received an excellent rating with many first and second place awards.

My cell was clean and orderly as ever, but this time I failed the clean inspection. Why? It was something personal with her because I was the grievance clerk. The very first thing she said when she entered my cell was something derogatory about my grievance work. She arrogantly said, "What's the matter you run out of grievances?" I was simply doing the job as prescribed in SCDC Policy 300.2, and I became a target for retaliation.

Warden Cepak and A/W Mack are relatively new here, and they seem to have a cold malice towards prisoners. I've heard employees and prisoners say A/W Mack has a hatred for men. Both, Cepak and Mack, are trying to maintain a strong lead on Governor Beasley and Commissioner Moore's get tough on prisoner policy.

Everyone here, guards and prisoners, were shocked that I failed the inspection. - The punishment for this is the loss of: out-of-cell time, phone calls, visits, weekend showers, and canteen privileges until the next weekly inspection. I was on lockdown for eight days. I wasn't allowed to call my lawyer or family. My family visit was canceled. My mother and son were coming to visit we. I hadn't seen my mother since October 1994, and I hadn't seen my son in nearly a year.

Prisoners who are in population are not put on lockdown for failing a clean cell inspection. Furthermore, death row prisoners who are charged for possession of drugs or violent behavior are not denied visits and telephone calls. - I wrote a letter to the Inmate Grievance Coordinator, Mr. Dennis Dunlap, and a letter of resignation to, Ms. Harriette Fowler, the Administrative Assistant for the Warden.

South Carolina prisons are predominately managed and populated by blacks. The white prisoner is the minority in the scheme of prison management and racism is quite evident. The prison system is geared for blacks, so the white prisoner fits in essentially when education or some special skill is required.

SCDC staff took the grievance clerk job as a threat to their absolute authority; thus, they would not let me out my cell as they would a floor sweeper.

As the Inmate Grievance Clerk for death row, I assisted inmates as a clerk when they filed a grievance / complaint. I hoped it would be a pretty good job. No one in the past had ever really set the system up according to SCDC policy and made it work. Unfortunately, I learned that staff didn't want it to work, and I became a target of retribution.

Reflections Upon A Sunny Day

A/W Deck took a special interest and made a determined effort to seek retaliation. To keep the IGC job was to ask for more retaliation, so I gave it up.

On March 28, 1995, our visiting policy was changed. I'm not allowed to set up visiting appointments anymore; furthermore, Mr. Duck can no longer schedule visits. All visits must be scheduled by Dr. David J. Lowman, Visiting Coordinator for Broad River Correctional Institution. Mr. Lowman coordinates visits for over a thousand prisoners in prison population. He cannot be contacted by inmates on death row, and he never visits this building. Family and friends have difficulty getting in touch with him to schedule an appointment and the long distance calls are expensive; moreover, visiting days and hours were reduced.

On April 11, 1995, A/W Mack sent a guard to shakedown/search my cell during the recreation period. The guard told me she sent him to search for grievance records.

One of the guards told me on April 16, 1995, that he didn't like all the prison changes, and he said when something happens they [officials] are going to ask, "Why?" The following morning, the tension exploded in prison population and there was a riot. Five guards were stabbed and three hostages were taken. The prisons were put on lockdown. The hostage takers requested a media interview. Eleven hours later, they spoke with reporters and released the three hostages unharmed. — I suspected that the prisoners were protesting the cancellation of AA custody, work release, furloughs, and changes in visitation, but they were only concerned about their dreadlock hair being cut.

Death Row had nothing to do with the riot, but we were locked down for two weeks and denied showers, warm food, phone calls, sick call, etc.

On May 9, 1995, death row was put on lockdown status because Michael Moore was being confirmed as Commissioner.

On May 15. 1995, fifteen men were put on lockdown. LT Mazyk and another woman were looking in cells during lunchtime. I was put on lockdown because I had a calendar and a picture of Bethany and Rebekah on my locker. — The Inmate Disciplinary Action Report stated that I was charged with: "Creating a Health Safety or Fire Hazard."

The water here is very tainted with strong chemicals and the air quality in this place is causing a lot of health problems, e.g., itchy eyes, sore throats, sinus trouble, earaches, etc. I've never had so much ear trouble in my life. I can't get the medical care I need, so I've been suffering for a long time.

Officer Hudson stopped the afternoon Bible study I was sharing with Robert Nance. There was time for poker games but not for a Bible study. Robert started coming to my cell during the morning recreation period and we continued the study. We joined [volunteers] Al Bozard and Bill Cogdill On Wednesday mornings.

On June 4, 1995, Bobby Holmes got into a fight with the guards. Everyone was punished for Holmes' actions. On June 5, 1995, Associate Warden Pris Mack eliminated a dozen jobs in this building. She had the steam tables, the milk machine, salt, pepper, and plastic utensils removed. We have to drink hot and sour milk now, because we no longer have a way to refrigerate the five-gallon containers. Our food is brought to us in a [roach wagon] food cart. The portions are smaller. The trays are dirty, and the food is cold. Gravy is often in a solid form.

The telephones have been malfunctioning ever since the new system was installed. Ten-minute telephone calls are often cut off in four minutes. Requests for repair falls upon deaf ears.

Reflections Upon A Sunny Day

On June 29, 1995, Officer Ray told me to pack my stuff. I asked him why I couldn't pull the time in my cell like J.D. Gleaton did. He said, "It depends on who you are." I asked if it was A/W Mack, and he smiled. - The lockup cells had been occupied for weeks but somehow they made room for me.

I was served lockup papers and charged with POSSESSION AND/OR ATTEMPTS TO OBTAIN CONTRABAND (PG 28). I was moved upstairs to cell 244, and confined [lockup] in Administrative Segregation.

I was informed that this was my first offense; that it was a thirty-day sentence and I should be released after one-third of the sentence had been served. SGT Brice said if it goes over twenty days I should know who's behind it. He asked me if I'd ever met anyone that mean before. I was locked on a tier with county safe keepers who were waiting trial; with two inmates who where on protective custody; with one inmate on administrative segregation, and with one inmate who was on lockup pending investigation. - This was a violation of there own rules.

RE: SGDC Inmate Guide 4.10 E (2) (a) on pg 29 states the following; (2) The following is a list of articles which are hereby designated contraband: (a) <u>Any item which was not issued to the inmate officially</u> or which cannot be purchased by him or her in the prison canteen, or which has not been authorized by the Institution dead.

July 8, 1995, was my tenth day on lockup one third of the sentence. RE: SCDC inmate Guide 4.5 (2) pg. 19 states the following: (E) Review and release from Administrative Segregation will occur after one-third (1/3) of the sentence has been served provided that the inmate has committed no additional offenses, with the exception of those offenses listed in Section 4.8 while serving the sentence. (There were no additional offenses.)

On July 11, 1995, I had to wear handcuffs to visit with my attorneys from the Resource Center.

July 18th was my twentieth day on lockup - two thirds of the sentence. My efforts and the efforts that were made in my behalf, regarding my release, failed.

On July 26, 1995, the SCDC 19-1 Lockup form was brought to me for signature. Someone dated it 7-27-95 for me. I noticed that the accusing officer signed his narrative on July 25, 1995 – twenty-nine days after my lockup. The text and disposition section of the SOC 19-1 Form, describing the search and items found (e.g. spy binoculars) was very slanted and distorted. I wished to speak with the adjustment committee to give them the true facts.

On July 27, 1995, I spoke with the Inmate Representative. I told her what happened. She was interested in knowing if I were pleading guilty. She said the best I'd get would be time served; that there would be a continuance, which would take another month. I saw where this was going and told her I was pleading guilty.

On July 28, 1995, (30 days) Jr. Duck brought me a waiver form hoping the release process might speed up. At 11:09 p.m., the SCDC 19-1 Form was brought to me for final signature, but I wasn't released.

On July 29, 1995, (31 days) Bud spoke with an officer and got me off lockup. During my thirty-one days on lockup, I was not permitted to purchase anything from the canteen. I was not allowed to purchase personal hygiene items, nor was I issued these items. I was denied showers and three legitimate medical requests were denied. I was locked on a tier with county safe-keepers, and SCDC guidelines and policies regarding lockup were disregarded.

The cashless system has not stopped the drug sales or poker games here. We are permitted to purchase canteen goods on Monday and Wednesday mornings, during the recreation period, and the canteen computer breaks down frequently. I miss having cash to give to charity, to give for a child's birthday, to purchase office supplies, and to pay for photos taken in the visiting room.

The new telephone system has been terrible. The recording states that it will be a 15-minute call but it never lasts over 10 minutes. After dialing the 0, area code, and phone number, a very loud and hateful sounding voice says, "THIS WILL BE A 15 minute call". Then a voice says, "Enter your personal identification number." The volume is greatly reduced by the recording devices and you can barely hear a voice say give your name at the sound of the tone. You can't hear the call being made so you have to wait and see if your call was accepted. There's a constant hum on the line and when your party does come on the line the volume is reduced at least by half. Sometimes a recording will say, "You have dialed an unauthorized number," even though it's an approved number on your list. And, everyone is having problems with the phone disconnecting a conversation in the middle of the call. The recording says in a harsh loud voice, "THIS CALL IS TERMINATED! YOU DIALED YOUR NUMBER IMPROPERLY!"

Lawyers used to enter the cellblock to talk with and answer the questions of the men, and use the attorney conference room for private meetings. A/W Mack stopped all of this. Attorneys have to come in like visitors now and use the visiting room or one of the rooms in that area.

Magistrate Judge Carr, who was originally appointed to hear my case, would have overturned it. I feel certain of this. Two weeks before the case was to be heard, Judge Carr was replaced by Judge McCrory, who was the prosecutor [of Sly] in York county. The new judge didn't review and rule on my case; he prosecuted me with an extraordinary long distorted brief. He requested a Summary judgment from the Court and it was granted. In doing this he skipped me through the District Court [an important step] completely.

Attorney General Charles Condon recently went to Washington, D.C. and succeeded in cutting off federal funds to the Post Conviction Defender Organization of SC.

I am in the 4th Circuit Court of Appeals. A firm of lawyers in Washington D.C. put a brief together to appeal the Summary Judgment, i.e., my being denied review by the District Court. I've not been given any encouraging news. And, I have noticed that the judges are predominately pro-death and are inclined to be indifferent on important issues, such as, ineffective Assistance of Counsel or Incorrect Court Instructions to the Jury.

I long to live the new life I've been given in Christ, beyond prison walls, in freedom. I possess love, spiritual knowledge, and wisdom that I never had before. In Christ I am so much better equipped to be a servant, a brother, a husband, a father, and so much more.

Sylvester [Sly] Adams has exhausted all of his appeals. Governor Beasley turned down his request for clemency. Sly was taken to the execution room and killed by lethal injection on August 18, 1995.

After the execution, I saw David Bruck, John Blume, and a few others on TV giving a calm sensible argument against the killing of prisoners. While watching the program, they showed Governor Beasley's reply to the death penalty. His face was twisted and contorted in anger as he supported killing; using the sane words used by AG Charles Condon. Governor Beasley looked like he had murder in his heart.

Reflections Upon A Sunny Day

I personally solicited people to vote for David Beasley. I'm sure I am one of many in prison who heard him profess his Christian values. I didn't expect Mr. Beasley to be lenient with prisoners, but I did expect those values to reach into prison, i.e., some love, compassion, and forgiveness. — The present administration is saying, no prisoner has any redeeming qualities; that he is to be killed or locked away forever and never be forgiven.

Governor Beasley had a chance to show mercy without really sticking his neck out and hurting his political career, for Sly had a number of issues, e.g., the trial errors, his retardation, the victims family was against the execution, and two jurors were against the death penalty. Mr. Beasley has shown his true colors. If he wouldn't give Sly clemency, there's little chance of anyone else receiving mercy.

On September 13, 1995, A/W Mack denied the Resource Center lawyers access to their clients on death row. It was Christina's last chance to see me. She was doing some investigative work on my case and wanted to share it with me before leaving for home in England.

On September 19, 1995, I started leading a morning Bible study and prayer group. Bud Von Bohlen, Mitchell Sims, Robert Nance, and Andy Smith meet in my cell at 8:30 A.M. and study for an hour. On Wednesday mornings we join our friends, Al Bozard and Bill Cogdill, who take time off from work to share with us.

On September 21, 1995, during the last 15 minutes of the recreation period, I returned to my cell to get ready for a shower. I noticed a man and a woman walking straight to my cell. It was the woman who had us put on lockdown for two days for having Bethany and Rebekah's photo on my locker. The woman wanted me to step out my cell while she went through my belongings. She had a hateful attitude. After looking under my bed and in my locker, she arrogantly said, "You got a lot of stuff, what is it?" They were files and court transcripts. My cell was the only one checked downstairs. Later in the day, Mr. Duck stopped by my cell. While he was talking with the guys in this corner, he informed me that the same woman had some long forms filled out and had turned them in to A/W Mack. He also said A/W Mack asks about me. He said it burns her up that I don't do anything to get busted for.

When I called home on September 27, 1995, Joey answered the phone. It was the first time since 1990. He told me that my mother was very sick. The doctor she went to didn't know what was wrong with her, but he thinks her condition may be a result of her taking lithium. Besides having a bad kidney infection; she can't walk without holding on to something; she can't straighten up; she can't hold her head up, and there's something wrong, with her heart.

Within my family my mother has been the only one to stick by me; the only one to visit me; the only one to provide for my welfare; the only one to remember my birthday or Father's Day. If it hadn't been for her I wouldn't have any family connection.

I need people who care about me. Since August 1991, volunteers have brought my mother to visit me twenty times. Joey came with her only two times. My friend, Jennifer Long, visited me fifty eight times. She even came to see me during her break from missionary service in Mexico. Ken Ritchie visited me forty six times on weekends, and his wife, Cathy, and children, Bethany and Rebekah, visited me fourteen times. Since their move to NC in 1993, it's a 4 1/2 hour one-way drive for them to visit me. My sister, Loretta, lives only 2 1/2 hours away and she visited me only one time and it was for only fifteen minutes. - Besides my mother, my Christian friends are my family. They are the ones who care about me; the ones who send me little gifts and letters and ask me to call them collect every week. They are the ones who make me feel wanted and loved.

I found out Saturday morning, October 7, 1995, that my Appeal was turned down. Bud brought me the Charleston News clipping. It said, "A three-Judge panel of the 4th U.S. Circuit Court of Appeals unanimously ruled this week that the trial and sentencing of Kornahrens were 'free from constitutional defect.'" The courts decision didn't surprise me. Now my case will be submitted to the U.S. Supreme Court - the last Appeal. Heaven is looking better every day.

Governor Beasley hired Michael Moore from Texas and made him the Commissioner to implement his agenda; to make prison... prison with insensitive cruelty. His "get tough" attitude has permeated through his chain of command. I'm eating cold and raw food, and I can't get proper medical treatment. I've needed medical help for months. Men here suffer with toothaches for weeks until they have to pull their own teeth.

Medical requests regarding kidney infections, earaches, etc., are put on hold for weeks or totally ignored. Within the present administration there is no one to turn to for help. All Beasley and Moore are interested in is having prisoners jump briskly through proverbial hoops for them to make them look good. There's no problem with control here. Commissioner Moore made a News announcement stating that he was moving the population of death row to another prison some fifty miles away but is leaving the electric chair here for executions. His reason was: He doesn't want the guards here to [be attached] have any feelings of care or concern for us.

When Mitch mentioned me in prayer Monday morning, October 9, 1995, Bud burst into tears. He cried so hard that he buried his face in my bath towel.

One October 9, 1995, I received a letter from my attorney. He sent information regarding the Court denying my appeal. There was a 23-page report attached. On page 2, Circuit Judge Williams said, "Kornahrens never contested the fact that he committed these gruesome crimes. Instead, in all stages of this proceeding, he has challenged the degree of his guilt and debated the proper penalty for his crimes..." - The present attitude of the courts is if you admit your guilt...the wheels of justice are greased. The Court's statements were indifferent to the errors and their evidence *was* distorted.

The general public doesn't know what's going on in government, the military, or it's prisons. What does a U.S. citizen really know about political assassinations, propaganda, disinformation, covert operations of the CIA and other agencies, the sale of weaponry, the arming of nations, the profit of war, nuclear & biological weapons research, space wars, the survival of the elect, the profit of prison industry, the cruel and unusual beatings, rapes and hangings by prison officials, the power achieved in death penalty politics, and the plain truth about the death penalty?

A few years ago, I heard several guards talking about a warden at the Women's Correctional Center who traded favors for sex with hundreds of women, that is, until one woman finally brought the abuse to light. The warden wasn't even fired. He got a slap on the wrist and was moved to another institution.

As for the governor, he has been making speeches on getting tough on crime and making prison-prison. The governor is saying that he wants prison to be harder with more suffering. Even if he based his theory on the prisoners who don't care about anything, e.g., the young blacks who act like savages and those who think only of drugs, he doesn't know what it's really like in prison. The people who really suffer are those who have remorse for their crime and want to avoid undue complications, serve the time, and be an asset to society.

Commissioner Moore says he is 45 years old, but he looks a lot older like someone who has made a career out of inflicting pain and suffering. One of the first things he said when interviewed for the position was, "I believe in an eye for an eye."

Incorrigible prisoners should be controlled, but all too often it's the prisoner who's bent on evil that is catered to and given the best privileges. Why are the most violent prisoners given the longest leash to inflict pain and suffering on others? Why are drug dealers pampered? Why is a known child molester, who has a dirty record, given work release [AA Custody] to prey on yet more children? And, why is it that a degenerate prisoner, who is an immense pain in the side of the prison institution, given parole... and the hard-working well-behaved prisoner turned down?

You can put a badge, uniform, or a fancy title on anyone, but it doesn't make him a good person. All-to-often, newfound power only frees the inhibitions of the prejudiced, the racist, and the sexist to be cruel and sadistic to those subject to their authority.

The policy in prison is punish everyone for the actions of one. Regretfully, the state laws that are being passed are doing the same thing.

The Broadacres Baptist Church volunteers visited death row on October 26, 1995. They have faithfully visited once a month for over ten years. Bill Inman, Betts Davis, and Naida Knotts are the few who have persevered in this ministry.

By order of the Governor, BRCI has copied the Texas twelve- hour employee shift, and he said we will be in prison uniforms by the first of the year. — One of my attorneys, Donna Taylor, went to school with David Beasley. She didn't like him in school, and she was against his race for the governor's seat. She wrote to one last week and said, "Yes, even I have been disappointed at how right I was about Beasley. He was and apparently remains a shallow politician who only mouths Christian virtues, while possessing none at all. Things do not look good for Corrections for the rest of his term."

On October 26, 1995, I received a letter from my attorney, He said, "Enclosed is a copy of the Petition for Rehearing that has been filed on your behalf. I would expect a ruling on the Petition some time in November, although sometimes it takes longer for a ruling on whether to rehear a case." The issues addressed in the Petition were based on (1) Skipper v. South Carolina, in which the Supreme Court reversed a death sentence because of the exclusion of prison guard and expert testimony that the defendant would adapt well to prison life (2) and the ineffective assistance of counsel claim. The Court Panel's decision on this issue is marred by a stark internal contradiction.

Prison has never been a playground for me. I have suffered and hurt more than you can imagine. I'm not talking about the cold food and showers, but being confined in a cage locked away from everything and everybody. There are thousands of things that people take for granted everyday that I miss dearly.

On November 13, 1995, during my recreation period, my attorneys, Ray McClain and Donna Taylor, showed up. We sat at a table in cell 104 and talked. Ray started telling me about the Appeal. I listened until I got confused. I asked if he was talking about the application for rehearing to the 4th Circuit or the U.S. Supreme Court. He asked if I had received his letter. I hadn't. The request for rehearing was denied. He was talking about the Appeal to the U.S. Supreme Court. He was telling me that the Court didn't have to review my case. We talked about the time frame. He said they may execute me in the summer of 1996.

Reflections Upon A Sunny Day

On November 28, 1995, Bobby Holmes (b) got into another fight with the guards because his first appeal was turned down. Lieutenant Moore took it upon himself to personally punish us for his actions. He started strip-searching us before and during our visits with family and friends, and he forbade us to carry our Bible or anything else to the visiting room.

James Tucker (w) is still at MSU (20 months) on lockup for throwing a ½ cup of warm coffee on a guard. The guard testified against Tucker in his death penalty trial and taunted Tucker into a reaction. If Tucker wants fresh air, he is put in a tiny case and he has to wear a leather collar around his neck with a chain attached to it. Larry Hall (w) is still on SSR status (12+ months) for attacking a guard with a hairbrush.

There is no justice in this world. One politician's slap on the wrist is another man's prison sentence. The rich and famous are exempt from the laws that apply to the poor and common. Law enforcement is corrupt at every level, and the scales of justice is blindfolded and covered in blood. There is no truth in this world. Lawyers are professional liars and their expertise is expected. Politicians are renowned liars and society accepts it as a joke. All the schemes and lies, and the world loves it. Pilate said, "What is truth?" Clinton claims truth! Beasley professes truth! But, they wouldn't know truth if He was looking them in the face. There is no forgiveness in this world. Sue thy neighbor if he trespasses against thee; seek revenge and punish with all thy heart is the American way. There is no love in this world but love for money, power, and ungodliness. - It's not supposed to be that way!

There are people who feel that prisoners should suffer more; that being in prison is not enough. I've seen guards antagonize and torment prisoners simply because the prisoner is a prisoner. I've seen SCDC staff and associates treat prisoners with contempt as if they were a disgusting parasite. I have even seen prison volunteers do this. And what I am saying is, there are so many people who feel like they have to or need to do their part in giving a prisoner another kick in the butt while he's down. - This is the way of the world, and they kicked Jesus when He was down, too.

Michael Torrence, Robert South, and Cecil Lucas mentioned to Robert South that I was concerned about where he may be spending eternity, he doesn't believe in the sovereignty of God; that He has the right to test us, nor does he believe in Jesus. Robert believes in reincarnation, and his concept of heaven is having a log cabin isolated in the wood with a marijuana garden. He uses a few Bible verses, which he had misinterpreted, to justify his use of drugs. I shared the correct interpretation. I heard from Bud that Robert appreciated my concern, but he prefers his interpretation of the Bible verses.

There have been many changes this year, and I have recorded them for your reading; that you may know what goes on behind prison walls. I long to be with my family and friends but my thoughts have not been focused on my circumstances but rather on God's Word and my relationship with my Lord and Savior. I've learned to be content and the Holy Spirit has surely comforted me in all circumstances.

The legal system is like a system of gates that shut like one-way turnstiles, and you can't go back in once you've come out. If the trial attorney does not raise an issue or make an objection, the higher courts say the defendant has waived his rights to raise the issue later on.

Introducing these issues later will almost surely evoke "abuse of the writ" from federal court. The court wants to protect itself from defendants filing issues piecemeal, which would keep cases before the courts indefinitely.

Reflections Upon A Sunny Day

In the past, defense attorneys used to be able to count on the federal courts to monitor and check errors and abuses in state courts. It was the authority of the federal court, which put legal teeth into the civil rights movement in the 1960s. If it had been left to state legislatures to enact social legislation on their own, Jim Crow might still be the law of the land today. Then in Gregg v. Georgia in 1976, the high court, by removing the constitutional protection against capital punishment essentially said that if states wanted to kill their citizens, they wouldn't stop them. The Court interpreted the Constitution as saying that putting someone to death was not forbidden by the Eighth Amendment, which forbids cruel and unusual punishment. The political motive behind this decision was a power struggle between the Federal Government and state's rights – that old struggle, as old as the Constitution itself. Southern states were mad as hell about the federal enforcement of desegregation in the sixties. And then they were mad as hell again with the Furman v. Georgia ruling in 1972, which said the application of the death penalty was 'arbitrary and capricious', which looked like the Court might permanently overturn the death penalty. The South has always been a proponent of strong land-and-order measures, mainly to keep blacks in line, and they were not about to let the fed in Washington tell them how they could or couldn't punish their criminals. They prevailed.

In recent years, they're so interested in speeding up executions that it doesn't seem to matter that they're running roughshod over people's constitutional rights. They keep tightening procedural requirements so that it's harder and harder to get a hearing in death penalty cases. Clients might have the most substantial issue in the world-even new evidence of innocence-but the courts say, "Sorry, filed too late," and refuse to hear the case.

It's rare nowadays in capital cases, for the courts to concede that defense attorneys are ineffective. There are cases where defense attorneys in capital cases have actually shown up for trial drunk, or so ill prepared they told the judge they didn't know what they were doing, and even then the appeal courts wouldn't concur on ineffectiveness of counsel.

The high court's stringent standard of judging ineffectiveness of counsel now puts the burden of proof on a defendant's appellate attorney to demonstrate that defense counsel blunders directly affected the jury's verdict, and that minus those blunders the jury would have returned a different verdict. But how are you going to demonstrate that, of all the variables in a case, a mistake of the defense counsel caused the jury to render a certain verdict? The Court just comes back and says that the attorney's mistakes were "harmless error" and the jury would have returned a guilty verdict anyway. Every person is supposed to have a constitutional right to effective assistance of counsel, but the courts, by imposing such impossible procedural structures, have reamed out that right to an empty shell.

Reflections Upon a Sunny Day-1996

Depression - everyone experiences it at one time or another. When we lose a loved one it's normal for someone to grieve or get depressed for a little while.

Among human illness, mental illness is the least understood by people. It's easy for people to accept the need for medicine when someone suffers diabetes, angina, ulcers, asthma, etc., but when the need is for depression, mania, anxiety, etc., it's taboo.

A great sadness enveloped me at a young age and it lasted for long periods at a time. It was clinical depression. I lost interest in everything and there was no happiness in my life. Depression came often and it was never diagnosed or treated. Between the gloom of depression came hypo-mania. Hypo-mania can make you feel like you can do anything. Endless energy, quick positive imaginative creative thinking, etc., are some of the effects. The high feels good but if a person can't control his behavior during a period of hypo-mania he can get himself into trouble - even jail.

Mania - is more severe than hypo-mania. It's a form of insanity in which there is wild behavior; excessive desire for something; uncontrollable and violent passion. - According to Dr. John DeWitt, who was the SCDC psychiatrist for BRCI, he said I was experiencing depression and mania at the time of my crime.

I requested a jury trial, not to deny the crime, but to present the mitigating circumstances, that is, to explain how such a terrible thing like this happened. (Runyon failed to call my witnesses,) I was not arraigned for robbery, rape or any other aggravating circumstance. I remember reading about motive in my transcript. There was no motive for the crimes, Why? Because I was sick. (Runyon failed to have me properly evaluated, and he failed to call my doctor (Dr. Diane Hamrick) to court.

On January 2, 1996, I received a letter from the Covington & Burling law firm. They said the Supreme Court accepts very few cases, and that it is unlikely that they will grant any particular petition for certiorari including mine.

On January 10, 1996, I began six weeks of radiation treatment at The Center for Cancer Treatment and Research at Richland Memorial Hospital in Columbia. I was chained and escorted by armed guards to the hospital each day. - My treatment was complete on February 21, 1996. My mouth was so sore and raw that I could hardly talk, so I waited a week before resuming the Bible study I was sharing with Bud, Hitch, Robert, and Andy.

On March 7, I received a letter from, Ray McClain, my attorney in Charleston. He said, "The Supreme Court will only review a case if the decision will address issues that will help courts around the country resolve questions that have been in dispute. Therefore, the Petition for Certiorari does not seek review of all questions in your case, but only the procedural.

On June 26, 1996, our exercise/weight machine was removed from the building.

On June 28, 1996, a building shakedown [search] was conducted. TV's, radios, and typewriters were handled roughly and stripped open.

My radio was damaged. Many were damaged and broken by the rough treatment. Some cells were checked lightly, others were hit hard. My cell was thoroughly searched and left in disorder. Four items were confiscated from me. Two of the items (stapler & three hole punch) were issued to me by the Inmate Relations Coordinator [IRC] in 1991, and I have used them in plain view ever since. The other two items (toy opera binoculars & plastic camera) were forwarded from the SCDC Mail Room to the Edisto Unit and they were issued officially by a SCDC officer. The toy binoculars were issued to Freddy Singleton, and I bought them in 1992 for .50 cents. They were in plain view. Over a dozen officers have seen them and judged them for just what they were - a toy. The plastic camera was a cheap promotional gift sent from a photo reprint company about a year ago. I put it in my canteen box and essentially forgot about it.

Later, SGT Brice came to my door to talk. He didn't mention anything about the camera but did mention that A/W Mack had a personal interest in me.

Reflections Upon a Sunny Day-1996

"But a man who commits adultery lacks judgment; whoever does so destroys himself. Blows and disgrace are his lot, and his shame will never be wiped away; for jealousy arouses a husband's fury, and he will show no mercy when he takes revenge." (Pr 6:32-34)

When I read these verses in 1985, I wondered about them and all that had happened. The life I lived was unbearable and it took two years for the debris and confusion in my mind to settle so that I could think straight, and God opened my eyes so that I could see and understand.

In 1975, my wife ran off with a man while I was on active duty in Mississippi. Then in 1977 my wife tormented me with the long affair she had with Jon. With all my strength I tried to save our marriage. I didn't have any help, and I didn't know Jesus. I wasn't prepared or equipped for what was happening.

In 1978, my wife introduced me to Jon and Beverly. She couldn't get enough of being with Jon. (In 1995 I was given court transcripts that revealed Jon was put in jail for beating and threatening to kill Beverly in 1979.) Having been overwhelmed with my wife's threats and her adultery, I pulled a gun on her in 1980. She told me she didn't love Jon; that she was breaking off the affair. The stress and worry was having such an affect on my mind that I was seeing Jon's face on billboards.

Reflections Upon A Sunny Day

In 1981, I caught my wife and Jon together. Years of pain and anger boiled to the surface. I was half out of my mind. I put a beating on Jon that he'll never forget (When I escaped in 1988 he caught the first plane to Ohio.) but I didn't have murder in my heart. He thought I was going to kill him, and he begged for his life. I told him to leave my wife alone. "Yes sir Mr. Kornahrens," he said. And I want you to get out of town. "Yes sir, yes sir Mr. Kornahrens," he said.

I was charged with Assault and Battery with Intent to Kill. He may have left and my wife may have settled down if it hadn't been for the lawyers and the laws in this state. As a man I was not equal as a parent. I couldn't have my children, and the law took their side. With the mighty arm of the law, Jon and my wife used it like a lethal weapon. From 1981 to 1985 it was non-stop harassment and torment. They broke me. Pages 89-90 of my autobiography explain how the stress affected my body and mind.

I was subconsciously preparing myself for suicide and if I had slammed my car into a tree or I had jumped off the Cooper River Bridge, what would people have thought. Some would have said, "Well he had a lot on him." Others would have said, "If I had known something was wrong maybe I could have helped." Either way they would have concluded that I wasn't able to think or reason properly. As it turned out, the fine line between suicide and homicide was crossed. The unbearable pain I suffered was real to me.

In a sick state of mind, as if I were watching it happen in a dream, lives were lost. And, no one concluded that I was out of my mind. No one can understand another person's pain unless they have experienced it.

About the Author

Fred H. Kornahrens III grew up in South Carolina in an abusive and unstable household. He later joined the military and married Patti Jo Wilkerson. The couple had three children, but Kornahrens's mental instability led to a tragic crime for which he was sentenced to death.

The foreword for Reflections upon a Sunny Day was written by Joseph Wilkerson Kornahrens, the eldest child of Fred H. Kornahrens III, and M. Scott Steedley. Steedley is the founder of the nonprofit International Center for Sustainability. He was born in South Carolina's low country and hopes to pass on to his four children an appreciation of the region's beauty and cultural heritage.

www.ingramcontent.com/pod-product-compliance
Lightning Source LLC
Chambersburg PA
CBHW020327240426
43665CB00044B/722